SUB 4:00

SUB 4:00

Alan Webb
and the Quest
for the Fastest Mile

CHRIS LEAR

RODALE

Notice

This book is intended as a reference volume only. Mention of specific companies, organizations, or authorities in this book does not imply endorsement by the publisher, nor does mention of specific companies, organizations, or authorities imply that they endorse this book.

Printed in the United States of America
Rodale Inc. makes every effort to use acid-free ∞, recycled paper ♻.

Book design by Drew Frantzen
Interior photographs © 2002 by Alison Wade/New York Road Runners (One to go, Just did it, Too close to call, Off and running, and The Sage Expressway)

Library of Congress Cataloging-in-Publication Data

Lear, Chris, date.
    Sub-4:00 : Alan Webb and the quest for the fastest mile / Chris Lear.
       p.   cm.
    Includes index.
    ISBN 1—57954—746—X hardcover
    ISBN 1—59486—056—4 paperback
    1. Webb, Alan. 2. Runners (Sports)—United States—Biography. 3. University of Michigan—Track and field. 4. Michigan Wolverines (Track and field team) I. Title: Alan Webb and the quest for the fastest mile. II. Title.
    GV1061.15.W43L43 2003
    796.42'092—dc21   2003006295

Distributed to the trade by Holtzbrinck Publishers

2 4 6 8 10 9 7 5 3 1 hardcover
2 4 6 8 10 9 7 5 3 1 paperback

THIS BOOK IS FOR MY PARENTS,
GENE AND SUZANNE LEAR,
AND FOR MY WIFE, SHAWN,
WITH DEEPEST LOVE AND GRATITUDE.

CONTENTS

FOREWORD

As I consider the years gone by, I see God's hand at work in my life. I am not a believer in fate or chance; I believe that each of us is created by God for a specific purpose. Those like Alan Webb, Nate Brannen, Kevin Sullivan, Paul McMullen, Tim Broe, and even myself were purposefully wired with that special blend of strength and speed that the mile requires. We were born to run.

I am fairly confident that no one, not even myself, ever thought that I would amount to much in the world of athletics. In my preteen years, I was even cut from the church baseball team. But running brought something new to the table—a sense of belonging and eventually the taste of success that left me wanting more.

My running career began ingloriously; I dropped out of my first cross country workout. But 2 years later—years of sweat, tears, frustration, hard work, and incredible success—I emerged as Jim Ryun, the runner. At 17, I made my first Olympic team at 1500 meters, and my picture appeared on the cover of *Sports Illustrated*.

In 1965, at age 18, I found myself at a starting line on a June night just after my high school graduation. In the year since the Olympics, I had become even stronger and more confident.

To my left on that warm San Diego night was Jim Grelle, the American record holder in the mile. To his left was Peter Snell, the double gold medalist from the Olympics the year before. My race plan was simple: stay near the front, then make a move with 300 meters to go and hold off Snell and Grelle.

As the race progressed, I made my move as planned. I held off Grelle and, miraculously, Snell. I hit the tape first in 3:55.3, a new American record. All I could do for the next 30 minutes was sit on a bench with a towel clenched between my teeth. I had never hurt so much in all my life. I didn't know it then, but my 3:55.3 would become a high school record that would stand for 36 years.

When Tim Danielson and Marty Liquori broke 4 minutes in consecutive years after me, it seemed only a matter of time before my record fell. But with each passing year, it became more than a mark. For American high school runners, the 4-minute mile suddenly became a barrier. For most of them, my record seemed beyond even their wildest dreams.

Then, in June 1999, something happened: My sophomore mile record fell to a young man named Alan Webb. The next year, he scared 4 minutes with his 4:03, and then came his 3:59 on January 20, 2001. One barrier down, one to go.

In May 2001, I was in Kansas at a Wichita East High School track reunion when I received the call about Webb's record run. I must confess, I felt a twinge at seeing my record go. But more than that, I felt great joy for Webb; he had faced the barrier and broken through it. And at the end of those brief 3 minutes and 53 seconds, he moved from stellar high school athlete to America's future hope for the mile. It is a heavy mantle to wear. It is something that must be embraced, for it has its own unique pressures. The failures seem that much greater, the successes that much sweeter.

Webb's first year out of high school somewhat echoed my 1972 season. It is not a year I would ever wish to relive. The highs were extremely high, the lows extremely low. From one week to the next, I could run a 3:55 mile or a 4:07. Without a doubt, the lowest point was the 4:19 I ran during a race televised to a national audience. I still vividly remember walking from the track, waving off the press, and finding a tree to beat on with my spikes.

However, it was out of this crucible of events that I became the man I am today. It is through the struggle that often we find the reward. I have no doubt the same will be true for Alan Webb. I'm not saying that he will never again have a year like he had in 2002. Competitive running is filled with too many variables to make such a statement. Webb tasted necessary failure that year, as we all do. Life is not a constant state of living on the mountaintops.

That fact, for me, is the beauty of Chris Lear's *Sub 4:00*. He takes us inside the tumultuous world of competitive running. It is never just about the races; I always felt the races themselves comprised about 10 percent of my running career. It is about the preparation, the outside pressures, the mental game, and, most important, those few fleeting moments when we are in the running zone and everything is effortless. This reality was clear in Lear's first book, *Running with the Buffaloes*, and it shines through again in *Sub 4:00*.

Congressman Jim Ryun
Lawrence, Kansas
March 2003

ACKNOWLEDGMENTS

O n a brisk, drizzly evening in late spring, I was riding shotgun with Michigan freshman Sean Moore when conversation turned to running for Michigan. Moore said, "You know, most of us had choices; we could have gone to schools with nicer weather, equal academic reputations. When it comes down to it, we're at Michigan for one reason: we're here because of Ronnie."

Count me in, too. From this book's inception, in the fall of 2001, to the end of my stay in Ann Arbor, in June 2002, Ron Warhurst was unflinchingly honest and cooperative. The season played out differently than anyone could have imagined, and I'm sure there were instances when he wished I would eat that damned tape recorder or when he wanted to be rid of my presence. To his credit, with nothing to gain, he never made me feel unwelcome. On the contrary, he made me feel at home, and for the vast majority of my stay in Ann Arbor, kept me laughing. I am truly indebted to him.

I am also grateful to the core group of milers who welcomed me into their lives and are at the heart of this book. Kevin Sullivan, Tim Broe, Paul McMullen, Nate Brannen, and Alan Webb could not have been more gracious or more cooperative. Not only are they spectacular athletes, they're also stand-up guys. I'll cherish my memories of the time I spent with them and look forward to crossing paths with all of them in the future. Special thanks to Tim Broe and Vanessa Bell for their friendship and for miraculously coming up with extra chicken or a plate of pasta, time and again.

The rest of the Michigan track family was just as kind to me in my months in Ann Arbor. Trainer Will Turner and ace physiotherapist Pete Kitto helped mend me when I broke down. The Michigan track staff—Fred LaPlante, Ricky Deligny, James Henry, Anne Takacs-Grieb, Karen Harvey, and Mike McGuire—were a joy to be around. The same can be said for the Michigan team. I first met Michigan runners Nick Stanko and Drennan Wesley when they ventured to Boulder, Colorado, for a summer of run and fun in 2001, and we quickly forged a friendship. Their friendship and insight into the tides of Ann Arbor and their assistance during my stay were incalculably helpful. Thanks too to the entire Michigan track team, particularly the middle-distance and distance runners with whom I spent so much time. I'd be remiss if I didn't list those I haven't already mentioned by name: Brian Berryhill, David Cook, Dan Cooke, Tom Greenless, Ryan Hesselink, Kevin Lamb, Tarn Leach, Mark Pilja, Terrence Rindler, Kevin Rogan, Rondell Ruff, Dave Sage, Jeremy Schneider, Phil Stead, Brian Turner, and Mike Wisniewski.

Along the way, many people graciously shared their time, insight, and hospitality. Some received scant mention in the final draft, but I valued their time and contributions just the same. Thanks to Kalli Warhurst, Bill Martin, Bruce Madej, David Crabtree, Andrew Ladd, Todd Snyder, Katie Treveloni, Nick Harp, Jill McMullen, John Mortimer, Brian Diemer, Greg Meyer, Dr. Jon Cross, Ian Forsyth, Scott MacDonald, Gerard Donakowski, Andy Downin, Matt Downin, Dave Monti, Josh Rowe, Toni Berryhill, Rick Berryhill, Kathy Berryhill, Adam Goucher, Ryan Bolton, Diane Broe, Jason Broe, Les Gauwitz, Ed McGraw, Matt Holthaus, Chris Graff, Elizabeth Graff, Steve Scott, Bernard Lagat, Hicham El Gerrouj, Abdelkada Kada, Ibrahim Aden, Jason Vigilante, John Cook, Scott Raczko, Jorge Torres, Ed Torres, Steve Slattery, Dathan Ritzenhein, the Webb family, Peter Grinbergs, Abdi Abdirahman, Jason Lunn, Todd Klein, Todd Williams, Anthony Famiglietti, Alison Wade, Marcus O'Sullivan, Ryan Hayden, Adrian Blincoe, Jason Jabaut, Nic O'Brien, Scott Tantino, Jon Fasulo, Tom Parlapiano, Del Hessel, Steve Holman, Seneca Lassiter, Marty Liquori, Don Kopriva, Dan Wilson, Scott Davis, and Josh Spiker. And to anyone I may have accidentally missed, thank you!

Thanks to Susan Reed, PJ Mark, and the folks at IMG.

Thanks to the crew at Peaberry Coffee in Boulder for enduring my squatting self for months on end.

One shot. Sometimes that's all we need. Thanks to Mark Wetmore for giving me mine. And thanks to Larry Laconi, whose faith in *Running with the Buffaloes* brought it to the big time. If not for their help a few years ago, I never would have had the opportunity to do this book.

Then there are my friends, who along with my family encouraged and counseled me in countless phone conversations; Scott Anderson, Cael Davis, Andrew Goldstein, and Robert Johnson were particularly helpful. To my other friends and mentors too numerous to mention, I offer a heartfelt thank-you.

This book has benefited greatly from the tireless effort, good humor, and stewardship of my ace editor, Alisa Bauman. I'm privileged to have worked with her. Thanks, too, to the staff at Rodale, especially Steve Madden, for supporting this project.

The love and support of my family have been instrumental in any success I have had. My parents, Suzanne and Gene Lear, and my siblings, Frederique and Tim, have always been my most ardent supporters. Thankfully, we can all now laugh about hocking books on chilly autumn afternoons at Holmdel Park. I'll never forget it (not that they'd ever hesitate to remind me!). I owe Tim special thanks for being an insightful first reader.

Last, I'd like to thank my wife, Shawn Lear. When I went to Ann Arbor, she held down the fort and planned an amazing wedding with the help of my family and my wonderful mother-in-law, Denise Feeney. In August 2002 we tied the knot in front of many of the friends and family who mean the world to us. My memory of her entrance at the end of the aisle is priceless; she literally took my breath away. For her support, patience, and love, I thank Shawn from the bottom of my heart.

INTRODUCTION

PERFECTION

In November 2001, I went to the University of Michigan in Ann Arbor to see how Alan Webb and Nathan Brannen, the first-ever pair of high school sub-4 milers to attend the same university, were handling the transition to collegiate running.

At the time, Webb was already a household name, tagged with the illusory title "America's next great miler" by a sports press desperate for another world-beating U.S. miler. On the other hand, Brannen, a Canadian, was flying under the radar, despite credentials that rivaled Webb's. On that brisk autumn weekend, I watched them practice. While Brannen struggled, Webb performed a stunning workout that trumped anything else I had ever seen.

Webb had come to the university to run for Michigan's famed coach Ron Warhurst, mentor to guys like Brian Diemer, the last American middle-distance runner to win an Olympic medal, and Greg Meyer, the last American to win the Boston Marathon, and to train alongside Brannen and fellow world-class runners Tim Broe, Kevin "Sully" Sullivan, and Paul McMullen.

But on that fall day, none of the aforementioned runners were even remotely within hailing distance of Webb. Clearly, Webb had made great strides since capturing the nation's fancy the previous spring in the Prefontaine Classic. I wondered then how his newfound strength would translate to the track come this spring, when he was once again running his specialty, the mile—or its 109-meter shorter and more commonly run metric cousin, the 1500 meters*— under the watchful eye of an impatient public and a ravenous sports press. And I wondered how Brannen and his cohorts would respond to the challenge.

Early in March 2002, as Webb was about to start his first track season as a Michigan Wolverine, I moved to Ann Arbor to learn what had gotten him this far and to see firsthand, in the company of North America's greatest conglomerate of middle-distance talent, what would happen next.

Yet Alan Webb's story starts long before March 2002. It also starts long before January 13, 1983, when he was born. It actually dates back to the 1960s, when someone named Jim Ryun was about to be known as "America's greatest miler."

---

*Outdoor tracks switched from their traditional 440 yards in circumference to 400 meters during the 1970s and 1980s. USA Track and Field (USATF) went metric in 1974 (outdoors) and 1987 (indoors); the National Collegiate Athletic Association (NCAA) switched in 1976 (outdoors) and 1984 (indoors). Although the mile is still run, particularly indoors, the 1500 meters is more common. According to track legend, the 1500 is now run because at one time, the French used 500-meter tracks. For symmetry's sake, three-lap, 1500-meter races were run in place of the mile. Soon, even though tracks became standardized at 400 meters, 1500-meter races became the norm internationally, resulting in an odd 3¾-lap race.

AMERICA'S GREATEST MILER

On a warm evening in June 1965, Jim Ryun, wearing the white singlet of his Wichita East High School track team, took his place in lane 5 at Balboa Stadium in San Diego to compete against the world's greatest milers in the AAU (Amateur Athletic Union) Championships, which served as the U.S. national championships. On his left, in lane 4, was Jim Grelle, an NCAA mile champion who had set a new American mile record of 3:55.4 in Vancouver a week earlier. Next to Grelle, in lane 3, was Olympic 800- and 1500-meter champion and 800 world record holder Peter Snell of New Zealand, the preeminent middle-distance runner of the day.

This was not Ryun's first race against Snell. Three weeks earlier, at the Compton Relays in California, he entered a mile against Snell, intending to match the Kiwi's finishing burst over the last 220 yards. But when Snell launched into his finishing kick, he left Ryun behind.

In the intervening weeks, Michel Jazy of France lowered Snell's world mile record from 3:54.1 to 3:53.6, attracting even more attention to the showdown in San Diego. Ryun and his coach, J. D. Edmiston, formulated a plan to counteract Snell's wicked kick.

In order to beat Snell and Grelle, Ryun would have to outsmart them. If he beat Snell to the punch and began his finishing kick from 300 yards out, they reasoned, he might not be able to sustain it to the tape. They had to force Snell to go wide, but how? The answer: Ryun was to hold back early in the race and get in position on the third lap.

The first half-mile went according to plan. Ryun conserved his energy in the back of the pack of eight runners through the first two laps, passing the half-mile mark in 2:00.5. The crowd roared when Czech miler Josef Odlozil picked up the pace and shot into the lead from fourth. Instantly, the runners strung out behind him. Sensing the importance of the break, Ryun moved into third behind Grelle. Snell moved, too, right off Ryun's shoulder.

They held those positions to the final lap, which Ryun reached in an unimpressive 3:01.4. Each of the four contenders had excellent finishing speed, but none was as fearsome as Snell.

Ryun would have to execute his plan perfectly if he hoped to win.

Odlozil began to fade, so Ryun nonchalantly swung wide on the turn to be able to smoothly shoot past Grelle and Odlozil. He quickly moved past Grelle, then Odlozil, into the lead just as he reached the backstretch. The crowd erupted at the sight of the skinny teenager taking the lead over the imposing, muscular Snell.

Now the plan required patience. To kick from here would be suicide, for he would tire before the tape and be reeled in by Grelle and Snell. He would have to withstand any challenge down the backstretch while saving some energy for a final burst down the homestretch. He picked up the pace on the backstretch, keeping all challengers at bay. On the curve, Grelle went after Ryun. Time to go. Around the first half of the turn, they battled shoulder to shoulder. Snell was forced out to lane 2 to match their challenge.

They hit the homestretch nearly three abreast. All that was left was to drive full-out to the tape and hope that the extra ground Snell and Grelle were forced to cover on the turn would prove the difference. The crowd roared for the skinny teenager.

Snell churned past Grelle down the straightaway in pursuit of Ryun, who could see his awesome stride to his right. And Grelle refused to give an inch. Thirty yards from the finish, it was still a three-man race. After running the last quarter in a blistering 53.9 seconds—a record pace for such a fast race—Ryun hit the tape. His time of 3:55.3 established a new American record, a mile time that would later become the standard by which promising American schoolboy milers were judged.

Jim Ryun was 18 years old. A year later, as a freshman at the University of Kansas, he set a world record of 3:51.3.

THE LAST AMERICAN TRACK HERO

Fast-forward to May 2001. The world record in the mile, set by Morocco's Hicham el Guerrouj, is now an astonishing 3:43.13. Since Ryun, only seven men have had the honor of holding the world mile record. In 1975, John Walker of New Zealand became the first man to run under 3:50 when he ran 3:49.4. A trio of Englishmen—

Sebastian Coe, Steve Ovett, and Steve Cram—followed, and in 1985 Cram held the record at 3:46.3.

Then the Africans took over in earnest. Noureddine Morceli of Algeria dominated the mile in the early 1990s and lowered the record to 3:44.39 in 1993 before El Guerrouj made the record his own 6 years later.

Africans—Kenyans, Ethiopians, Moroccans—now dominate the middle-distance and distance events. East African–born runners hold 83 percent of the all-time fastest times in events ranging from the 800 to the 10,000 meters. Most American distance runners have ceased to compare themselves to them, content with the dubious distinction of being first non-African or first North American in the world's toughest track competitions.

American spectators have long since stopped caring about track and field. What little fanfare the sport receives in the United States is reserved for 100-meter sprinters such as Tim Montgomery, the world's fastest man, and Marion Jones, the world's fastest woman. If you asked average Americans to name a current elite miler, probably less than 1 percent could come up with a name.

When did it all go wrong? Track pundits will say it was in 1967, 34 long years ago, which was the last time an American schoolboy broke 4 minutes in the mile. For 3 consecutive years, beginning with Ryun in 1965, an American schoolboy did it. One year after Ryun, in 1966, Tim Danielson of Chula Vista, California, broke 4 minutes. Then in 1967, Marty Liquori of New Jersey's Essex Catholic High School ran a 3:59.8, good for seventh at the national championships in Bakersfield, California. Ryun won that race, too, in a world record 3:51.1, 0.2 second under his previous best. Times were good.

And then . . . nothing. Thirty-four years of futility made Ryun's high school record of 3:55.3 seem both heroic and unassailable. With no home-grown stars to look to for inspiration, it's no wonder track was in a funk.

Enter Alan Webb, a glimmer of hope, the glimmer who seemed destined to become America's next great miler.

Webb, a runner from South Lakes High School in Reston, Virginia, was Ryun's opposite. Ryun was tall, gawky, reticent, and unathletic, taking up track as a last resort and then plying his trade with the ardor of a farmer, earning each progression with an unstinting and voracious training regimen: twice a day, every day, week after 110-mile week. Webb was short and stocky, gregarious and self-assured, with remarkable athletic talent to boot. He excelled at everything from soccer to basketball, winning the state 3,200-meter championship as a freshman while devoting most of his training energy to swimming, in which he held Olympic aspirations.

Despite his lack of devotion to the sport, Webb had started to cause a stir among track fans. He had beaten Ryun's sophomore class mile record with a 4:06.94 in the spring of 1999. In April of his junior year he anchored the South Lakes distance medley relay team to a second-place finish at the Penn Relays with a 3:59.9 leg of 1600 meters, which converts to a 4:01 mile. No high-schooler had ever run faster at Penn.

The watch was now on for Webb to go sub-4.

THE QUEST FOR A SUB-4

Webb went for it at the Herbster Track Classic in a high school—only invitational race. He won the race but fell short of his goal, running 4:03.33. The experience proved invaluable for Webb and his coach, Scott Raczko.

"There were lots of good lessons learned there, because there was lots of publicity before the race and it was a little overwhelming to him," Raczko says. "4:03 was a great time. It was an open PR [personal record] for him. But at the same time, there was an injury coming on, and we didn't pick up on it until the following week. It's funny, when Alan was doing strides before the race, we were standing there thinking something was just not right, he had a little hitch. A week later, his piriformis injury came up."

Not wanting to further aggravate the injury, Raczko pulled the plug on the season. Still, the sports press began looking at Webb as The One.

A successful cross country season culminated in late fall of his senior year with a second-place finish in the Foot Locker National

High School Cross Country Championships. Webb took a short break and resumed training on Christmas Day.

After just a few weeks, he started to show fine form. Raczko called Ian Brooks, race coordinator and announcer for the elite miles at the New Balance Games, to be held at the Armory Track and Field Center in New York City on January 20, and told him to book Webb for the elite mile, with one stipulation. "Based on our experience at Herbster, we needed to keep this 100 percent quiet. I didn't want him disappointed if he didn't do it [run a sub-4]. The only reason he'd be disappointed is if other people drummed it up. If he ran 4-flat or something, that's a PR and a high school record. That'd be a big success."

Tuesday of race week, Webb ripped a tune-up workout, running a 600 in under 1:30, a couple of 400s in 56 and 57 seconds, and a couple of snappy 200s in cold, windy conditions. Raczko and Webb both felt he had the fitness to run a sub-4 at the end of cross country and that all he needed was a few quicker workouts to sharpen up. At this point, they weren't worried about times. More than anything, Raczko wanted to see how he looked. He wasn't disappointed. "When he is on, he is freaking rolling. After that workout it was like, 'Pssst, that's the deal, he is ready.'"

Webb's participation in the race was such a highly guarded secret that not even his fellow competitors were aware of his entry until the hour of the race. Sub-4 miler Matt Holthaus was already stretching, well into his warmup, when the New York Athletic Club's Paul Mascali told him Webb was in the race. Until that moment, Holthaus was utterly at ease, readying for an inconsequential rust-buster for the year ahead. "But when they dropped that bombshell on us," he recalls, "I immediately got butterflies in my stomach. I thought, Oh, brother. No one wants to get beat by a high-schooler."

Still, Holthaus and fellow sub-4 miler Scott Anderson were dismissive of Webb's chances. As seasoned post-collegians, they'd competed against highly touted high-schoolers such as Sharif Karie and Jonathan Riley in well-publicized attempts to go sub-4 in recent years, and all fell short. Says Anderson, "We figured this was the same old routine."

It took exactly one lap for Webb to erase that notion. "He at-tacked that race right from the first lap," Holthaus remembers. "He didn't defer to us older guys at all. He just went right with the rabbit. We knew then that he meant business." Running their season openers, Anderson and Holthaus took a more measured ap-proach. With each lap, they steadily cut into Webb's lead and waited for him to falter. He didn't.

Finally, they got within striking distance. With Kenyan Leonard Mucheru galloping away uncontested and Webb on 4-minute pace, all eyes were on him and the race for second. Holthaus and An-derson picked up the pace, and with one lap to go were down by only 5 meters. Holthaus says, "That woke both of us up, and then the whole pride thing came into play. We both caught up to Webb going into the final curve. I was in the inside lane, and as we came off the final turn, I felt like I had another gear, but I was boxed in. I thought, Oh, man, it'll be horrible to lose it like this, but luckily I asked Scott to move out a little bit, for whatever it was worth, and they drifted out just enough to open a little room on the in-side." To Holthaus's relief, he managed to sneak past on the rail and run clear to the finish. Webb summoned his own pride, though, to hold off a hard-charging Anderson all the way to the end, fin-ishing third.

Pandemonium ensued. Webb had done it. Not only was his 3:59.86 the new national high school indoor record, it was also the first-ever indoor sub-4 by a schoolboy. As soon as the news broke, Webb became the personification of hope. At last, an American runner had emerged with the talent and the chutzpah to close the chasm that existed between American milers and Mucheru and his fellow Africans.

TAKING DOWN RYUN'S RECORD

When Ryun broke 4 minutes for the first time, in the spring of his junior year in high school, his life changed. "Suddenly, having run 4 minutes as a high school junior just a month beyond my 17th birthday, there began to be instant national recognition. In another 3 months, *Sports Illustrated* would, incredibly, choose me for their

cover, and from that moment on such notoriety followed me wher-
ever I went. Hardly a day went by when some Kansas paper or
magazine did not run some kind of story on 'the amazing kid from
Wichita.' Letters and phone calls began to pour in, and in one sense
my life ceased to be my own."

Webb's experience mirrored Ryun's. Raczko says, "From that
point on things were different in terms of what attention Alan got.
From January 20 through June, not one day went by without some
type of media request." The question was obvious: Could Webb
take down Ryun's record?

By late May, Webb was physically ready to take a shot at Ryun's
record in the Prefontaine Classic in Eugene, Oregon. He had
demonstrated that he had the strength. At his district meet in Virginia, he recorded one of the most remarkable triples in high
school history when he won the 1600 in 4:06 after going out in 2:14
for the first 800, followed by a swift 49 seconds for the open
quarter and capped with a 1:49 for the 800. And he proved to
Raczko that he had the speed in his last workout when he ran 6 by
400 meters in an astonishing 54 seconds. And then he did one
more. Raczko loosened the reins, letting Webb cut loose only in the
final straightaway. He ran a 52.

The more pressing question was whether Webb was mentally
prepared to go out and race the likes of Hicham el Guerrouj and
Olympic bronze medalist Bernard Lagat. El G, as El Guerrouj is
called, promised a hot race when he declared his intentions to van-
quish former world record holder Noureddine Morceli's time of
3:50.86—the fastest time ever run outdoors in the United States.
The field, full of Olympic finalists and 3:50 milers, would be
fighting turf battles of their own. Unlike Ryun in 1965, Webb had
no pretensions about beating the world's best milers. He hoped
only to be in the mix and have a shot at Ryun's record.

So Raczko worried, "Was it safe to tell Alan to hang in the back
and be concerned only about his pace? As competitive as he is, that
is something I really had to put in his mind and instill in him. I
even told him, 'You'll probably be in last place after the quarter, but
that's okay if you're running your pace.'"

Raczko had Webb visualize any number of scenarios so he'd be ready for them all. By race day, Raczko sensed Webb was ready. He knew Webb wouldn't back down because of all the big-name athletes in the field. He read Webb's demeanor for telltale signs of his mental state: "A lot of kids in that position, they're like, Whoa. He was nervous, but it was a positive nervousness. He gets excited. He can't wait to go. That's a real key."

Across the country, many of the nation's top collegiate milers huddled around their televisions to watch the race unfold. Villanova's duo of Ryan Hayden and Adrian Blincoe had the afternoon off and tuned in to watch. At best, they thought Webb would run 3:57, and perhaps 3:56 if everything played out perfectly.

Webb lined up in the middle of the field. The pre-race favorites, El G and Lagat, were at the end of the line, right next to the rabbits (runners who set the pace for a few laps before dropping out). Immediately, the rabbits bolted for the lead off the start. El G and Lagat went right behind them. Webb was engulfed by the pack as he shot for the turn. Halfway around the bend, he'd been safely shot out the back door, with only miler Ibrahim Aden behind him.

By 400 meters, the rabbits had gapped the field. El Guerrouj led the milers through in 54.9 seconds, with Lagat off his right shoulder. Webb, having been passed by Aden, came through in last, looking extremely relaxed and at ease—and on pace at 58.1.

Down the backstretch, Webb passed two-time U.S. Olympian Jason Pyrah. He continued on pace toward the half-mile mark, making up ground on the pack as the pace slowed up front. He hit the half in 1:57.7, right on the back of the pack—and on pace.

On the curve he passed Aden, exerting no additional effort but maintaining his rhythm. He settled in behind Canadian Olympian Graham Hood on the backstretch, biding his time. He maintained his position down the homestretch and moved toward the outside of lane 1. He hit the final lap in 2:58.

Webb then exploded around the corner and instantly started flying past his competitors. Meet announcer Scott Davis could barely contain himself. "I can still see him moving out at the start of that fourth lap and moving past those guys like they were standing still," he remembers. "I remember blurting out something like, 'El G has come through in 2:55,' and then 'look at Alan Webb!' "

In their dorm at Villanova, Hayden and Blincoe went haywire. They were out of their seats and yelling for Webb.

All told, Webb passed a half-dozen world-class milers around the turn and down the backstretch, including defending NCAA champion Bryan Berryhill of Colorado State. Berryhill couldn't believe his eyes. "I saw that little bastard fly by me, and I thought, Come on, I'm not that bad. A high school guy just passed me? But I couldn't close it. He was flying. He took everybody by surprise there."

Webb continued his surge on the final curve, passing Adil Kaouch of Morocco and Raymond Yator of Kenya. Davis stopped announcing altogether. "When it's that noisy up there, there's no sense. When a Hayward crowd gets that worked up, there's no sense trying to talk over them."

Webb hit the homestretch in fourth, with only El G, Lagat, and Michigan alumnus Kevin "Sully" Sullivan ahead of him. Sully didn't hear the crowd and had no idea who was behind him. He just wanted to win. He picked up the pace in the homestretch and flew by Lagat.

Webb started feeling the effort down the homestretch, and Kaouch rallied to his shoulder. Ahead, Sully kept closing on El G, but the gap was too large. El G won and Sully crossed in second. Webb and Kaouch battled for fourth, gaining on Lagat. But Lagat was just out of reach and crossed the finish line as Webb and Kaouch approached in tandem, right on his heels. Kaouch leaned for the finish and just edged Webb for fourth.

Webb staggered across the line, mouth agape, and wobbled a few steps before regaining his composure. The television announcers were in shock at what they'd just seen. They awaited the scoreboard display of Webb's official time.

As everyone waited, El G walked over to Webb and pinched his earlobe to get his attention. He gave Webb a congratulatory hug and raised his arm with his toward the west grandstand at historic Hayward Field. And then the crowd roared. The television announcer screamed, "YES!" And Webb smiled as he watched his time flash on the scoreboard: 3:53.43.

Davis bellowed out the news that Ryun's record was history. He then glanced down press row and saw one reporter after another with tears in their eyes. "They just never thought they'd see something like that," he says.

At Villanova, Blincoe and Hayden sat stunned. Their reaction was just as visceral, just as immediate. For the next hour, they were glued to the couch, trying to digest what they'd seen. Only after the initial shock wore off did they dare to consider the next logical thought: How, then, do you possibly top that?

MARCH

CHAPTER:01

STARTING OVER

I arrive at the University of Michigan during the first week of March 2002, at the beginning of the outdoor track season. A handful of athletes will compete at the NCAA Indoor Track and Field Championships in Fayetteville, Arkansas, in a few days, but for the vast majority of collegiate and post-collegiate runners in the United States, the spring outdoor track season has arrived.

Only it doesn't feel like it in Ann Arbor, Michigan. Old Man Winter is hanging on something fierce.

Practice starts in an hour, at 3:30 P.M. After a 2-day cross-country drive, I'm loath to spend any more time driving my little jalopy around campus. So I walk to the athletic department to try to catch Michigan coach Ron Warhurst before practice. I find his office door open, and, as I peek in, I spot him hunting and pecking at his keyboard.

I knock. He turns, "Christopher!" He grins broadly and waves me in. I take a seat on his couch beside a rag-tag pile of old newspaper clippings and track magazines. I notice a few All-America plaques on the wall from Warhurst's early days at Michigan. I know they're hardly representative of his total haul: In his 27 years with the university, his athletes have won 94 All-America honors in cross country and track and field combined.

Warhurst looks as I remember him from my visit last November, when I traveled here for an initial visit to talk up my book project and get everyone on board. As we chitchat about my trip and his runners, I listen to his deep baritone voice, gravelly from years of smoking. His laughter erupts freely and often in an infectious cackle. An ex-Marine, Warhurst has both the authoritative air and the incisive wit of a drill sergeant, and he brings a drill sergeant's old-school approach to his coaching. He coaches on feel and instinct and tests the limits, both psychological and physical, of his athletes. Yet at times, he's also remarkably collegial.

On his desk sits a framed wedding photo of him and his wife, Kalli. It wasn't too long ago that Coach Warhurst thought he'd die a bachelor, but now, this May, at age 59, the decorated Vietnam vet will become a father for the first time.

For fatherhood, he's had practice. In coming months, I'll hear from multitudes of Michigan trackmen, some of whose names I see on the wall above me, who will tell me how Warhurst not only coached them to great performances but also helped steward them to manhood.

Also in the next few months, Warhurst will face the greatest challenge of his career, one that will test all the assumptions and tenets of his three decades of coaching. That challenge will revolve around Alan Webb, his newest track sensation.

ALAN WEBB: MAKING A COMEBACK

The phone rings. Warhurst takes the call and I duck out. I walk briskly across the parking lot from the athletic building to the University of Michigan Indoor Track Building to await the arrival of Webb and the rest of the Wolverines. The building is like a large airplane hangar, and, at first glance, I think I'm alone.

I notice a couple of old bleachers. As I walk past them, I notice movement out of the corner of my eye. "Hey!" Webb yells to me from beyond the second set of bleachers. Although practice won't start for another half-hour, Webb is already here, stretching to ready his body for the upcoming workout. He springs up, bounds over, and greets me warmly.

Webb didn't compete this past winter due to a nagging Achilles tendon injury that first flared in December, persisted through the winter, and finally forced him to take a 2-week layoff from running. As we chat, I give him a once-over, searching for signs that this training break has softened his powerful physique. I see no marked changes from when I saw him in the fall. And I'll never forget what I witnessed then, 5 months ago.

It was in November 2001, the week after Webb won the Big Ten Cross Country Championships. He was preparing to run the NCAA regional qualifying meet en route to the NCAA Cross Country Championships. Webb's teammates told me that he had been demolishing workout after workout all fall, consistently running times that boggled the mind. Yet I was still unprepared for how indefatigable and indomitable he looked.

That day, I watched in awe as Webb ran a better Michigan (a workout that Warhurst's harriers have been running for some two decades) than anyone else ever had. The Michigan tests the range of a runner's talents, requiring the speed to devour track intervals of 1 mile and 400, 800, and 1200 meters, plus the stamina to endure punishing 1¼-mile road runs between the track intervals. Essentially, they run *hard* for just under 7 miles, with little break between repeats.

With extraordinary control, Webb ran incredibly fast splits of

4:19, 0:54, 2:04, and 3:06 for the track work. He raved afterward about how much he had progressed since he ran his famed 3:53 mile (in the Prefontaine Classic), how in just half a year he'd made huge strength gains while preserving the ballistic speed that allowed him to run a 54-second 400-meter sprint while his teammates could manage nothing faster than a 58. "I felt so in control of my stride," he said after the workout. "I've never felt that much in control of my body, ever, even last year at the end of outdoor [track season]."

It seemed that attending Michigan was agreeing with Webb, propelling his running to yet another amazing level.

Coach Warhurst was just as excited about Webb's progress. Although Webb's fall training was designed to prepare him to run 10,000 meters—not the mile—at the NCAA Cross Country Championships, he had adapted so well to the training and had such natural speed that Warhurst knew Webb could go on to stun the world with a much faster mile time.

"He can run a 4-minute mile right now," Warhurst told me after that spectacular workout. "So? I'm thinking [he can run] under 3:50. Everyone else in the world wants to know when he will run under 3:50. Well, it's gonna come, it's gonna happen, but I don't want it to happen next week. I want it to be at the NCAA outdoor 1500 or at the Penn Relays or in the summer. The summer is the key. I have to train him not only to represent Michigan. I have to train him to represent the United States."

To train Webb to reach his potential, Warhurst planned a series of workouts to test both his mental and physical limits. "Basically, I want to see how far he can go without breaking down, and I want to see how he responds to the training. He's going to get faster by getting stronger to sustain the basic leg speed. It's simple, simple for me. And it basically starts with cross country to develop the strength."

Then, in December, Webb's success began to unravel. After pushing hard, he injured his Achilles. He battled the injury throughout the winter.

I know that now he fears another layoff. Spring track season is *his* season. The mile is *his* race. He doesn't want to do anything to his body that would jeopardize this.

So, at the track building, I find him cautiously easing back into his running regimen. Today's task: 4 miles. This is child's play for him, but he's clearly excited to be running again. I watch him as he completes his pre-run stretches. Webb moves from one drill to the next with vitality, a boyish sense of excitement. As I marvel at his intensity, I realize that his previous accomplishments have done little to satiate his drive. Rather, they've whetted his appetite for more.

KEVIN SULLIVAN: WORLD-CLASS MILER

Webb, of course, isn't the only one here for practice. Over on the far turn, quietly going about his own stretching regimen, is 1998 University of Michigan graduate Kevin Sullivan—"Sully" to all who know him. Although he now volunteers to help coach the middle-distance and distance runners, Sully is an athlete first and a coach second. A world-class miler, he finished fifth in the 1500 meters in the 2000 Olympic Games.

He's one of three professional world-class middle-distance runners now training with Warhurst in Ann Arbor, and he's one of the main reasons that Alan Webb decided to attend school and run track and cross country here. Of course, Coach Warhurst had wooed Webb by cultivating a relationship with his high school coach, Scott Raczko. But because Sully and other top milers already trained at Michigan, Webb knew he would be training with the best sub-4-minute milers in the country. That could only help him achieve his dreams.

Sully's a quiet guy. He's so reserved and unassuming that he's easy to overlook, especially next to Webb, who, as the *It* guy in American track and field, commands the media's attention. Sully's anonymity in the United States is also a product of his nationality: He's Canadian. That he is a Canadian star in a sport that barely resonates with his hockey-mad countrymen makes him obscure enough to Canadians, let alone Americans. But anonymity suits his temperament. Sully trains not in hopes of fame or celebrity. Rather, he trains for the singular purpose of beating the world's best milers. He dreams of climbing a few places higher at the 2004 Olympic Games than he did in 2000, high enough to land a cherished spot on the podium. The coterie of world-class runners at Michigan is here, in large part, because of Sully.

A native of Brantford, Ontario (best known as the hometown of hockey god Wayne Gretzky), Sully entered the University of Michigan in 1993 as the most sought-after recruit in North America. Before going to Michigan, Sully, at age 18, ran a sparkling 3:39.11 in the 1500 meters—equivalent to a 3:56 or 3:57 mile—to win the bronze medal at the World Junior Championships (for athletes 19 and younger).

Warhurst's signing of Sully was a remarkable coup. Since his first year as coach at Michigan in 1974, he had distinguished himself as the orchestrator of one of the nation's premier distance-running programs. He could boast of coaching myriad NCAA All-Americans in events from the 3000 meters on up. His athletes include NCAA champions such as Brian Diemer (3000-meter steeplechase, 1983) and John Scherer (5000-meter indoor, 1989, and 10,000-meter outdoor, 1988 and 1989). Moreover, his cross country teams excelled year after year. From 1974 to 1992, his teams won four Big Ten titles in cross country, qualified for the NCAA Championships 13 times, and finished in the top 10 at the NCAA Cross Country Championships five times. Although Warhurst had certainly coached sub-4-minute milers, his forte was developing distance runners.

Sully single-handedly erased any notion that Warhurst couldn't develop milers. At Michigan, he won the NCAA indoor mile title twice (1995 and 1998) and the outdoor title once (1998). Moreover, he did it while also excelling on the world stage. After his sophomore track season in 1995, he competed in the 1500 meters in the World Track and Field Championships and finished fifth.

Upon graduation in 1998, Sully signed a sizeable endorsement contract with Reebok, yet he remained in Ann Arbor under Warhurst's tutelage. He was rewarded for his decision to stay. In July 2000, in Oslo, Norway, he ran his fastest mile—3:50.26.

TIM BROE: SUB-4 MILER

By the summer of 2001, two other professional middle-distance runners had gravitated to Ann Arbor to train alongside Sully. The first was Illinois native and University of Alabama graduate Tim Broe. Broe won the NCAA steeplechase title as an Alabama senior in 2000 and then missed the U.S. Olympic team by the barest of margins, finishing fourth at the Olympic Trials, just one place away from making the team.

Broe signed a contract with Sully's agent, Mark Wetmore, shortly thereafter, and when he asked who should guide his career, Wetmore suggested he give Warhurst a call. They began collaborating by fax and phone, and Broe's running took off.

In January 2002, after several training stints at Michigan, Broe moved to Ann Arbor to train full-time with Sully directly under Warhurst's supervision and serve as a volunteer assistant coach. He proceeded to go on a remarkable tear. On January 27, he ran a 7:39.23 at the Adidas Boston Indoor Games, breaking the U.S. indoor 3000-meter record of 7:39.94 set in 1989 by Steve Scott. Scott still holds the American mile record (3:47.6) that he set in 1982.

On February 9, Broe won the USA Cross Country Championship in the 4-K. And on March 1, he won the 3000 meters at the USA Indoor Track and Field Championships in 7:50.09, then came back a mere 2 hours later to finish third in the mile in 3:58.81, only 1 second off the winning time.

Although he's heading south for a vacation tomorrow, I expect Broe to show up at the indoor track in just a little while.

PAUL MCMULLEN: MISSING IN ACTION

While I await Broe, I don't hold out much hope of seeing Warhurst's most quixotic charge, Paul McMullen. McMullen was a fierce rival of Sully's as a collegian when he competed for Eastern Michigan University, just miles down the road in Ypsilanti. Like Sully, McMullen went on to run professionally, earning high praise for making the finals in the 1500 meters at the 1995 World Championships, where he finished 10th, and for qualifying for the U.S. Olympic team in 1996.

In 1997, McMullen suffered what appeared to be a career-ending injury when his right foot slipped under a lawn mower, severing parts of two toes and cutting through his big toe to the bone. He feared he was finished, but only a year later, he returned to win the U.S. indoor mile title in 3:55.81.

In June 2000, however, after finishing a dispiriting 10th in the first round of the 1500 meters at the Olympic Trials, McMullen decided he had had enough. He didn't run again until January 2001, when he began jogging to lose some of the girth he'd gained in the intervening months. As his fitness progressed, though, so did his ambition, and in April 2001, he called Warhurst to see if he could come to train with Sully at Michigan.

Warhurst obliged, and over the next 3 months, McMullen followed Warhurst's program to the letter while dieting to get back into racing shape. He began his comeback with a 3:48.51 time for the 1500 at the Len Paddock Invitational in Ann Arbor on May 11, 2001. From then on, he cut his times as rapidly as he dropped his weight. Although with Warhurst for only 4 months, he ended his phoenix-like summer track campaign with another 10th-place finish at the World Track and Field Championships and new personal bests of 1:45.71 for 800 meters and 3:33.89 for 1500 meters.

In late October, after a well-deserved rest, McMullen reappeared at the indoor track building, 25 pounds heavier and ready to begin his buildup for the 2002 summer campaign. Soon afterward, however, he injured his right upper gluteus muscle and vanished from sight. He hasn't trained with the Michigan team since. I wonder if, or when, I'll see him again.

I wander over to Sully and soon discover that while he's attired in full tights, jacket, and gloves, he may not join Webb for a run this afternoon. On February 17, Sully ran a 1500 in Birmingham, England. During the race, Morocco's Hachlaf Abdelkader shoved him in the back, and he landed awkwardly on his right foot, jamming his hip. His lower back has been sore ever since, and no matter what he does, he can't seem to shake the pain. That the pain appears only when he's running makes it a bit more confounding, but since an athlete of Sully's caliber often has acute aches and pains, it's something he's just monitoring for now, not something to cause him sleepless nights.

NATE BRANNEN: WINDING DOWN

At 3:30, Webb's roommate, Nathan Brannen, enters the gym. While most of his teammates are heading out for a 10-mile run, he's hooking up with Webb for an easy 4-miler. It's odd that their paths are crossing today, because they're heading in opposite directions. While Webb is preparing for the spring campaign, Brannen is winding down his training after a superb indoor season. In 2 days he'll be deplaning in Arkansas, to run the mile at the NCAA Indoor Track and Field Championships.

Neither Webb nor Brannen could have envisioned this scenario at the end of November. Webb had just completed a fall cross country campaign that drew raves from start to finish. He dominated his opposition all fall, won the Big Ten title, and finished 11th at the NCAA Cross Country Championships—a superb performance for a miler.

While Webb continually exceeded any notion of what his limitations might be, Brannen languished in the back of the pack. In November, when Webb ran times of 4:19, 0:54, and 2:04 in the Michigan, Brannen ran relatively pedestrian times of 4:39, 0:62, and 2:12.

For Brannen, the repeated beatings were tough to swallow. He had arrived on campus with impeccable credentials of his own. He, too, was a sub-4-minute miler before he ever sported Michigan's maize-and-blue, block-M singlet. Yet nearly all of the attention, from both Warhurst and the media, centered on Webb.

While Webb's sub-4 miles at South Lakes were heavily publicized, Brannen's sub-4 run as a high-schooler in Canada received scant attention from the U.S. media. And truth be told, an attempt at a sub-4 mile was an afterthought for him; his focus was on the 800 and 1500 meters. In the 800-meter final at the Canadian National Championships, Brannen amazed his compatriots with a sterling second-place finish in 1:46.6. In the process, he defeated 2000 Olympian Zach Whitmarsh and earned a spot on the Canadian team for the World Championships in Edmonton in August.

"That race," says Brannen, "opened new doors for me. And it opened people's eyes as to who I could race against." Among those he impressed was the meet director for the following week's Halifax Invitational, who invited Brannen to his meet to run the mile. Brannen agreed to go as long as they also invited his teammate Matt Kerr, a former star at the University of Arkansas, to rabbit (set the pace) for him.

Brannen decided to try to be the third Canadian high-schooler to go sub-4. Although the meet attracted plenty of media attention locally in Halifax, the setting was markedly more low-key than when Webb took down Jim Ryun's record at the Prefontaine Classic in June 2001. Brannen lined up for the mile, the last race of the evening, with only a sparse crowd on hand to support him. Yet, "everybody knew what we were trying to do; they were cheering us on," Brannen says. "They definitely wanted to see a 4-minute mile, so that was pretty cool."

Brannen entered the race planning to run consistent 60-second laps, called even splits in track jargon, for three laps before kicking home on the last lap to sneak in under 4 minutes. But, flushed with adrenaline, he found his plan immediately going awry. Kerr nervously skittered through the first lap in 56 seconds, with Brannen right on his heels. The quick lap left Brannen "hurting big time" and doubting that he would have enough in the tank at the end of the race.

Brannen regrouped as Kerr settled into the 60-second pace on the second lap. They slowed even more through the agonizing third lap, yet due to their early pace, they still hit the ¾-mile mark at 2:58—under 4-minute-mile pace. With lungs searing and legs burning, Brannen went for it. He took off.

"I got to 300 [meters] to go and I just started rigging [fading]," he told me. He was all alone, racing only the clock to the line and slowing with each step. He grimaced as he bore down on the final straightaway. The clock turned to 3:59 as he approached the line, and then, what seemed like a long instant later, he crossed it.

Brannen collapsed to the track, uncertain of the verdict and too tired to care. For 10 or 15 minutes, he lay in pain, waiting to hear the official verdict. Finally, the announcement came: "It's official. It's a sub-4-minute mile!" The crowd went crazy. At 3:59.85, he'd made it by the slimmest of margins.

Two months later, on August 4, Brannen's career reached its zenith when he represented Canada at the World Track and Field Championships. Other than the Olympic Games, there is no greater track competition than those championships.

"That day," says Brannen, "was easily the most nerve-wracking day of my life." That Canada was hosting the event in Edmonton only compounded his anxiety. He warmed up on the track behind the main stadium before being called to the first check-in. Surrounded by the world's best half-milers, Brannen stretched and jogged to loosen up.

Finally, 2 or 3 minutes before his race, he was granted access to the track to perform a few strides. In an instant, his 800-meter heat at the World Championships would begin. He moved to his box in lane 5 as they began announcing the competitors. More than 70,000 fans, mostly Canadian, filled the stadium to capacity. They announced Brannen, "and it just went nuts in there. I put my head down, and I thought I was gonna cry. It was just amazing. It was the weirdest feeling I'd ever had. It was everything all mixed into one: nervousness, excitement, just a feeling I'd never had in a place I'd never been in."

Only four runners advanced to the finals that day, and Brannen finished fifth. Yet he managed to beat the defending NCAA champion, Botswana's Otukile Lekote, a student at South Carolina University. He took solace in that. He also managed to hang in with the world's fastest half-milers. It proved he had the physical gifts and the gumption to compete with superior athletes in track's toughest crucible.

As he left the track that day, he had one thought: "In 2003, I'm coming back [to the World Championships], and I'm making the semi. There's no way around it." A few weeks later, flush with confidence, he was off to the University of Michigan—and a disappointing cross country season.

DISAPPOINTMENTS AND DECISIONS

Brannen debuted at Michigan in the fall with an acceptable 18th-place finish at the Great American Cross Country Festival in North Carolina, but at the Michigan home meet, in front of his trusted coach of old, Pete Grinbergs, he "got demolished."

He searched for an end to his poor form. He looked for redemption at the Big Tens a week later. It didn't happen. Webb once again ran away with the laurels, while Brannen trudged home in 40th. It crushed him. "That was the lowest point I've ever been. I wanted to stop. I didn't want to run nationals. I didn't want to go and embarrass myself. I wasn't even in the top five [on the squad]," he explained.

He began to revisit his decision to attend Michigan. In his junior year in high school, he was certain he would go to Arkansas. Without a doubt, Arkansas had the richest middle-distance track tradition in the NCAA. But it didn't have the academic reputation of some of the other schools that were courting him. Michigan was close to home, and its academics were top-notch.

He'd already met Coach Warhurst at the Canadian National Track and Field Championships a year earlier. Says Brannen, "I saw Kevin [Sullivan] at the meet with an old scraggly guy with this blue Michigan hat that looked like it must have been 5 years old, and it was on the side of his head. I was thinking, Who's the old dude? Is that his dad or is that the Michigan coach? I warmed up, and right before the meet he said, 'Good luck, Nate, and Go, Blue.' I realized that must be Ronnie."

He instantly liked Warhurst. "I figured Ron must be doing something right to keep one of the best runners in the world after he graduated. I knew he had to be a decent coach." The enticement to attend Michigan became stronger and stronger. Says Brannen, "I kept hearing we might get Tim Broe, Paul McMullen, and Alan Webb, in addition to all the other guys there. I thought, What better place to go than Michigan? You have five of the best runners in the world there, plus a coach who kept Sully around." Collectively, the group would be the strongest middle-distance training group in North America.

But that fall, beaten and fatigued, Brannen wasn't sure he wanted to stick around Ann Arbor. It was a feeling that one of his teammates—Alan Webb—would also come to experience in the months of the spring track season.

The fall cross country season ended disastrously for Brannen at the NCAA meet, when he finished a dismal 180th. He had had enough. He spoke to his old coach Pete Grinbergs and told him he wasn't sure he'd made the right decision and that he wanted to come home.

Now, put yourself in Grinbergs' shoes. There's a joke among professional coaches in Canada that goes, "Us guys in Canada, we're really only high school coaches." It underscores the fact that after years of toil, Canada's top runners invariably head south and accept scholarships to run for American universities. It pains Grinbergs because he knows how to coach; he's coached Olympians, national team members, you name it. But more often than not, his best talent "is gone at the most important developmental time in their lives. It's really hard to let them go."

"You realize that with the best ones, there's a powerful force out there and you're only part of it," he told me. "When they make it to the Olympics, they have at least a dozen voices giving them input. You have to abdicate control, wait for your moments, and then get in there. My focus with my athletes is not only on the training but also on individuals, psychologically and spiritually, so they become independent and empowered."

And so Grinbergs listened to Brannen. As he did, he thought, If Nate's not willing to put up with a little adversity, what the hell is going to happen? The coach told him to stay put. Things would turn around. He was convinced Brannen would find his groove during the indoor track season. But to do that, he had to regain his belief in his own gifts. In Grinbergs' opinion, this would require one monumental step: "He had to dispel this myth about Webb."

Brannen went home for Christmas determined to regroup and turn things around. For 3 weeks, he trained with his old teammates and had fun. He returned to Michigan with a renewed sense of purpose.

Says Brannen, "That was the turning point—just getting out of here for a bit and training with my old coach again." He proceeded to tear through the winter indoor campaign, set indoor personal bests of 1:48 and 4:01 in the 800 and mile, and qualify to run both events at the NCAA Championships. Moreover, he found his body responding to Warhurst's training. The same strength workouts that had put him under during cross country were now empowering him.

COURAGE, STRENGTH, AND BRAVERY

Now, 48 hours before the NCAA Championships, Brannen runs through Ann Arbor's streets at an effortless 6-minute-mile clip, with Webb at his side. He knows he's back on track toward cementing his reputation as one of the finest middle-distance talents in the world. No longer is he plagued by the doubts that consumed him through the fall. Yet, in the back of his mind, he still wonders if he can measure up to Webb. If Webb hadn't injured his Achilles early in the winter, forcing him to redshirt (not compete and retain the season of eligibility to be used in a 5th year) the indoor season, he might have some answers.

For now, Brannen does his best to excise these thoughts from his mind. His focus is on running the mile in Fayetteville in 2 days, in a race that will go on without Webb.

In a flash, Brannen and Webb are back at Ferry Field, the University of Michigan outdoor track. The good news is that Webb ran freely, without pain in his Achilles. The bad news is that Brannen felt an ache in his left foot. He shrugs it off and heads to the track to do some quick 200-meter repeats, his final tune-up before the NCAAs.

Webb, meanwhile, hits the weight room, a facility the Michigan trackmen share with some of Michigan's other teams, for a hard lifting session. It's here, as Webb strips down to a sleeveless T-shirt, that I see the vast strength gains he's made in the weight room during the winter. For a middle-distance runner, his arms appear titanic.

That's not all that catches my eye. On his right shoulder is a freshly inked black tattoo, a Chinese character that looks like a runner in full flight.

I ask about it. Webb tells me that he recently went to a tattoo parlor with Brannen and fellow Wolverine freshman distance runners Tarn Leach and Sean "Seanymo" Moore to participate in what has become a rite of passage for Warhurst's boys. Sully started the tradition as an undergrad when he tattooed a Canadian flag with a Michigan block M atop it on his right hip. Distance runners in each subsequent class have emulated him, getting variations of his block M tattooed onto their right hips.

Brannen, Leach, and Moore all took their turns in the chair, having their loyalty to Coach Warhurst, Michigan, class after class of Michigan harriers, and each other inked into their skin. Webb chose to forgo branding himself with the Michigan M and in its stead had a large black Chinese character tattooed on his right shoulder. He tells me the tattoo stands for courage, strength, and bravery.

Indeed, I think it does take those qualities to find one's own way and take the road less traveled. In the ensuing months, as Webb fights to reclaim his standing as the world's preeminent young miler, he'll find he needs all of them—courage, strength, and bravery—in spades.

CHAPTER:02

THE AGONY OF DEFEAT

J ust 2 days after meeting Webb and the other runners at
Michigan, I'm off with Nate Brannen and Coach Ron Warhurst
to Fayetteville, Arkansas, for the NCAA Indoor Track and Field
Championships.

Because of his Achilles injury during the winter season, Webb
didn't qualify for this meet. But Brannen did, running a 4:01 mile in
February at the Adidas Boston Indoor Games. He's Michigan's lone
representative in Fayetteville. Tomorrow, he will compete against

the 15 fastest collegiate milers in the country. And Webb is back in Ann Arbor.

Moments after waking the following morning, Brannen sits on the couch in the living room of his two-bedroom suite at the Residence Inn. He thinks about his upcoming event and tells me that he feels slightly relieved, as he's running in the second of two heats this evening. The top three finishers in each heat and the runners with the next four fastest times will advance to tomorrow's final. Since Brannen is running in the second heat, he'll know precisely how fast he needs to run to advance. Should the first heat go slowly, a fast early pace in the second will ensure that virtually all the competitors in that heat advance.

Several hours later, at the track, Brannen gets some ice and electric stimulation therapy for his tender left foot. Despite daily treatment, the pain along the top of his foot has continued to worsen. It was severe enough a few days ago to cause him to do his last session before nationals—a set of three 200s—in his training flats instead of his spikes.

That session impressed Warhurst. When Brannen finished the last 200 in 24 seconds, his fastest 200 since the World Championships last August, Warhurst shook his head and looked at his watch in disbelief. Brannen looked so relaxed, no different from when he runs 200s in 28 seconds. That workout gave the coach his first glimpse of Brannen's tremendous acceleration. Brannen, however, didn't share Warhurst's enthusiasm. He complained that he felt flat, that he "didn't feel any pop." Had he worn spikes, he might have felt faster.

The soreness has allowed doubt to creep into his psyche. He's entering the most significant competition of his collegiate career, and he feels a touch flat. He wonders, What if I'm not sharp? What if it's not the shoes? What if I'm just not on my game? He tries to expunge these thoughts from his mind.

As Brannen undergoes therapy, Warhurst scans the heat sheets for the first time and begins to formulate a plan for Brannen. A short while later, Brannen finishes his treatment and heads out the door for a mile jog to test his foot. It's not good: He feels a shooting pain each time he toes off. Determined to give it a go tonight, he prays that pre-race adrenaline and some ibuprofen will mask the pain. Now, though, he's concerned. "It's the worst it's been yet," he says.

Later, in his room at the Residence Inn, Warhurst looks at the start list for tonight's mile one last time. He then calls Brannen and asks him to come to his room to discuss strategy.

Running in the second of two eight-man heats with Brannen are two runners from Weber State, Jeremy Tolman and Joel Atwater; Warhurst believes they hold the key to Brannen's fate. He tells Brannen that Alabama's stellar Kenyan, David Kimani, and Stanford's Don Sage are both doubling tonight and running the distance medley relay after the mile prelims. As a result, both will favor a slow pace in the mile so they'll be as fresh as possible for the relay. The veteran of the field, 25-year-old German Christian Goy of Illinois State, is doubling in the 3000 meters, so he too can be expected to prefer a dawdling pace.

Peeking over his reading glasses, Warhurst looks Brannen in the eye and says, "I bet the two guys from Weber State will team up to make sure the pace isn't too slow. If these guys know what the times are [from the first heat], I think these are the guys that are gonna want to make a run at it." The Weber runners are steeplechasers, runners who rely on their strength, not their speed. Therefore, they'll be unlikely to sit and wait for the race to come down to a kick.

Warhurst looks again at the sheet and thinks of Kimani, who must run four races in 2 days. He tells Brannen to shadow him tonight, if possible. "You gotta get on Kimani's ass. He's gonna want to get as clean a race as possible in this one."

Warhurst worries because he has no way of knowing what the competitors in the first heat will run. In years past, the field was full of familiar faces, and Warhurst had watched them often enough to know their tendencies. But he knows very little about this year's field, led as it is by unknowns like Eric Garner, a lanky sophomore from the University of Washington. Garner is the top-seeded runner in the first heat by virtue of his 3:58.93 mile at the end of March. That was his first-ever sub-4 mile, and Warhurst has no idea how he will react to the pressure of the NCAA Championships. As he looks at the list for heat one, the coach thinks that it will go slow, since there is a host of newcomers who probably won't risk fading off a fast pace, but then again . . .

Brannen matter-of-factly tells Warhurst, "I really don't care [what the first heat runs]. If I have to go 3:59, I'm gonna do that. If I have do 4:05, that's okay, too."

Warhust thinks about it some more and then focuses on how he wants Brannen to position himself in there. "The thing about it is, the field's not big enough that you get stuck behind a lot of people. But just stay off the curb, you know what I'm saying?"

Brannen nods.

"Then if someone makes a quick move and accelerates, and you're trapped, you gotta wait for the whole army to get by you, then do a real hard acceleration to get back in it. If you're off the curb when somebody moves, you can respond then instead of waiting to get around the curve onto the straightaway.

"You just want to be in position to use your speed in the end. And if there's a logjam with 600 to go, make sure you're in real good position. Don't be behind anybody. Run in lane 2 if you have to. You don't want to take a chance if the pace gets slow that you just get bumped at the end. I don't think it's gonna ever happen— I think you're too fast—but don't put yourself in a position where you have to panic and make a big run for it at the end. I mean there can be four guys coming down the straightaway side by side and I know who's gonna win. There's not a question in that."

Warhurst continues, going through a few different scenarios. Brannen sits impassively, listening. Finally, Warhurst leans forward and says, "Look, there's no reason to overthink it. No matter what they do there [in heat one] you just gotta beat the people in there [in heat two]. You just put yourself in position and run your ass off in the last quarter or 300. I don't give a shit. You just gotta beat the people in there."

LAST-MINUTE JITTERS

An hour before his heat, Brannen heads out for a 2-mile jog. If only he could fast-forward to race time. He hates the anxiety he suffers beforehand.

It's always the same. He thinks maybe he should just tank it and not make the final. Then he could stop worrying and just have fun. But these thoughts are fleeting. Last year he ran huge races, like the Canadian National Championships and the Francophone Games, where he had to run trials and finals. Only once, at the World Championships, did he fail to advance. He takes comfort in the fact that at the Francophone Games, he ran what was at the time his fastest half-mile ever—1:46.9—just to make the final. He's run to the limit before in order to advance. He's prepared to do it tonight.

If only his foot didn't hurt so much. He can't believe he forgot to take his ibuprofen.

Brannen runs past several of his competitors on his pre-race jog. Among them, he passes Garner, the Washington Husky, and Goy, the stoic German, as he circles back toward the track center. He has no idea who they are.

He also sees a tall, thin Kenyan loping around the baseball diamond in his running sweats. Brannen recognizes the figure in an instant. It's Alabama's David Kimani. He knows all about Kimani, thanks to Tim Broe.

Broe loves to tell stories. Whenever he runs with the guys, they know they're in for an earful. One of his favorite subjects is David Kimani. Broe raced him often while Kimani was competing for the University of South Alabama and Broe for the Crimson Tide. It's with reverence that he calls Kimani his "Kenyan Kryptonite."

Thanks in part to Broe's stories, Brannen fears Kimani. Again he reassures himself of his ability to run whatever is necessary to advance to the final.

After his jog, Brannen retreats to the practice corridor to finish his preparation. He begins a series of butt kicks to warm up his legs. All around him, the top collegiate milers in the country are doing the same. There's more chaos and tension here than in the races unfolding on the track.

Brannen has to focus in the midst of all the activity. He slips on the headphones of his MP3 player, and in an instant he's eliminated aural contact with the outside world. He looks straight ahead and down at the track as he does his drills. Twenty minutes before race time, Warhurst walks back from the stands and leans down as Brannen sits against the wall.

"Remember, run through the finish like a cat with turpentine up your ass," he says. "Now, the last thing I'm gonna tell you is don't get boxed in on the curve. Stay wide on the curve and just run a real fast race. I'll tell you what you need to run when you get out there, but chances are, you'll already know what you need to run."

Brannen watches Warhurst leave the practice area. "I'm getting really nervous now, man," he says. He pulls his headphones back over his ears, leans back against the wall, eyes his track spikes, and waits.

JUST ONE GUY

The first heat goes slowly, with Eliud Njubi grabbing the third and last automatic qualifying spot in 4:06.9. Warhurst excitedly leans over the railing and reminds Brannen one last time to stay in it. If he beats one guy and is under 4:06.9, he's in the final. "Now stay off the curve and don't pass on the inside."

Brannen lines up in lane 2, between Weber's Tolman and Stanford's Sage. He gets out last off the start but hits the 200 comfortably in fifth place. As Warhurst expected, one of the Weber runners, Tolman, is leading the field. If it's a fast pace, both Weber State milers may qualify for the final.

Tolman passes the first quarter-mile in 58.7 seconds. Already it appears that the provisional four qualifiers will come from this heat. Tolman leads through the half-mile in 2 minutes even.

Brannen, a lithe 5'8" 128-pounder, is smaller than most of the other runners in the mile field, yet he has managed to hold his own on the outside of lane 5, expending little energy to maintain his position. Only four laps remain. (The indoor track at Arkansas is 200 meters, so the mile race is a shade over eight laps.)

Kimani takes over the lead after the half and slows the pace. Behind him, the pack bunches up. Although they are on 4-minute-mile pace, no one has dropped from the field. They are all keenly aware that, at this speed, they will all make the final— except one.

The pace continues to dawdle as Kimani slows it down before launching into his kick. They hit the 3/4-mile mark in 3:03. Now on the backstretch, the runners start maneuvering for position for the final lap. Brannen tries to move past the runner in front of him, but Georgia Tech's Brendon Mahoney, sitting off Brannen's shoulder, goes first. He traps Brannen between himself and the other runner. Brannen knows he has no choice but to sit and wait for Mahoney to finish his move before he can get out—whenever that moment arises. He tries not to panic.

Only 350 meters remain, and Brannen is now in last place, trapped. Around the turn he spies an opening. He tries to shoot the gap but it closes before he can complete the move. He then moves out to lane 3 on the curve to pass on the outside, but he's lost his momentum. He has been stopping and starting for the last three laps and has nothing to show for his efforts. Worse, the uneven effort is starting to take a toll. His arms begin to flail ever so slightly as he launches another attack.

Around the turn, Brannen again moves to the inside, and Chris Mulvaney of Arkansas, trying to hang on to his second-to-last position, pinches down into lane 1 to prevent the pass. Brannen loses his balance and stumbles right off the track. Again he's lost all momentum. He gets back on the track and chases Mulvaney down the backstretch, a good 2 yards behind the pack. His arms flail and his legs tighten drastically. He tries to regroup and get his form back together. Into the final turn, he manages to make a final desperate bid to pass Mulvaney on his inside shoulder. He's instantly ensnared in a thicket of elbows.

Brannen slows as all the others in the field stretch out toward the tape. He finishes last in 4:03.53. All seven runners ahead of him qualify for the final.

JUST ONE RACE

Exasperated, he tears his jersey out of his shorts and storms off the track toward the practice area with his fingers interlaced across his head. He bends his head down as he sits against the wall.

"All I had to do was beat *one* guy. I couldn't even beat *one* guy," he tells me. "I got knocked off the track and lost my stride and that was it. I was completely out of it. I was running all out and it felt like I wasn't even moving that last 50 [meters]." For all his experience, he ran like someone who's never been here before—like a freshman.

I head back to the stands to see how Warhurst is taking it. "All he had to do was stay on the outside. He tried to pass three times on the inside and had to back off and accelerate," he tells me. "He fartleked [changed speeds] the last quarter-mile. You can't do that when you're running 60-flat pace." He pauses and continues, "That's what happens when you're a freshman and you don't pay attention. You can't pass on the inside in indoor track. There's simply nowhere to go. He ran a 4:03 and the effort was probably more like a 3:56."

Brannen makes his way into the stands to see Warhurst before heading out for a jog. He sits beside him on the bleachers. Warhurst thinks of everything he told him—stay wide, don't panic, don't run behind anybody—and he knows there's nothing he can say that Brannen doesn't already know. So he just shakes his head knowingly, looks over at Brannen, and puts his arm around his shoulders, hugging him.

Brannen heads outside for his last run of the weekend. As soon as he sets off, a flash storm dumps water by the bucketful. Minutes later, soaked to the bone, Brannen laughs at the rain and takes flying leaps into every puddle. "Is that all you got?" he asks. One race does not a career make.

As the evening winds down, Brannen takes a call from Webb and tells him about his race and about Villanova's dominating victory in the medley relay. Webb reassures him that their time is yet to come. "Don't worry, Nate," he says. "We'll get 'em at Penn."

CHAPTER:03

LEAVING THE PAST
BEHIND

Nate Brannen isn't the only miler on Coach Ron Warhurst's mind down in Fayetteville this weekend. As he watches Christian Goy hold off David Kimani over the last 200 meters to win the NCAA mile in 4:00.26, Warhurst can't help but wonder what a healthy Alan Webb might have done to the field in that last 200 meters. If only they had held the championships at the end of the fall season, when Webb was in top form!

Warhurst wonders whether he'll be able to get Webb in the same top condition for the NCAA Outdoor Track and Field Championships in June. He's still at a loss to figure what he might have done differently last fall. He's not sure exactly what pushed Webb's body over the edge far enough to ruin his entire winter indoor season, but he suspects it had something to do with a particular workout Webb completed in mid-December.

WEBB'S ACHILLES' HEEL

It wasn't supposed to be a killer workout. Webb had just completed his first week back at running, just building his mileage again, running 6, 7, or 8 miles a day after taking a week or so off to recharge after the cross country season. Warhurst looked out his office window that afternoon and saw the sun shining brightly.

He told the guys, "We got some nice weather. Go do some hills. Go to the Arb and run two or three hills there and then three or four Harvards."

The Arb hill is a steady, winding dirt path that climbs a little over ¼ mile in Nichols Arboretum, an obscure little park tucked away in Ann Arbor's suburbs. The Harvards are run up Harvard Street, a steep 300-meter cul-de-sac no more than ¼ mile down the road from the top of the path at the arboretum.

Warhurst loves the strength and pop the hills develop in his runners. They've been running up and down these hills for years. And as early in the season as it was, Warhurst didn't have any specific time goals for them.

Webb went with the guys that afternoon and did a couple of Arbs and four Harvards. On the last Harvard, he felt the urge to crank it. He bolted up the last 100 meters of his final climb, and by the time he returned to Ferry Field, he felt some soreness in his Achilles tendon. Warhurst told him, "Okay. Just lighten it up, ice it. Don't run for a day or two."

The next 3 months tested the patience of both Webb and Warhurst, straining the translucent filaments of trust that bind coaches and athletes the world over.

What frustrated Warhurst the most were the constant glimmers of hope. Webb would run one day pain-free, then another, but then soreness would creep in and he'd take a couple of days off. He usually could walk or run on the leg, but when he ran hard, it would act up again.

And run hard he did. In mid-January, Webb did an excellent session with Tim Broe. He ran 4 by 1200 meters at a blistering pace, then followed that with four quarter-miles in 59 seconds. Afterward, Warhurst asked him how he felt, and he said, "It's okay." The next day, the pain had returned.

"That's the kind of rotation we were going through," Warhurst says. "It was never to the point where he told me, 'I can't run on it,' you know. He's telling me as we watch the rest of the NCAAs, 'It's kind of okay,' and I didn't really read it very well at the time, because I didn't know him that well, but he obviously has tremendous pain tolerance."

THE WINTER OF WEBB'S DISCONTENT

As the winter progressed, Webb got closer to his wits' end. All fall he'd been getting fitter and fitter, and by December he was dying to have it translate to the track. His anxiety mounted with each day off and each race skipped. Webb explains, "Everyone was saying, 'Alan, you have to be patient, you're not gonna lose anything, blah, blah, blah.' And I'm thinking, Yeah, I'm not gonna lose anything, but how long is this gonna take? Every time I got to a point where I thought it would be better, I would have the next time goal and it still wouldn't be better, and it just went over and over again, until I finally just took 2 weeks off with no running."

Brannen, Sullivan, and Broe, the guys Webb had come to Ann Arbor to run with and had run circles around in the fall, did not wait around idly for him to heal. That only compounded matters.

As Webb's downtime grew ever longer, he began to question when he'd suffered the injury. Sure, he had blasted that last 100 at the Harvard that day in December, but he'd run that hard tons of times. Running at that pace was nothing new. "I know it didn't happen because of one workout," he says.

So when did it happen? Perhaps he'd been injured in the fall and it simply took a while to show up. "I think that cross country [season] was just really stressful," he says. "We trained really hard. We got a lot accomplished, but it might have been a little bit too much."

As the days wore on, his winter season vanishing, he turned to Warhurst, searching for a plan. He didn't get it. "It wasn't good. Many, many times I just had no idea what I was supposed to be doing, you know. I didn't know how long to take off running, I didn't know what workouts I was supposed to be doing or how I was going to start running again." He pauses, then adds morosely, "What steps was I gonna take to start running—that's what I wanted to know."

As a rule, Warhurst doesn't dispense such information. Other than general advice such as "get in the pool" or "get on the bike," he won't tell an athlete what cross-training to do when injured. He doesn't map out a schedule for a runner to follow until he is back on his feet. Some, like Webb, crave this guidance. But at Michigan, athletes are expected to do some things on their own, and this is one of them.

At a loss for what to do on a day-to-day basis to get back to running, Webb turned to his high school coach, Scott Raczko, for assistance. Says Webb, "I called him and talked to him a lot because he just knows the specifics of it. I would talk to him about exactly what I was doing for cross-training and what I was gonna do to start running again. He was really good about that. Coach Raczko's also really knowledgeable about the physiology of running—what is good and what is not good, generally. [He knows] the high-risk things you can do in running, and the low-risk things. If I ever have a question about that, I know I can talk to him about it."

PAST AND PRESENT

Webb trusts his former coach mostly because Raczko successfully dealt with the first debilitating injury in his running career, a hip strain that caused him to forgo a shot at a sub-4 mile his junior year of high school. Calling it quits then, when Webb was on the brink of such a historic feat, was a difficult decision.

Webb had just run a 4:03 mile, then his fastest time, at the Herbster Track Classic in North Carolina when the injury first surfaced. Coach Raczko watched him doing strides before the race. "We were standing there thinking, Something's not right; he's got a little hitch. You could tell," he says. The injury continued to worsen after that, hobbling Webb so much that he actually lost the 800 meters at the Virginia state meet, running a mediocre 1:51.

Raczko and Webb had already accepted an invitation to run the Prefontaine Classic in Eugene, but Raczko decided to pull the plug. He wasn't willing to mortgage Webb's future for a short-term gain. According to Raczko, "It was a disappointment to Alan, but the nice thing was that we were able to convince him that he had to look long term. We told him, 'Next year you can get all your goals, run in these meets, etc. We're not going to let this stuff happen next year.'"

Webb's hip injury also came on the heels of the best training of his life. Raczko remembers the injury occurring after "a phenomenal week of training. It was one of best training weeks ever." As he searched for the cause of the injury, Raczko discovered that Webb had hurt his hip after they had simultaneously raised the volume and intensity of Webb's work in the same week. Raczko vowed not to repeat that mistake in Webb's senior campaign. He didn't, and the rest is history.

Now, history was repeating itself. Once again, Webb had been injured while putting too much strain on his body—but Warhurst didn't have the base of knowledge that Raczko had. All fall Warhurst had been testing, pushing, pulling, and prying, searching for those limits whose parameters Raczko already knew. So now Webb wonders if he would have been in such a predicament if he had stuck with Raczko and simply stayed to train with the man who engineered his rise to uncharted heights.

GROWING UP

Raczko was not alone in helping Webb cope with his Achilles injury. Throughout the winter, Webb leaned heavily on his father for psychological support. Steve Webb, a Yale grad, is an economist for the World Bank and a former economics professor at the University of Michigan. Alan says, "My dad is really good at calming me down and helping me think through things. He's just a creative guy; he has good ideas." Steve's unwavering support of his son would become apparent through the spring as he appeared at venue after venue to watch Alan compete.

Yet no one, not Raczko or his father, could rid Webb of his malaise. His injury consumed him, affecting every facet of his life, including his schoolwork. At a school the size of Michigan, it's easy to get lost in introductory classes with hundreds of students. Webb had his share of gigantic classes in large lecture halls, but he also had a year-long writing workshop, a class with only about a dozen students, with Nick Harp, a first-year lecturer in the English department. Since the start of classes in September, Harp had gotten to know Webb more intimately than any other professor, in that odd way that college professors do: in small weekly installments.

When Harp met Webb, he had yet to catch wind of his stature (although he frequently heard his female students remarking about how Webb had "hot legs"), but he was impressed. "He struck me right off as confident and bright and enthusiastic." When he found out who he was dealing with, he worried: "I thought, jeez, this guy's in his freshman year of college, he's away from home, he's dealing with all the standard stuff that any college freshman is dealing with, but this guy, you know, is on David Letterman, too."

He saw Webb's gregarious nature, his love of the spotlight, early on. The first few classes were held in a computer lab, and the students had access to the Internet. There, "Alan would consistently bring to the attention of the class some of the latest headlines about him. It was kind of like he would make himself the center of attention very briefly in his classes." Harp laughs as he recalls the incidents. Like his students, he got a kick out of it, but on another level he felt it was a manifestation of Webb's insecurity—an insecurity that all college freshmen tend to share. Harp says, "That indicated, I don't know, something . . . that this is part of the difficulty of the transition in some way."

Harp doesn't follow track, so through the winter he had no way of knowing the specifics of Webb's troubles, but he sensed that something was amiss. "I got the sense that there was stuff he was really wrestling with." The quality of Webb's work started to decline, as did his preparation for class. He handed in one assignment very late and turned in another only after Harp convinced him that a poor grade was better than a zero. They talked it over, and Webb explained "how he was under some pressure. He didn't go into it, but throughout I can see that it's consistently been a pressurized environment," Harp says.

Harp felt that Webb's stature and notoriety must have had something to do with the marked change in his disposition. But he also felt that in another sense Webb's struggles, whatever they were, were part and parcel of the maturation process that all freshmen undergo as they learn to make choices for themselves. He says, "I'm sure he's got good coaches and counselors, but ultimately, he was like every other 18- and 19-year-old around here who is having to make decisions for himself, and I sensed that."

Harp sensed Webb's inner turmoil when his Achilles failed him, virtually robbing him of his identity and sense of self. And in early March, when Webb began running once more, Harp sensed that, too. "Finally, things seemed to normalize."

MOVING ON

Now, in mid-March, with the outdoor season laid bare before him, his Achilles mended, and his muscles once again hardening to meet the demands of his task, Webb is prepared to forget the winter and ignore the fissure that reached to the very foundation of his relationship with Warhurst.

The process of moving on began recently when Webb met with the coach to map out a schedule, right there in black and white, with daily and weekly mileage figures and workouts with target times for Webb to control. The schedule provided him with enormous peace of mind. "Now I have a plan, a sheet with what I'm going to do, and we're not going to get ahead of ourselves," he says. He's excited, if cautious, about regaining the fitness he had in cross country.

He monitors his Achilles daily, and for the next month he'll care for it with the attentiveness of a mother with her newborn child. "I'm keeping an eye on things because I don't want to go through this all over again," he says. "I'm in the homestretch. In terms of fitness, I'm at 60 percent right now, but I feel I can get to 100 percent quickly."

Webb understands that the path from 60 percent to 100 percent fitness is rarely straightforward. It's more likely to be circuitous, replete with potholes and obstructions.

I have dinner with Webb in mid-March at a burger chain in Ann Arbor. I ask him how fast he might have run a mile in December.

"Gosh, it would have been fast, I can tell you that," he answers.

No doubt Webb would have won the mile at the NCAAs if they had been held before he was injured. But they weren't, and so Webb, Coach Warhurst, and I look to the future.

CHAPTER:04

THE WAR DOG

Whether Alan Webb would come to feel at home at Michigan remained to be seen. However, whether Ron Warhurst coached Webb for just 1 year or for 4 or 5, he had already earned the attention of the running community simply by getting the star miler to attend Michigan.

That Webb decided to attend school and run track and cross country at Michigan, after entreaties from virtually every university in the land, was a tribute to Warhurst, who is affectionately known in the Michigan athletic department as "the War Dog." Webb and his roommate, Nate Brannen, formed the first-ever pair of freshman sub-4-minute milers to attend the same university.

Signing the two runners is considered one of the greatest recruiting coups of recent times. Yet as recently as a decade ago, Warhurst wouldn't have invested the time or the energy to land them at all.

It wasn't that he couldn't recruit. He was and is an excellent communicator. While other coaches of his generation lament how drastically different kids are nowadays, Warhurst, at 59, relates to his athletes as well if not better than he ever has. He has an uncanny ability to relate to them on their level, whatever that may be. Nor was Warhurst's decision not to chase the nation's finest runners a sign of sloth or indifference.

The reason he wouldn't have gone after such a highly touted pair years ago was that he was filled with self-doubt and couldn't stomach the risk inherent in the task—the risk of rejection. To understand the genesis of that self-doubt, you'd have to roll back 35 years and place yourself in Warhurst's shoes, in his midtwenties, squatting in a hooch in mud and water and slush in the badlands of an area the Marines called the Arizona Territory, 20 miles southwest of Da Nang, Vietnam.

'NAM

He didn't have to be there, a Marine in Vietnam in 1969. Unlike others, who lacked the financial, educational, or social wherewithal to avoid conscription, Warhurst enlisted.

He had finished graduate school and a year as graduate assistant coach at Eastern Michigan University in June 1968. He found himself with a degree in physiology, a passion for running, and no job—or job prospects. At night on the news, he'd see reports of the raging war in Vietnam. He pictured himself there, charging up hills like John Wayne in *The Battle of Iwo Jima*, conquering the enemy and returning home a hero. He could almost hear the Hollywood soundtrack in the background when he envisioned the scene.

Moreover, the soldier's life appealed to him. A distance runner accustomed to running 80 to 90 miles a week, he wouldn't have any problem tackling the hills or running through the bush. To excel as a soldier, he'd have to use the same physical and mental attributes that made him a successful runner: toughness, endurance, discipline, and courage. War was not a race; a soldier's life included an infinite amount of risk. But that's what appealed to him. Thinking of war as he did, and being a bored, adventure-seeking 25-year-old with no job, no wife, and no fear, he enlisted in the mother of 'em all: the Marines.

Seven months later, in February 1969, Warhurst landed in Vietnam to begin his 13-month tour. He wasn't supposed to be there so soon. He had yet to complete jump school, but the Marines needed replacements.

It took one mission in the field to rid him of any illusions about war. The first time out, humping in the field, he looked the typical rube. "I was right out of boot camp and I was gonna be prepared. I had a hundred pounds of shit in my pack when I went out humping the first time."

That first night, Warhurst grabbed his shovel, dug a 6-foot hole, and dumped most of his gear in it. He decided to carry only the bare essentials. "I got rid of those extra boots, the extra jersey, extra top, extra pants. Eventually what I ended up carrying was a tiny backpack."

At night on missions, Warhurst's squad dug foxholes and sat in a circle with a diameter of maybe 50 meters. This war was unlike any other in U.S. history. There was no front line of 500 or 1,000 men pushing ahead while others rested in the rear. Instead, squads of 20 or so men moved constantly here and there in an effort to find and kill as many Viet Cong as possible. This meant there were no safe havens for the Marines in the field. Says Warhurst, "There was no downtime. You were aware that something could happen, would happen, and did happen at any given time."

Even when resting or sleeping, the troops were on edge, listening for the telltale signs of an ambush. One evening, while sitting in the circle, Warhurst heard rustling about 100 yards away, followed by *THUMP, THUMP, THUMP*. Instantly, he knew three mortars were coming. While the mortars flew, the Viet Cong started attacking the machine gunner, firing in his direction. Warhurst and his buddy, Beaner, ran to help the gunner, a friend of Beaner's. As they moved, flares illuminated the night sky, and they could see the Viet Cong moving toward them across a rice paddy.

Warhurst heard the whistling noise of a mortar bearing down on him. "Beaner, get down!" he yelled. He hit the ground and felt a burning sensation on the side of his head. Moments later, he felt his warm blood pouring down the side of his face.

Beaner yelled to him, "Are you hit? Are you hit?"

"Yeah," Warhurst said, patting his head to see if it was intact, "I'm hit in the fucking head." Moments later, he breathed a sigh of relief. "Beaner, Beaner. It's okay! It's okay! It's all there."

Today, Warhurst can still point to the scar on his head. He received a Purple Heart for that wound, another for a shrapnel wound to the shin that hospitalized him for 3 weeks, and a Navy Medal of Commendation for courage under fire.

Yet he feels undeserving of his first Purple Heart. "That was a cheap one, you know. Some guys are getting their asses blown off for a Purple Heart, and I just get dinged." He feels fortunate to have escaped with his body and faculties intact.

Like others, Warhurst returned from Vietnam and promptly stowed his uniform in the back of the closet. For him and his fellow soldiers, reintegration into society was devoid of the catharsis that veterans of all previous U.S. wars had experienced.

For several months after his return, alienated and isolated, Warhurst idled, whiling away the hours with drink. After a couple of months, he wanted to go back. He was bored and angry.

For all its inherent risk, Warhurst's Vietnam experience was thrilling and wholly enervating. Compared to the Technicolor phantasm of the Arizona Territory, his existence at his parents' new home in the New Jersey suburbs seemed two-dimensional and black-and-white.

Warhurst was rescued from his ennui by a friend who'd just been accepted in the economics department at the University of Michigan and asked Warhurst to join him. Hell, yes.

MOVING TO MICHIGAN

Once there, Warhurst returned to what had sustained him prior to his stint in 'Nam: He laced up his shoes and he ran. Temporarily unemployed, he quickly plugged himself back into the running scene, tagging along for runs with University of Michigan and Eastern Michigan athletes. One of the first people he met was Jon Cross, a 2-miler who ran 9:18 as a high-schooler in Belleville, Michigan.

Cross matriculated at Michigan and forged a friendship with Warhurst his freshman year. On weekends, Warhurst would pound the pavement with Cross and his Michigan teammates. He was back to doing something physical. For all the alienation he felt from society in general, here he was welcomed back as one of the boys. He escaped into the pure physicality of the endeavor, with each mile a rite of purification, a cathartic act.

He'd stick it to all the young bucks, and they loved it. He became a mentor of sorts to them, viewed as he was by guys like Fred LaPlante, then a middle-distance standout for Eastern Michigan and now Michigan's sprint coach, as "the local running guru."

One year later, in 1974, when the Michigan cross country coaching job opened up, new head coach Jack Harvey asked the guys for their thoughts. They wanted Warhurst. Coach Harvey was sold but for one nagging doubt. He said to Warhurst, "I just got one question. I understand you have a drug problem."

"What?"

"I understand you smoked pot."

Warhurst didn't blink. "Yeah, I smoked pot in Vietnam. Did the person who told you that also tell you I killed seven people?"

"No."

"Well, what do you think is more morally wrong, me smoking a little pot in Vietnam, or killing people? I mean, are you making a moral judgment here?"

"No," Harvey, the gargantuan ex-shot-putter replied. "I just wanted to know. The job is yours if you want it."

Warhurst didn't hesitate: "I'll take it." The job was his, for

$5,800. It didn't sink in until he returned home. "I said, 'Holy shit, I just got the job at Michigan!' I had no clue what that really meant, the impact of it."

In Jon Cross, Greg Meyer, Mike McGuire, and Bill Donakowski, Warhurst inherited a foundation on which to build a program. And he threw himself into the job, running with the guys and often running to and from work, a backpack over his shoulders, beads and hair flying to and fro.

Most mornings, he would get to the track at 7:30 and do a morning run with Meyer. Meyer recalls those days fondly. "When we'd run every morning and then slide down [to the Delta Restaurant] for coffee or breakfast afterward, very little of our conversation was about running. It was more about life or just every other thing. Being one of his early guys, and being a person who bought into everything he told me to do, built the trust. We knew each other very well. We knew how we thought. It was just one of those things. It clicked over that period of time."

It clicked, all right, to the tune of three Big Ten cross country championships in Warhurst's first 3 years. In no time, he had proved he could coach with the best out there.

According to Meyer, Warhurst's interpersonal skills helped elevate the program to championship heights. "My personal philosophy, after all these years, is that everyone is gonna get their cardiovascular stuff done a certain way, but believing in what you're doing and keeping that focus is what I think determines success. A lot of people can post great workouts, but if you come out of there still doubting yourself and worried about what's going on, you're not going to run as well. Ron has the ability to help build confidence; a lot of people don't. With him, when he said you were ready to go, you felt you were ready to go. When you take that doubt out, it allows you to run a lot better."

As the years passed, Warhurst compiled one successful season after another. Yet despite his success, he was haunted by the memories of Vietnam.

To medicate his fractured psyche, he turned to booze and cigarettes (a vice he picked up in Vietnam). While other coaches spent their evenings recruiting, Warhurst spent his at Fraser's Pub, a smoky sports bar in Ann Arbor. Every once in a while, in spite of his lax recruiting, Warhurst would get a gem, like Brian Diemer, a 1983 Michigan grad and the 1984 Olympic bronze medalist in the steeplechase.

Each year, Warhurst's workouts hardened Diemer. And yet, Diemer feels Warhurst's talent was more in working on an athlete's mind than on his legs. His words echo those of Meyer. "Warhurst was always very instrumental in making me believe in *me*. He showed a belief that I could do it, and I took that and ran with it. He sat me down before [the Olympics in] '84 and told me he thought I could medal." Diemer trusted the coach, and in the Los Angeles Olympic Games, he won the bronze—to date, the last Olympic medal won by an American distance runner.

STRAIGHTENING UP

For Warhurst, the inspiration to quit smoking came unexpectedly in 1993, in the form of an acute asthma attack that ended in a visit to the emergency room. After that scare, he never smoked another cigarette. Later, inspired by his wife-to-be, Kalli, he gave up drinking cold turkey. Overnight, a 20-year routine of going straight from the track to Fraser's Pub abruptly ended.

Freed at last from his dependency on alcohol, he found he no longer needed the emotional crutch it once provided. Moreover, the hours he had spent daily at Fraser's were now a blank canvas. Ready at long last to handle whatever came his way, he began to fill some of those hours on the phone—recruiting.

He started going after the best talent out there, and lo and behold, they came to Ann Arbor. Unquestionably, Sully's arrival in 1993 got the ball rolling. Then in 1994, John Mortimer, runner-up at the National High School Cross Country Championships, committed to the Maize and Blue.

Mortimer's first year at Michigan coincided with Warhurst's first year of sobriety. "I think his coaching improved dramatically from there on out," Mortimer says. "And his recruiting also improved dramatically. He didn't spend any time doing things that would be detrimental to that."

In 1997 and 1998, Sullivan and Mortimer led the Wolverines to their first back-to-back Big Ten cross country titles since Warhurst's harriers three-peated from 1974 to 1976. And both years, the teams finished fourth at the NCAA Cross Country Championships, making them Warhurst's best-ever squads.

Warhurst's new hands-on approach was most evident with his recruitment of Webb. In July 2001, at the beginning of the summer recruiting period before Webb's senior year, Warhurst was the first coach to call him.

Within a week, Warhurst was in Webb's living room in Virginia for a home visit—also the first coach to make the trip. Webb felt wanted. During the visit, Warhurst immediately offered Webb a full scholarship to Michigan, the school he'd grown up rooting for, in the town where he'd formed his earliest memories when his father had taught economics at the university.

Webb, of course, received other offers, but Warhurst was the first to offer him a full scholarship—something that Webb, like many kids, viewed as the fulfillment of a lifelong dream. "It meant a lot to me," he remembers. "It was my first time going through that, so it was sort of special."

Warhurst's success with Sully, Webb says, "gave Warhurst validity, an established record with another miler." As the weeks went on and they continued to converse, Webb felt more and more comfortable with Warhurst. Of course, he considered other schools, eventually winnowing the list of contenders to Michigan, Stanford, and William and Mary.

CHOOSING MICHIGAN

By November, Webb was ready to decide. He'd spoken at length about the decision with his high school coach, Scott Raczko, and his father. He decided to become a Wolverine. He signed that month, in what is known as the early signing period. (The NCAA permits recruits to accept scholarships early during a short window of time in the fall. Otherwise, they accept offers beginning in April.) Nate Brannen would join him in the spring.

In the end, Warhurst was much more proactive in his courtship of Alan Webb than he was years earlier with runners like John Mortimer, who contacted Warhurst himself. Yet his sales pitch never varied. Mortimer believed Warhurst when he told him on his recruiting trip, "Come to Michigan, and you'll be great." Mortimer watched Sullivan's progress and Scott MacDonald's 2-year transformation from a 4:15 high school miler to a sub-4 miler, and he signed to run for the Wolverines.

Five years later, Warhurst delivered the same message to Webb and Brannen. Like Mortimer, they keyed on Warhurst's success with Sully and came to believe that the coach could use his craftiness and intuition to take them to Sully's level.

They came to Michigan expecting to be next. With only one season remaining in their freshman year, however, Webb is still somewhat riddled with the doubt that surfaced this past winter. Only time will tell whether Warhurst can conjure the formula for success that will take both Webb and Brannen to their fastest miles and best races ever.

CHAPTER:05

A TEAM IN TURMOIL

After Alan Webb broke Jim Ryun's high school mile record at the Prefontaine Classic last year, Sully caught up with Ron Warhurst. He looked at his coach and grinned. "We're gonna have fun next year, aren't we?" Together they envisioned monster workouts with Sully, Webb, Nate Brannen, Paul McMullen, and Tim Broe swapping leads, burning up the track, synergistically rising to the top of the world.

Well, that was the plan all right, but, now, approaching the ides of March, Warhurst finds himself dealing with a team in turmoil.

Brannen is taking a week off to rest his sore foot and making doctor's appointments to have it examined. Sully, Warhurst's ironman, has been unable to shake a literal pain in the ass. Broe, fresh off an American 3000-meter record, is heading back to Alabama for a few weeks with his fiancée. She wants warmer weather so that she can hit the links to prepare for the upcoming Futures Tour, a minor league tour of the LPGA.

As for McMullen, he's still MIA.

That leaves Webb. And he's not in the best shape, either. Against the odds, he must now claw himself back to fitness alone, an unwelcome prospect when Ann Arbor's daily weather has shifted little from dark, gloomy, windy, bitter and "stay inside, stupid."

PLANNING A FUTURE

With no control over the climate, Webb fortifies himself the only way he knows how: by controlling his workout regimen. For him, that means leaving absolutely nothing to chance. A few days ago, he constructed this plan by meeting with Warhurst to map out the next 6 weeks of his training.

Webb and Warhurst now refer to the 6-week training block from March to mid-April as a mini–cross country season, replete with many of the same workouts, such as 1000-meter hill repeats at Nichols Arboretum (Arbs) and Warhurst's famed Michigan, that Webb dominated in the fall. Punishing himself over the same hills and runs will leave no doubts as to his fitness; it will be quantifiable, in black-and-white.

While he certainly isn't starting from scratch, Webb has lost a significant amount of the strength and fitness that he gained through cross country. So, in drawing up the 6-week training block, Warhurst focused on workouts that would help build the fitness and confidence Webb possessed last fall, when he won the Big Ten Cross Country Championships and finished 11th at the NCAA Cross Country Championships.

Yet, not wanting to compromise Webb's training or subject him to any unwarranted criticism from the press, Warhurst and Webb made another crucial decision that day. Webb will not race himself into shape, as many milers returning from injury do. Ferry Field, the Wolverines' outdoor track, will be his proving ground. Only when Webb has demonstrated sufficient fitness away from the media's inquisitive glare will Warhurst send him to the wolves.

They penciled in the Mt. SAC Relays in Walnut, California, on April 20 as Webb's opening race. It's unheard of for collegiate runners, especially freshmen, to automatically qualify for the NCAA Championships right out of the gate, but given Webb's extraordinary skills, he and his coach have now fixed their sights on accomplishing just that in Walnut. Should Webb not qualify in his debut, he will have three more shots, the last at the Big Ten Championships on May 18 and 19.

THE FIRST WORKOUT OF THE PLAN

Webb's road to the NCAAs begins today, March 11.

He steps onto Ferry Field for what seems like the first time in ages to run a set of pedestrian quarters (400-meter repetitions) in 70 seconds each (a 4:40-mile pace). "Slow," he says sheepishly to no one in particular as he performs an active stretching routine before his workout. "I hope nobody watches." He can't remember when he's done a workout this slowly; freshman year in high school, *maybe*.

He takes solace in the fact that this past weekend's NCAA indoor mile final was won by Illinois State's Christian Goy in just over 4 minutes. That the NCAAs were won in a rather mediocre time, tactical affair or not, significantly buoys his confidence. Even if he never reaches top fitness this season, he knows he doesn't have too far to climb to compete with the collegians.

Webb effortlessly coasts through the exercise on the track, hitting his last several quarters in 66 seconds apiece. But his day is far from over. He views running as but one piece in a comprehensive training program that begins with an active stretching routine, proceeds to the track for a run, and continues on some days in the weight room with a vigorous lifting session that would put some collegiate football players to shame. Other days, instead of lifting weights, he moves on to a series of hurdle drills (often performed by sprinters to develop their speed) and concludes, without fail, with some final strides on the track before departing for home.

He does none of this willy-nilly. As he began his comeback, Webb spent hours developing his off-track training program. Now, he has the program planned all the way through the USA Outdoor Track and Field Championships in late June.

It's the same grueling off-track strategy he used last fall to run a successful cross country season. Indeed, senior distance runner Drennan Wesley was amazed one day by how long and how hard Webb worked. That day, at the end of a track workout, Wesley heard Webb invite Nate Brannen to run some additional strides before heading back to their dorm.

The rest of the Wolverines were long gone, and Brannen passed. Webb looked at Wesley and said simply, "It's lonely at the top," before running off to do his strides.

Lonely, indeed. Webb often concludes his training 45 minutes to an hour after the other Wolverines have gone home. Often, Brannen and the other freshmen have already finished supper by the time Webb returns to the dorm.

Hard as he works, Webb is no masochist. His injury last fall and winter taught him that he must recover in order to reap the fruits of his labor. So, now, this March, he allows himself a luxury few top collegians do—a day off every Sunday. He's the only Wolverine with such a schedule.

ANOTHER TRAINING PARTNER DOWN

As Webb coasts through his quarters on the track, Brannen waits at the medical center in Schembechler Hall, the football facility named after legendary Michigan football coach Bo Schembechler, for a doctor to review x-rays of his sore left foot.

The doctor arrives and goes over the films. He tells Brannen about a cloudy spot on his second metatarsal, precisely where his foot aches. On the x-ray, the doctor shows him distinct lines that outline his healthy bones. He then explains that cloudy spots are generally signs of activity within the affected bone. Granted, he says, a spot could be a benign indicator of blood accumulating in an area that's inflamed, but he tells Brannen that he's almost certain it's a stress fracture. He orders a bone scan to confirm the diagnosis and tells Brannen not to run.

The next afternoon, Brannen's teammates learn the news as they stretch at 3:15 P.M., clad in running tights, hats, and jackets. Brannen saunters over in baggy sweatpants. Just by looking at his attire, they know something is up. Nick Stanko, the cross country captain, speaks for the lot of them: "How's the foot?"

Brannen tells the story to his teammates. I can tell that he's clinging to a more optimistic outlook, in spite of the doctor's dire diagnosis. "He's 90 percent sure it's a stress fracture," Brannen says.

Warhurst arrives at 3:30, backpack slung over his shoulder. He smiles at Brannen with thumbs up as he sees him.

"Good news?"

"No."

Warhurst considers the consequences. If it is a stress fracture, Brannen will be out for 3 to 4 weeks. Missing time in the preseason, as Webb had, is one thing, but missing 4 weeks in the midst of a season is crippling. Rare is the athlete who can do that and return to compete at a high level.

Should Brannen miss 3 weeks, he'll return to training April 1. Warhurst estimates that it will take at least 2 more weeks for Brannen to get back to his regular training routine. That leaves just 2 weeks to ready him for the Penn Relays, a meet Warhurst has been pointing toward since the day Brannen signed with Michigan. He'll also have only 5 weeks to prepare for the Big Ten Championships.

Then again, Brannen could miss 4 weeks. That's a perfectly reasonable amount of time for a stress fracture to heal. If he goes without training for that long, Warhurst doubts he will be able to participate at the Penn Relays. In that scenario, Warhurst tells me that he would entertain the possibility of encouraging Brannen to take the entire season off.

I know that Brannen's redshirting would put Warhurst under

fire. Rival coaches would undoubtedly use it against Michigan in the recruiting process. "Michigan," they'll tell recruits, "why would you want to go there? They got the top two milers in North America last year, and what happened? They both got injured. What's that tell you?"

Brannen doubts he'll be out long or that a 3-week layoff will affect him. "I was gonna take a week off anyway, and I'll get in the pool," he tells me optimistically. "I should be able to maintain quite a bit of fitness." He's determined not to dwell on it or pout. He wants to deal with the diagnosis and move forward.

In contrast, Webb's injury this winter was, for him, a dire situation that led him to seriously question Warhurst's methods. Brannen displays no such doubt. In part, that's because he has decided to stay at Michigan for 5 years, meaning he'll have to redshirt a season somewhere along the line anyway. And if he has to miss this season, one in which there is no World Championships or Olympics, he tells me he won't be crushed.

Still, Brannen wants to run. As he faces weeks of exercising in a pool to rehabilitate the fracture, he can't help but wonder, "How did it happen?"

As he and I and Rondell Ruff (a fellow freshman middle-distance runner also "pooling it" with a stress fracture) walk across the track toward the pool, Brannen speculates that his injury is due to too many sessions of running in spikes on Michigan's unforgiving indoor track. Under Pete Grinbergs, his club coach in Canada, he rarely trained in spikes. This winter, he tells me, he trained in spikes all the time at an intensity he'd never experienced. His face betrays no emotion as he concludes his thoughts. "It's just the constant pounding going around in circles. I should've known this was gonna happen."

NOT ALONE

Sully can relate to Brannen's predicament. He's struggling with his own body woes. From his vantage point, working out on an elliptical trainer in the varsity training room, he has a bird's-eye view of the pool and can see Brannen and Ruff doing their pool work.

The elliptical trainer is one of the godforsaken cross-training machines on which Sully's quickly becoming quite proficient. He could ride the exercise bike, but he detests it, and the elliptical machine, which provides a rough approximation of the running motion without any pounding, is a better simulation than anything other than pool running. He's been running in the pool occasionally for variety's sake, but he finds that he just can't get his heart rate high enough to get a good workout. So the elliptical it is.

As Sully moves his feet in circles, he glances out the room's tinted window at Ferry Field. That only a thin pane of glass separates running on the track from being in the training room is not lost on him. He tried running over the weekend but covered only 1½ miles on Saturday and 2½ on Sunday. In each instance, his glute tightened up and he was forced to call it quits. In lieu of running, he's been going like mad on the elliptical machine, averaging 2 hours a day—1 hour in the morning and another in the afternoon.

Motivating himself to head to the track this afternoon to exercise on the elliptical trainer was no easy task. For weeks he's been hammering away, hoping that he would be running again soon and representing Canada in Dublin, Ireland, at the end of March at the World Cross Country Championships. Now that carrot is gone.

He called the Canadian Track Federation yesterday and forfeited his spot on the squad. Although a miler by trade, Sully has loved cross country since his earliest days as a junior, especially when he has occasion to represent Canada, which he views as an honor of the highest order.

Should his injury not heal, jeopardizing his summer season, Sully will start to worry. Since graduating from Michigan he's run for Reebok, and his contract expires at the end of the year. Over the past several years, he's noticed a very disturbing trend. Reebok's been dumping all of their marquee athletes. "Their big thing last year was to re-sign [pole vault world record holder] Stacy Dragila, and they didn't do that. They didn't re-sign [world shot put champion] John Godina. They're not re-signing anyone," he tells me.

In the cutthroat world of track and field, you're only as good as your last race.

"I think I've done enough," he says, "to get something from

somebody. It's just a matter of how much, and that depends on how I'm running."

Cross-training alone won't get Sully back on track. He knows he must complement his track work with regular massage and physical therapy sessions. Most world-class runners have regular physiotherapists to attend to their various aches and pains, and Sully is no exception. Since the 2001 World Championships he's been a regular patient of Peter Kitto, a physical therapist at the Michigan Sports Medicine and Orthopedic Center.

Paul McMullen introduced Sully to Kitto, a perpetually wise-cracking Detroit Red Wings nut, last summer. McMullen heard of Kitto through a mutual acquaintance and went to see him to work on his perpetually sore hip flexors as the World Championships approached. Several sessions later, the excitable Kitto had fixed him, and McMullen, Kitto recalls, was saying, "Oh, man, you're the juice."

On Friday afternoon, Sully visits Kitto, hoping for every ounce of that juice. He lies on a massage table in the therapist's office and explains his troubles. Plying Sully's hamstrings with his fingers, Kitto wonders aloud what could possibly be happening. Sully's muscles feel loose and supple, leading Kitto to speculate that maybe his ailment isn't muscular. He suggests that he get an MRI.

Nevertheless, he digs deep into Sully's hamstrings and upper glutes, searching for telltale knots. It is then, when Kitto digs his fingers deeper into his upper glute than Sully thinks humanly possible, that his sense of humor is a distinct asset. When the pain's unbearable, Kitto cracks off a one-liner and has Sully laughing and crying simultaneously.

Kitto wrestles with Sully's ailment as he works. He can't understand why, after all the ultrasound, massage, ice, and electric stimulation, Sully's regressing. He chews on it throughout the session. He concludes that the pain may be lingering due to Sully's exhaustive cross-training regimen. He advises Sully to take 3 days of rest, with no running, stretching, lifting, or treatment. Just 3 days of nothing. If he doesn't respond, they'll check with Kitto's partner, Dr. John K. Anderson, for more testing.

Sully nods his consent. While he lacks the trademark compulsiveness of the never-miss-a-day distance runner, he's still susceptible to that twinge of guilt runners feel about taking time off. Nevertheless he listens, because he too is at a loss, and he trusts Kitto implicitly.

REHABBING WEBB

Kitto is but one of a diverse cadre of support personnel for Warhurst's men. After Webb's quarter workout, he and Warhurst pay a visit to Dr. Glenn Miller, a chiropractor (or "bone-bender" in Warhurst-speak) at the Ann Arbor Chiropractic Clinic.

Dr. Miller leads Warhurst and Webb from the waiting room into his office. Last weekend, Webb visited him for the first time and was fascinated to discover his unknown imbalances and weaknesses. A chiropractor in Virginia had fixed his hip when he injured it during his junior year in high school, and ever since he's been sold on the merits of chiropractic work. He hopes working with Dr. Miller will keep him from suffering any more injuries this season.

As Dr. Miller treats Webb, he speaks of neural pathways and body balance while using a variety of machines that look as if they're straight out of a Sharper Image catalog. Already, he says, he sees progress in Webb's alignment from last weekend. He adjusts Webb's neck as he stands, positioning it just right before cracking it, and then performs various tests by pushing and pulling on his arms to see if he's in balance. Satisfied with the improvement in strength on Webb's right side, he says, "You're just turning into a badass, aren't you?" In time, Brannen will also see Dr. Miller, who will apply a Chinese oscillating machine to help increase blood flow and thus promote the healing of Brannen's foot.

A day later, Dr. Miller's at the track, observing Webb as he performs a long set of 1000-meter runs with only a 200-meter recovery jog between repetitions. He eyes Webb's hips as he rounds the track to see if they are aligned properly, and he likes what he sees.

So does Warhurst. Webb ran his first interval 4 seconds slower than planned, but the wind is howling and he's wearing his clodhoppers to ease the strain on his Achilles, making his quick tempo all the more impressive. He proceeds to pick up the pace on each successive interval. Warhurst smiles as he watches Webb (whom he calls "the bandito" today for wearing a bandanna as a headband) set off on his third interval. "He's way fitter than he thinks he is."

Webb goes faster, running 2:48 on his fourth 1000. He walks for a while, gathering a few more precious moments of rest before jogging slowly to start his last 1000-meter effort. Warhurst was only looking for 2:50s today, so he speaks to Webb before he launches into the last one. "That's good. Your rhythm is good. No need to go faster." Then he talks to me and Dr. Miller as Webb rounds the far bend. "Patience is a virtue, boy. Not many youngsters understand that, but I think he's getting a feel for it. Time will tell."

Webb comes through the quarter in 64 seconds, 3 seconds faster than usual. He's going for it. Warhurst cheers him on as he passes the half-mile mark, mouth agape and visibly suffering, "That's the look. That's the determination." Webb closes in 32 seconds, his fastest 200 meters of the day, and finishes the 1000 in 2:44.

Afterward, Webb, while not ebullient about his effort, concludes that it bodes well for the season. "It's a step in the right direction. Give me a few weeks and I'll put spikes on and I'll do some eye-popping workouts." The clouds roll in as Webb talks, blanketing the sky in a muted gray pallor. Instantly, the temperature drops precipitously, and Webb's temperament mirrors the change. As Warhurst makes for the indoor track, Webb tells me that it was his intention today to run each interval at a successively quicker pace. "I think Ron gets a little carried away with the tempo stuff. Maybe if I was a 10-K runner, but . . . I like to do progressions. That way you're always getting a stimulus, not getting stale."

I wonder if Webb continues to feel a lingering dissatisfaction with the way Warhurst's workouts are structured. Before long, the seemingly innocuous fissure in the dam of their relationship will increase exponentially, and all the pent-up emotions will burst forth, requiring them to rebuild the dam from scratch.

As the days pass, Brannen, too, experiences mixed emotions. He waffles back and forth from accepting his diagnosis to believing that his foot is not fractured and that he'll be back running 2 weeks from the day he rested after the NCAAs, no more. His desire to be back so quickly stems in part from the psychological void he feels when he's away from the team.

THE VERDICT

Brannen's wait for a bone scan ends on March 20, in the midst of his second week off. He heads to University Hospital with Michigan trainer Will Turner. As they walk through the hospital corridors to the nuclear medicine room, neither betrays his nerves. Brannen's foot has been feeling fine of late, and both he and Turner expect the bone scan to confirm that the injury was just an inflammation of the soft tissue in his foot.

As Dick Nelson, the nuclear medicine technologist, slides the pallet on which Brannen lies so that his feet are positioned under the gamma camera, he explains what he'll be seeing on the monitor above his left shoulder. Nelson explains that if a bone is fractured and trying to repair itself, more gamma rays will be deposited there, and the fracture will show up brighter. Conversely, if a bone is no longer actively trying to repair itself, the image will show nothing unusual.

They take the scan and wait $2\frac{1}{2}$ minutes to obtain a sharp image.

Moments into the first scan, Brannen sees the injured area of his foot alight on the monitor like the North Star. He stares impassively, wordlessly, and unavoidably at the monitor, like a motorist driving by the scene of an accident. As they shift his foot from one position to the next, his gaze never wavers. As each subsequent image appears, Brannen hopes the bright dark spot will just disappear. In each instance, his metatarsal fracture glows fiercely. At last Brannen breaks his silence. "I was hoping to run tonight, tomorrow," he says weakly, knowing full well it will be some time before he's chasing Webb in the mile.

By 3:30 the following afternoon, Warhurst stands outside, bundled up in a parka and his omnipresent Michigan ball cap, resolutely weathering a storm that has blanketed much of the Midwest as it intermittently sends blinding sheets of snow across Ferry Field.

Inside the field house, there is a small training room with a couple of tables and a few hot tubs. Having concluded his warmup, Webb sits in a hot tub, heating his calves and Achilles while mulling over today's task—10 repeats at 600 meters. He wears a tight Dri-fit shirt with "South Lakes" emblazoned across the chest, and his biceps, triceps, and shoulders press against the fabric, the result of a winter of consistent lifting and time off his feet. Webb will run outdoors today, foul weather be damned.

If only he felt more rested. Despite designing his school schedule with Fridays off, he was up this morning at 7:30 to ready himself for a camera crew at 8:30. That the crew is here at the behest of USA Track and Field, shooting a segment on him for an interactive video that they'll have at the USA Track and Field Hall of Fame, is of no consequence to him. "I scheduled Fridays off so I could sleep in," he says, exasperated. "I mean I scheduled it. Shit."

At the track, Webb dives into each repetition, bursting off the line like a sprinter coming out of the blocks, leaning forward, pumping his legs in short, quick strides, and straightening up slowly after that. "Very nice!" Warhurst yells as Webb flies through the quarter-mile split of his fifth 600-meter repeat in 64 seconds. Warhurst's been tuning in to Webb's arm carriage, "the key to his speed later on," and he's very pleased with what he sees.

On the sixth, Webb's effort becomes audible. "Haaa, haaa, haaa," he puffs. Engine cranking, he removes his headband. "Save the gloves for the last two," Warhurst tells Webb, knowing he'll need any last bit of extra motivation there. Hurting, Webb tells Warhurst he'll need his help.

Webb dives into the seventh interval without hesitation, and then the eighth. In each he battles his own blood chemistry down the final straightaways, perceptibly raising his knees ever higher as lactic acid floods his thighs.

Warhurst watches Webb walk slowly in lane 1 on the far curve. There are two 600s to go, and Warhurst can see that he is spent. The plan was to hit 1:36 to 1:38 through eight repeats, and Webb has hit his splits on the nose. Now he walks, knowing he must run even faster to hit 1:35 for the last two. It's a certainty that the lactic acid will flow quicker and more voluminously through his system on the next interval than on any prior one. Webb wonders if he can take the pain.

Still, it takes an irritant to get a pearl, and Webb sets off determined to maximize that which he can control—his effort. When he begins, it's 24°F, and -12 with the windchill. Despite the cold, Webb runs like a metronome, nailing his splits on the nose in swirling winds, snow, and the occasional cloudless sky. It seems as if Webb, like other great runners, has a clock in his head that helps him set his pace perfectly.

Warhurst knows this is when milers are made. In freezing conditions, with no one to key on and nothing but your mind to get you through the din of your screeching nerve endings. "If this doesn't make you starchy," he says, breath visible, "I don't know what will."

The gloves come off. The sky, sunny minutes earlier, is now black. Webb attacks the last interval with calculated abandon, hitting the 200 mark a full second faster than in any prior interval. His cadence stays steady through the quarter before starting to slow ever so slightly. Warhurst yells at his charge: "Come home, boy! Move your arms!"

A spent Webb windmills his arms across the line. Moments later, he knows he hit time by the slimmest of margins—1:35.91— and he knows he's done. "That's it. I'm totally wasted."

THE LIGHT AT THE END OF THE TUNNEL

Later, after jogging, and too tired to lift weights, Webb hits the indoor track and does a series of strength exercises, variations of pushups and situps, while high school teams file into the track building for an invitational meet being held there that evening. They stare at Webb from afar, fully aware of who he is but too intimidated to ask for an autograph. Webb pays them no mind, focusing instead on his exercises. He's disappointed with his effort, so high are his standards. A master of his stride when fit, his injury robbed him of that gift, and out there now he feels inanely clumsy. "I like to be in complete control of my stride, in control of my pace at all times. I'm just not strong enough yet." He works as he says this, each repetition a penance of sorts for him.

Finally, a youngster musters up the courage to ask for an autograph. Politely, Webb tells him he'll sign later, when he's done stretching. Outside the confines of practice, he'll readily oblige, but his time at practice is sacrosanct.

The next day, Webb runs the longest 9 miles of his life, feeling as if the wind is in his face every step of the way. After the run, he sits on a bench in front of his locker. He just wants his bed. If only he can find the energy for the walk back to his dorm. He pulls the hood of his sweatshirt over his head so that it completely covers his face and then drops his arms, exasperated. "Where's the light at the end of the tunnel?" he says, rising to his feet. "I don't see it."

CHAPTER:06

ESCAPING THE ABYSS

Michigan senior Drennan Wesley remembers the day Alan Webb showed his teammates he was for real. It was early September, and the Michigan men had just returned to campus from their preseason training camp in Glen Arbor, Michigan, and settled in to begin the academic year.

Their first workout back on campus was a series of long, grinding 1000-meter hill repeats at Nichols Arboretum—the Arb. Warhurst has been having his guys run Arbs, as they call the repeats, for years. Thus, the workout is useful for judging a runner's fitness relative to both his contemporaries and the giants of Michigan past.

It took Webb all of one workout to etch his name atop the list of greats who've run there. Sully had the record for the fastest run up the Arb, at 3:16. Webb ran in the low 3:20s on each of the first four intervals. On the fifth and last effort, he blasted a 3:15 to become "King of the Arbs."

One week later, the Michigan men did another set of Arbs. This time, Webb *started* at 3:15 and ran his last interval in 3:09. "That was the day," Wesley says, "Webb blew our minds. We didn't think that could be done at the Arb."

It wasn't just the times Webb posted that impressed the guys. It was also the manner in which he approached the workout. While most approached it with a certain sense of dread, Webb bounced around, loose and excited, ready to attack it like a race. "He brought a whole new attitude," Wesley says.

Webb's demeanor suggested to Wesley and his teammates that he "was running this for something besides just getting in shape." Watching him, Wesley saw a man with an attitude of, "Hey, I'm gonna really accomplish something today."

RETAKING THE ARB

Webb's demeanor now, on the last Monday in March, is entirely more business-like. Lacking the fitness to which he had grown so accustomed, he has lost the swagger from his step. In the fall, he approached workouts envisioning nothing but the fantastic possibilities of what lay before him. Now he has that claustrophobic feeling that comes when you see nothing but limitations, and his preworkout grim-faced earnestness is a reflection of this.

Today, Warhurst once more sends Webb to the Arb, the canvas of some of his most mind-bending works, to get an accurate picture of where they now stand.

For once, Webb will run this workout in the company of another sub-4 miler. Tim Broe returned from his brief trip to Alabama late last evening.

"I can't take this," Broe says angrily in the field house as they ready for the run. It's 24°F outside and snowing. "It [the weather] is hot and cold, and up and down, and left and right, and up my ass. It's ridiculous. I can't take it."

"That's because you've been babied your whole life," Sully tells him.

They leave the field house, and as Warhurst climbs into his SUV to drive to the Arb, Broe continues to complain about the weather. "You know what?" Warhurst says sarcastically. "Life is tough." Yet the coach is happy that Broe's back to run with Webb. For as much as he bitches, Warhurst knows Broe is as tough as they come.

He also knows that Broe will bring out Webb's best effort.

After many starts and stops—moving to Michigan and then retreating to Alabama—this past January, Broe rented a place in Ann Arbor and subsequently flourished, running an American record for 3000 meters that month. In March, he captured the 3000-meter title at the USA Indoor Track and Field Championships and, wanting to test himself further and send a message to his fellow Americans, doubled in the mile, finishing a remarkable third in 3:58.

Webb watched Broe tear up the boards during the late winter season, and it chafed him. As strong as he was, he'd taken a shine to Steve Scott's indoor 3000 record, set way back in 1989, only to see Broe snatch it before he even had a chance at it. Today, on the Arbs, Webb will get to test himself against the current standard-bearer of American running. Warhurst is hoping that Broe's presence will elevate Webb's excitement and expectations.

As Warhurst stands on the Arb's final 90-degree turn 100 meters from the finish, waiting for his runners to climb the hill for the first time, he examines the ground and notes the half-inch of snow. Thanks to the dirt underneath, there's plenty of traction, so Warhurst quickly dismisses any notion of Webb reinjuring his Achilles on the hill.

Broe rounds the final turn of the first hill attempt, 5 seconds up on Webb, springing off his toes toward the finish. His face is locked in a grimace, something Warhurst has learned to disregard. At first, Broe's pained expression had made Warhurst worry that he was pushing his runner too hard, but then he noticed that Broe grimaced whether he was running an 8-minute mile or a 4-minute mile. He learned to judge Broe's effort more by his respiration. Here, too, Broe is unique. Unlike Webb and most other runners, who can be heard exhaling, Broe's breathing is audible when he inhales. It's a short, shrill sound, almost like a whistle, and this is what Warhurst hears as Broe flies past him.

Despite the wind, snow, and poor footing, Broe runs his first Arb in 3:25. Webb, running controlled due to the snow, lacks the familiar pop in his stride, and he rounds the final bend of the second interval crimson-faced from the cold. His face is notably expressive, and, as he passes us, I notice his tight expression, an unmistakable look of disgust.

Warhurst had hoped Broe's presence would benefit both, but he suddenly realizes that instead, it's heightened Webb's frustration. Not wanting Webb to get any more discouraged, he changes tactics. As Webb jogs down past him, Warhurst tells him to call it quits and head back to the indoor track for some speedwork. Webb stubbornly refuses. "No. I'll stay here and run. I'm running so shitty anyway, who cares?"

Broe waits for Webb at the bottom of the hill and tries to settle the young buck. He reminds Webb that it takes time to build fitness. He tells him it took Sully 8 years to get his 1500-meter race time down to 3:31. Webb replies, "I don't want to wait 8 years. I want to run 3:25 [in the 1500] now."

Broe recognizes the tenuousness of Webb's mental state, and he decides to do something about it. They complete the next hill. On his way down, Broe approaches Warhurst and quietly offers his advice before heading for his next repeat. Taxed from the climb, he speaks in staccato bursts between breaths. "If I was you . . . I would seriously have him . . . go to the track . . . and do like four 400s . . . going faster and faster. . . . He's really frustrated."

Again, Warhurst offers Webb the option of heading back to the track. Again, Webb declines. "I'm gonna finish the workout."

In the fall, with Webb at the top of his game, Warhurst had thought nothing about his dogged determination to do it his way. Call it what you will—chutzpah, moxie, starch—Webb had had it then, and he has it now. But, feeling his oats, he didn't need Warhurst in the fall. His return to fitness is a much more delicate process, and he needs his coach's counsel.

Warhurst knows this, but having been twice rebuffed by Webb, he turns and heads back to the track. He won't stick around to watch Webb self-destruct. And while he's tempted to assert his will and insist that Webb go back, he refrains. He wants to let Webb make his own decisions.

After the workout, back inside the track building, Broe chats with Sully about his run at the Arb. Head hung low, Webb walks past and out the door toward the weight room. "Oh, well," Broe says as Webb exits, "he's got a lot to learn. I'm glad I've never run this before, because I'd be frustrated too if I'd run 3:10, and I was out there [now] running 3:25 or 3:30. He'll learn."

Webb releases his rage in the weight room, pouring his frustration into the weights, and in so doing accomplishes a goal he'd set for himself in the fall by benching three sets of 145 pounds 15 times. Later, doing shoulder presses, he unleashes a barbaric yawp just as a song on the jukebox fades out. All motion in the weight room ceases, and all eyes turn toward Webb in surprise. He moves on to the next exercise.

That evening, in his dorm room, Brannen overhears a tearful Webb having a long conversation with his father. It was, he says, "the worst I'd seen him all year."

He'd only seen Webb this demoralized once before. At the end of February, an injured Webb had a one-way ticket home for spring break. Brannen spoke intimately with him about the joys they could experience come spring, such as running the Penn Relays and winning NCAA titles. Brannen left for class the next morning unsure if he would see his friend again in maize and blue. He breathed a sigh of relief when he returned from class and Webb told him he was staying. Days later, Webb was back running, and things started looking up.

Now, at the end of March, Webb was again on the brink.

THE BEST MILER EVER

As a youngster in Virginia, Webb excelled at everything from soccer to basketball, but the sport in which he had Olympic aspirations was swimming. It came naturally to him. He started at 2 or 3 years of age, and by the time he was 6, he was already competing in the Reston swim league during the summer. He stood out immediately, and by age 8, he was swimming year-round. Like other kids, he continued playing other sports such as soccer and basketball, but swimming was the sport that took hold of him.

By age 11, Webb was swimming more and more often. He joined the Solotar swim club, and his swimming took off. He says, "I was like, Whoa, man, this is what I want to do. I got really, really into it. I started moving up in group levels into more intense groups, working out more. I quit playing soccer [after 15 seasons] because I wanted to concentrate on swimming. I basically quit everything for swimming."

By the time Webb was in eighth grade, he had moved up the ranks to the top tier of his club. Soon after, a gentleman named Paul Burgen became the club's head coach. With the coaching change came a change in Webb's mentality. "He was the first coach who got me to look big-time," he says. His teammates shared his aspirations. Sharing a lane with Webb was none other than Inge de Bruin, who would become a gold medalist in the 2000 Sydney Olympics. The competition was intense, and Webb kept rising to the challenge of older, faster athletes. He practiced twice a day, 6 days a week.

Despite his commitment to swimming, however, his gut told him to give running a try. He'd run some as a kid, with immediate success. His father, Steve, recalls his first race: "There's a run they did every fall called the heartbreak run. That was the first time I saw him run in a race. They go out on this 1.7-mile cross country run. He was already finished before the next runner was in sight. I thought, Wow, maybe he'll end up being a cross country runner when he gets to high school. Maybe he'll switch over from swimming. But I kept him in swimming."

Webb excelled on the track as well. They'd run the mile in gym class, and he ate it up. "I always got really excited about that," he remembers, "because it was *the* race." He set the school record in the mile in sixth grade with a 5:44 and again in eighth grade, when he ran a 4:58. A seed had been planted. Says Webb, "I wondered what I could do if I actually trained for it."

So when he entered ninth grade, he decided to give cross country a try. He excelled immediately and ended the season with a second-place finish at the state cross country meet. He thought of prolonging his season further by running the regional qualifier for the Footlocker National Cross Country Championship, but it would have meant delaying his swim season by an additional 2 weeks.

Webb wasn't about to give up swimming. He'd come too far and worked too hard to quit now. He ended his cross country season and went on to complete a breakout swimming season, barely missing the national qualifying times in all his events by mere fractions of a second. Later, those fractions of a second would turn out to make all the difference in the world.

Webb returned to running in the spring of his freshman year. Again, he excelled, winning the state 3200-meter title in 9:34 and posting a seasonal best 1600-meter time of 4:23. His performances were all the more remarkable in light of how little training he did. He says, "I basically ran 3 days a week. I would do the workout one day, and the next day my shins would hurt so bad I wouldn't run. I was sort of halfway training. But I was still so fit from swimming, the distance runs didn't really matter."

Soon after the season ended, Scott Raczko, a young, enthusiastic coach, was hired to take over the South Lakes cross country and track programs.

By that summer, Solotar had disbanded, so Webb joined many of his former teammates at another big swim club in the area, Pearl-Burke. The club boasted notables such as future Olympic gold medalist (and Michigan graduate) Tom Dolan. It was Webb's type of place. "I was like, You know, I want to be an Olympian."

But he couldn't quiet that voice inside his head that said, "Alan, you're a runner." And he had the results to go with it, not to mention the notoriety. "I had this gut feeling my whole life I was going to be good at running, but there wasn't a strong club system in running like there was in swimming, so swimming was what I did," he explains.

Nevertheless, he had to make a choice. Pursuing swimming would mean forfeiting running to train twice a day. Not ready to give up running or to close the door on his swimming aspirations, Webb petitioned the South Lakes school board for a special exemption that would let him train longer in the mornings and come to school late.

Here's where missing those qualifying times came into play: The school board denied his petition on the grounds that he wasn't a national-class swimmer. Webb thought some more about his relative ability in each sport and made the decision to commit to running. He figured that if he didn't do as well as he thought he could, he could always go back to swimming.

That's when the magic started to happen. "Pretty much immediately after I committed, I started to improve dramatically," Webb says.

Not that he was a polished product at that age. When he started working with Webb in the summer before his sophomore year, Raczko saw a kid who'd posted good times as a freshman but who needed a lot of work on his form. Webb's arms frequently crossed over the middle of his torso, and, while his leg mechanics were okay, he kept his legs low to the ground, almost shuffling—so much so that Raczko would describe him as a "lumberer." Raczko didn't have high hopes that he was looking at track's next big stud. He just set out to develop him. He searched for signs of Webb's capabilities.

The moment of truth came at the end of Webb's sophomore cross country campaign, when the team traveled to the state meet hoping that Webb would take home the title. He had been progressively improving throughout the fall, and the day before the state meet, he and Raczko went to check out the course. Noticing that the course's final, gradual uphill was deceptively long, they picked a spot later on the hill for Webb to start his final burst for the finish.

The next day, Raczko waited for his runners at about the 4-K mark. Two leaders emerged way ahead of the field, but Webb wasn't one of them. He passed a dispirited Raczko 200 meters behind. With the other two such an incredible distance ahead, Raczko resigned himself to the fact that Webb would be third.

But the other runners hadn't scouted the course a day earlier. As Webb covered the final kilometer, off in the distance he detected the subtle yet telling signs of runners in distress. From behind he could see their shoulders start to roll and their arms begin to flail. And he spotted that slightest change in cadence that indicated to him that in their quest to break each other, they were both out of gas, with ¼ mile still to go.

What happened next is legend: Against all reason, he won. "By all accounts," says Raczko, "Alan started kicking like a maniac." That race told Raczko all he needed to know. "It showed that he has the desire to win and the talent to make good on that desire."

Toward the end of his sophomore year, Webb had improved his best times to 4:13 for 1600 meters and 9:10 for 3200. With his cross country success and years of aerobic training (via swimming), he and Raczko figured he was a natural 2-miler. They set their sights on the 2-mile at the high school nationals.

Figuring that it's easier to add strength to a speed base than the reverse, they focused on developing Webb's speed with a steady diet of 1600-meter workouts and races. Throughout that spring, says Raczko, "Alan's capabilities in workouts just kept getting better and better," and his 1600-meter times dropped accordingly. As they entered the postseason, Webb still wanted to learn "how to run fast," so Raczko entered him in the 1600 at the Virginia state meet. They decided he would run the race as a sort of workout, running hard on the straights and jogging the curves. Despite using such unorthodox tactics, Webb won the race with his best 1600 time ever—4:12.

His performance at that meet was a revelation: Maybe he was a miler after all. He and Raczko ditched their plans to have him run in the 2-mile at nationals and entered him in the mile against a field of 4:10 milers. For Webb, running would never be the same.

The race was like a dream. Webb came through the 800 meters solidly in the pack in 2:07. With only 200 meters remaining, he was right in the mix. At that point, Brendon Mahoney blasted away from the field. Webb found himself stuck behind Dylan Welsh, a tall miler from New York State. By the time he passed Welsh, Mahoney was out of reach. Webb chased him all the way to the tape and finished second in 4:06.94.

Soon thereafter, Webb discovered that he'd knocked legendary miler Jim Ryun from the record books and established a new national sophomore class record. "Ever since then, I've just been so focused on becoming better," he says. "I've become extremely aware of how my body acts and how it responds to training. Before that, it was just the swimming mentality, you just go hard. Now I'm extremely aware of exactly what my body is doing when I am running."

No longer would Webb settle for second best. And no longer would he settle for winning. He set his sights on becoming the best. Ever. For a high school miler in the United States, that meant beating Ryun's high school record of 3:55.3 and becoming the first high-schooler to run a sub-4 mile since Essex Catholic's Marty Liquori did it in 1967.

During the spring of Webb's junior year, Raczko and his runner looked to make history at the Herbster Track Classic in North Carolina. Two weeks prior to that attempt, they ratcheted up the volume and intensity of Webb's track work. In doing this, they unknowingly upset the balance of Webb's tightly wound legs.

As Raczko watched Webb do his strides before toeing the line at the Herbster Classic, he detected that "little hitch" in his stride. While Webb's 4:03 mile fell short of the long-coveted sub-4 mark, it was still a personal best, and it left both with the impression that given the right conditions, a sub-4 was inevitable.

It took a week for Webb's "hitch" to develop into a piriformis strain. It impeded his stride to such a degree that he lost the 800 at the Virginia state meet. At that, Raczko decided he'd seen enough, and he pulled the plug on Webb's junior campaign. Webb's assault on the history books would resume in his senior year.

That year, Webb didn't have to wait long to reap the benefits of his diligent work and focus. On January 20, 2001, earlier in the indoor season than anyone had dared dream it could be done, Webb ran a 3:59.86 mile at the New Balance Games at the Armory Track and Field Center in New York City and became the first high-schooler ever to run a sub-4 mile indoors.

After that, the media crush began in earnest. Because Webb had run through the sub-4 barrier so early in his senior campaign, the media's attention immediately began to focus on whether he could take down Ryun's 3:55.3. As they had done throughout the year, Webb and Raczko stayed on-task. Says Raczko, "No workout was altered or changed for anything. Any interviews were always done outside of practice time."

The rest is history.

A HEART-TO-HEART

Two days after Webb's disappointing Arb workout, Warhurst calls Webb into his office, along with Sully and assistant coach Fred LaPlante. He knows that he needs to restore Webb's faith in the program and in himself before it's too late.

The coach listens for a while as Webb complains about everything—the weather, the training, and the collegiate system. He listens as Webb questions whether Warhurst can take him where he wants to go, which is not, he stresses, to the top of the podium at the NCAA Championships but to the top of the podium at the World Junior Championships in July.

Warhurst then blasts Webb for his dubious commitment to the program. Alluding to what he feels is Webb's reliance on his high school coach, he says, "If you think Coach Raczko can coach you better than I can, we're wasting our time. You can only serve one master."

Warhurst reminds Webb that he'd gotten him into the best condition of his life last fall. And after discussing how Webb's program differed a year ago, the coach agrees to make some minor concessions to suit Webb's concerns. To satisfy Webb's perfectionist bent, Warhurst agrees to give him precise target times, such as 1:30 for 600 meters, instead of a range, such as 1:30 to 1:32.

LaPlante, who has been silently taking notes throughout the meeting, then offers his two cents. Knowing that Webb is a student of the sport, he alludes to Steve Ovett and Sebastian Coe, two great British milers who electrified the track world in the early 1980s. Coe was trained by his father, Peter, an engineer, in a very controlled and scientific manner. It worked; he set world records and won Olympic gold. Ovett was trained by Harry Wilson, a "swashbuckling-type character," and he won Olympic gold as well.

Likening Warhurst's laissez-faire approach to training to that of Wilson, LaPlante suggests to Webb that by training under

Warhurst, he would gain more self-reliance because he would be in charge of directing the minutiae of his training. In this way, he would also gain confidence in his own decision-making ability— and that, suggests LaPlante, would translate into a greater ability to make split-second decisions come race time. Webb was successful in a Coe-like environment with Raczko, and now, LaPlante suggests, he can be equally successful under Warhurst.

Then Sully intervenes and says what matters to Webb most of all.

In 1995, after his sophomore campaign at Michigan, Sully finished a remarkable fifth at the World Track and Field Championships. Sully was the golden boy of Canadian athletics, and the Canadian sports press immediately started anticipating a gold run for Sully at the 1996 Olympics. The expectations were positively Webb-like.

Then, in the early spring of 1996, Sully injured his Achilles. It took a while to diagnose the extent of the injury. Ultimately, he required surgery and was forced to miss the 1996 Olympic Games.

Like Webb, Sully had never experienced a major injury before, and when he returned, he struggled. He'd put on 22 pounds in the interim. The guys on the team called him "Tubby" and crushed him daily. Sully was frightened. He did what he could. He persisted. Slowly, he improved, and eventually, he made it back.

Now, in Warhurst's office, Sully implores Webb to have faith in his own God-given ability. He stresses that it doesn't have to happen overnight, but he will get fit again, and he will become better than ever. If Webb will only have faith and let Warhurst guide his training, Sully assures him, he'll get back.

Webb takes Sully's words to heart. "Kevin's gone through it all," he tells me afterward, "with Ron specifically and the collegiate system, so it was nice to have his reassurance, just to get me back into it. I just got off-track a bit, but now I'm back, and I'll have a good workout tomorrow. It probably won't be my greatest workout, but that's okay."

Webb was now back in the fold for the first time since his injury. Time would tell whether Webb, like Sully, would come to bleed maize and blue.

Chris Lear

Armed and ready

Alan Webb prepares for a workout at Michigan's Ferry Field in April 2002, a few days before making his collegiate debut in the 1500 meters at the Mt. SAC Relays.

Chris Lear

Climbing the Arb

Tim Broe winds his way up the arboretum hill in late April.

Going to school

Broe grimaces as he sprints up
Ann Arbor's Harvard hill in late April.

Flying
Webb leads Nate Brannen through a 53-second quarter in
early May in their first workout together since fall.

Chris Lear

Chilling

In a tub full of ice, Brannen braces himself against the cold
after screaming through a 600-meter interval on May 1.

Last to first

With a commanding lead, Webb enters the final backstretch
of his preliminary heat in the 1500 meters at the
Big Ten Championships in May. Just 100 meters earlier,
he trailed in last place.

Chris Lear

Caught in the Webb
Brannen (right) begins to crack while Webb shows
no signs of distress during a mid-May workout.

Chris Lear

In sync
Brannen (rirght) and Webb check their pace as they tear through
a 600-meter interval at Ferry Field in late May.

APRIL

CHAPTER:07

THE RISING

On the morning of Thursday, April 4, Ron Warhurst walks into his office to check his e-mail and complete some last-minute chores before leaving for the airport with most of the squad for the Duke Invitational in Durham, North Carolina. He smiles when he spots Nate Brannen lounging comfortably in his chair. "Look at this," he says to me with mock exasperation, "I leave for 10 minutes and he's in my chair!"

Turning aside so Brannen can't hear him, he whispers, "I like that. I like that moxie."

Brannen tells Warhurst that while he's not cleared to run, his fractured metatarsal now has a bit of a lump on it, which means the bone is calcifying and healing quickly. If his foot feels good enough, he'll try running next week.

Warhurst's smile is that of a man who feels the tide has turned. Things couldn't be better.

When he checks his e-mail, he learns that New Zealand miling sensation Nick Willis, an 18-year-old with a 4:01 mile to his credit, intends to sign with Michigan. He reads a fax. More good news. It reads:

> I would really appreciate the opportunity to be a part of the wonderful group you have there. I have nothing but respect for you and the runners you have there and I know that I could improve both myself and there [sic] running with the opportunity to be a part of this phenomenal training group!
>
> Thanks for the time and I look forward to hearing from you, Bryan Berryhill

Berryhill is the 2001 NCAA mile and 1500 champ, and his fax is a welcome ego boost at a time when most of Warhurst's "studs" are on the mend. The coach's only lament is that he won't be here this afternoon to watch Webb run a Michigan, after the show he put on Monday.

After a month of continuous struggle, Webb returned to the big leagues with a bang. Fittingly, his breakthrough occurred at the Arb. He did four Arbs, starting at 3:20 and dropping to 3:14 on his last repeat. Moreover, he rediscovered the pop in his stride. Says Webb, "My form felt like it did in cross: fluid, effortless." Just as important in Warhurst's eyes is Webb's change of disposition. Upon seeing Webb smiling and laughing, senior Mike "Wiz" Wisniewski remarked to me, "Before, he wasn't sure where he was heading, but now he can see a clear path leading to somewhere."

THE MICHIGAN

At 3:00 P.M., the bus is idling in the parking lot. Webb jumps on board, slaps five with all the guys, and wishes them luck in North Carolina. Seeing this, Warhurst beams. "Looks like communication isn't a one-way street."

As much as they'd like to, cross country captain Nick Stanko and Mike "Wiz" Wisniewski can't share in Warhurst's jubilation regarding Webb. Because they're less than a week removed from a trip to Stanford, where they'll both run the 10-K, they aren't racing this weekend in Durham. Instead, they get to run the Michigan today with Webb.

Walking from the track building to Ferry Field, they watch Webb bound powerfully down the track on a final stride before getting it on, and what they see makes them queasy. "We're in big, big trouble today," says Wiz.

Webb's renewed swagger isn't the only thing that tips Wiz off to his intentions. There is a telling change in Webb's attire today, particularly in his footwear. Gone are the clodhoppers, replaced by much lighter racing flats—the same red Nike flats he wore in the fall when he torched the best Michigan ever with splits of 4:19, 0:54, 2:04, and 3:06. Also, for the second time since fall, Webb is running without socks.

Running without socks in racing flats a size too small makes Webb feel light and fast, and, more important, it allows him to literally feel the friction as he heats up the track.

Webb screams, "Ohhh! Yeahhh!" and charges into the mile. It takes only one lap to know that he has tossed aside any preconceived time goals. He finishes in 4:21, just off his personal record pace, and makes his way to the road for the "short" road loop, about 300 meters short of a mile. Wiz is next across in 4:28. He hurries across the pavement and catches Webb to head off for the road.

Back on the track, Webb heads into a 1200, clicking off precisely even splits to finish in 3:10. Despite managing a respectable 3:22, Wiz's ire is obvious. He immediately sets out to break Webb on the second road loop. Webb sits on Wiz's shoulder through the half before Wiz puts a few meters on him. It doesn't last. Webb closes the gap and they finish stride for stride, a few seconds ahead of the pace they set on the first loop.

Despite the arduous road run, Webb runs the next half-mile with abandon and finishes with his arms flailing ever so slightly, breathing "huh . . . huh . . . huh." Once across the finish, his concentration cracks and with it goes his form. His arms fly out to his sides and his head flies back in a desperate search for oxygen. Webb's reward for the internal fire raging through every muscle, from his shoulders down to his calves, is displayed on the face of his watch: 2:00.

Wiz still can't get rolling on the track, and he heads into the final road loop with one objective: to break Webb. After a short recovery, Webb matches Wiz stride for stride as they run the final loop at their fastest clip yet. This time, Wiz has enough in the tank to beat Webb by the barest of margins.

They walk together onto the track for one agonizing final lap. Before he left, Warhurst said he wanted Webb to hammer today. He had no idea Webb would run this fast.

Webb charges into the last lap as he always does, leaning into the turn with short, clipped steps. When they hit the backstretch, Wiz and Stanko are right with him. It's evident that the bank is empty; Webb is spent. At the 200-meter mark, he glances at his watch.

Stanko can't believe he's right on Webb's heels. A true distance runner, he has barely broken 2 minutes in the half. He waits for Webb to explode and gap him by a ridiculous margin. A hundred meters later, Stanko knows he has a shot at the improbable: beating Webb, even if it's on nothing more than an interval.

Webb feels Wiz and Stanko, poised and waiting, on his back. He thinks, Just hold on for 100 meters; I can't let them beat me. A combination of racing instincts and flat-out exhaustion overrule his thoughts. He starts drifting out toward lane 2, his arms flailing out from his sides.

Wiz can't believe Webb's doing the skeleton dance. Less than 50 meters from the line, he quicksteps past Webb on the inside of lane

1. Moments later, Stanko lopes past Webb's outside shoulder. As they pass him, Webb helplessly sinks ever lower and just makes it to the line before collapsing onto the track after undoubtedly the most painful 62-second quarter of his life.

He lies there moaning, too tired to care about the white strand of spit hanging from his chin. With great effort, he rolls onto his side, into the fetal position. Later, as he slowly makes his way to the locker room, my cell phone rings. It's Warhurst. I tell him of Webb's run. "Holy shit," he says. "He's fitter than I thought he was. He'll qualify for the NCAAs in his first race. You heard it here first. You tell him I'm very, very happy with his workout."

I track down Webb, who is walking toward the weight room, water bottle in hand, and I tell him that I spoke to Warhurst. "Was he pissed?" Webb asks.

LOOKING AHEAD TO MT. SAC

Early the following week, Webb travels to New York City to celebrate his high school record one last time. Over the previous year, he has been honored by any number of organizations for his record, but none of the other awards carries quite the prestige of the award for which he is now a finalist: the Sullivan Award, the Heisman Trophy of amateur athletics.

The Sullivan, presented by the AAU (Amateur Athletics Union), an organization that supports 32 sports and boasts of 500,000 athletes at the grassroots level, is meant to honor the top amateur athlete in America. As such, the finalists with whom Webb gathers on this evening at the New York Athletic Club are some of the best athletes anywhere. In addition to Webb, they include Mark Prior, a pitcher for the University of Southern California Trojans who was honored as college baseball's player of the year and drafted by the Chicago Cubs; Cal Berkeley's world record–setting swimmer Natalie Coughlin; and Sean Townsend, a world champion gymnast.

There is a fifth, quite unlikely, finalist: figure skater Michelle Kwan. There's no doubt her athletic achievements merit her inclusion in this coterie of athletes. The rub is that this award honors the top *amateur* athlete in the land. By anyone's definition, an amateur athlete is one who competes for pleasure and not financial gain. Kwan earns a substantial income skating in the Champions on Ice tour, but the skating federation, and thus the AAU, consider her an amateur because she doesn't compete in unsanctioned events.

Members of the media gather with the athletes for an informal press conference before the reception. One of the reporters asks Webb if he is surprised, given his youth, to be the sole track representative here. Webb pauses to consider his response and then says, "I thought I was the only guy who was an *amateur*, but . . ." At that, everyone assembled around Webb shares an almost conspiratorial laugh.

The ceremony itself proves quite anticlimactic. In his opening remarks, before any of the finalists have been introduced, AAU president Bobby Dodd lets slip, in a rapid-fire Southern accent, the following: "I think back to the great winner last year, Rulon Gardner, and what it meant to me to see him sit down and talk to the young people, and I see that tonight with Michelle and [catching himself] so many of the athletes here tonight . . ." Seated in the front row with the other finalists and their guests, Webb discreetly whispers, "Guess we know who won this one."

Later, in his room, Webb turns his thoughts to future conquests, in particular his upcoming race at the Mt. SAC Relays in California and the Penn Relays in Philadelphia, which he and Brannen have fantasized about for months.

For weeks after he began his comeback, Webb's legs felt weak and Jell-O–like when he ran. No longer. Yet he worries that he lacks the top-end speedwork needed to defeat some of America's top collegiate milers, such as Villanova's Adrian Blincoe and Stanford's 1500-meter Olympian Gabe Jennings, who are rumored to be in the field at Mt. SAC. At the same time, he knows it's time to throw caution to the wind and once again test himself in the crucible of competition. "I need that pressure of racing. [In a race] you *have* to run fast. . . . I just need to do that again."

Webb will get his first taste of racing this weekend, when he runs a 1200-meter time trial. One week later, on April 20, the real racing begins at Mt. SAC. With those two efforts under his belt,

Webb feels he'll be ready to thrill another Penn Relays crowd if he gets the baton in contention. As he sits in his suite, he fears that regardless which events he runs—the 4 by 800 or distance medley relay—he'll receive the baton while buried in the back of the field.

Of course, in a relay with Brannen, that would be unlikely. But yesterday, Brannen tried to run and discovered he still has a busted wheel. He won't try running again until next week, at which point he will have been out of commission for 5 weeks and have only 2 weeks to prepare for the Penn Relays. One of middle-distance running's cruel certitudes is that the fitness that takes months and years to acquire can vanish in a matter of weeks.

Brannen is an exceptional athlete who is capable, on 2 weeks' training, of running well enough on an 800- or 1200-meter leg to help get the baton around to Webb in decent position. But as Webb munches on fruit in his hotel room, he knows this scenario is growing exceedingly more unlikely by the day.

CHAPTER:08

MAN UP!

On Saturday, April 13, Tim Broe is at the track to watch Alan Webb run his 1200-meter time trial. He's his usual amiable self. On this morning, as on so many recent mornings, he has reason to be. He has blitzed a fartlek run around town that the guys call "O'Reilly," after a long-since-forgotten Michigan harrier, and while he shuffles around afterward like a bent old man, his ease of effort on O'Reilly has him feeling just a notch or two shy of invincible.

Life is good when you're in the zone.

This morning, Broe has come to see just how much progress Webb has made. Ever since the meeting in Warhurst's office in late March, he's seen a tremendous change in Webb's demeanor. Most telling for Broe was one afternoon, a few days after Webb blew up at him on the Arb, when the two of them went out for a 10-miler through the streets of Ann Arbor. Mid-run, during a break in the conversation, Webb quietly apologized to Broe for his outburst. Broe accepted the apology without hesitation, and in a brotherly manner stressed to Webb that they were there to lean on each other in tough times. On his way home that evening, Broe acknowledged to me, "That was very big of Alan to do that."

Now, 10 minutes before go time, Broe sits on the indoor track with Sully and Brannen, wondering how Webb's approaching this time trial. Minutes later, Webb walks past them and out the door, with his head down and headphones on. With that, they have their answer. Says Brannen, "This ain't no training run."

Before each race his senior spring, Webb followed a particular pre-race routine that concluded only after he'd put his headphones on and listened to Everclear's hit song "One Hit Wonder." He abstained from listening to the song throughout the cross country season, wanting to save it for track. Now, 10 long months since he last raced at the USA Track and Field Championships, the headphones are back on.

Webb won't be running alone. As most of the team congregates on the homestretch, placing side bets on how fast Webb will run, freshmen Sean Moore and Tarn Leach, junior David Sage, and sophomore Brian Turner line up at the start.

Everyone waits for Webb as he sits on the track by the 100-meter starting line, headphones on, changing into his spikes. At last, Warhurst tells one of guys, "Tell that yo-yo to get his earphones off and get over here."

All eyes are on Webb as he slowly jogs to the starting line, intermittently shaking out his arms as if to ready them for the coming onslaught of lactic acid. Warhurst would be content to see Webb run a 2:56 this morning, and he "wouldn't put a 52 or 53 past him." He knows that Webb has other plans. In the locker room earlier this morning, Moore, fresh off a Michigan on Thursday, bitched about how sore he'd be after this one. Turner, today's rabbit, then gloated, "That's too bad; all I have to run is 1:26 [for 600 meters]." Webb instantly corrected him: "1:25." He wants a 2:50.

Down the first backstretch, Turner and Webb have already separated themselves from the rest of the pack. Broe booms his encouragement: "Man up!"

In no time, Turner and Webb pass the 400-meter mark. "56.2," Warhurst yells. They continue past the 600 right on pace at 1:25. "Stay relaxed, Webbster!" Warhurst shouts.

After the 600-meter mark, Turner drops out and Webb turns it up a notch. Warhurst urges him to stay relaxed as he eyes him across the track and through the 1000-meter mark in 2:22. "Shit!" he says to Sully, "That little fucker might run 2:51!"

Into the final homestretch, Webb starts to tighten, shoulders rising and cadence slowing. Warhurst spots it immediately and, over the others' exhortations, yells to Webb to shorten his stroke and pick up his arms. Leery of Warhurst's notoriously quick trigger finger in practice, many of the guys have a watch on Webb. They click in unison as he crosses the line a full 100 meters in front of Moore.

The time is 2:52.6. Webb is jacked. He tried to pick it up over the last 150 meters and isn't sure whether that made him decelerate further, but he doesn't dwell on it. He went in wanting to run his last quarter in 57 seconds and fell only 1 second short. Besides, it's his first-ever practice race, so it's "an infinite personal best!" And he did this at the end of a 71-mile week, tying his longest week ever . . . and . . . and . . .

He keeps finding reasons to be satisfied with his effort, sifting through the stats of his training log that he knows by heart, then analyzing them within the context of what he's done. For once it seems he has managed to satisfy his most demanding critic—himself.

But he's not done. While the others begin their cooldown, Webb puts his training shoes back on and hits the track for 300-, 400-, and 600-meter repeats at 4-minute-mile pace. As Warhurst watches him manage the task without a hint of strain, he speculates about how this will translate next week at Mt. SAC.

Excitedly, he says, "There's not a doubt in my mind that he can run 3:55 [for the mile] right now, which means if the pace is right out in California he'll run 3:40 [for 1500 meters], maybe under if somebody gets it going."

Webb's as excited, if not more so, by the implications of his run. He comes over to Warhurst after the workout and joyously exclaims of his 400-meter effort, "That 60 [seconds] felt like walking!"

Back and forth they chat with unrestrained optimism, Warhurst telling Webb he believes he can run 3:54 to 3:56 right now and Webb speculating that if he can do that now, then in 8 weeks he can—not should, not might, but can—run 3:48 or 3:49.

Warhurst says nothing to dissuade him, and for good reason. For months now, he has endured public and private criticism of his handling of Webb. If Webb doesn't set the world on fire this spring, he knows he'll be catching the heat. Webb's progress is as much a validation of his training as it is of Webb's fitness. So let Webb, who's as excitable as they come, use today as fuel for the fire. Hell, they're on a roll.

Ever the conservative, Sully sounds the one note of caution. Sitting on the locker room bench with Warhurst and Broe, he jogs his memory to place Webb's run in the context of what he's done in the past. The closest comparison he can make is from his freshman year, when 2 weeks after the cross country season he ran a 1200-meter time trial in 2:53. In his first mile of the season, he ran a 4:01.

Back from his cooldown, Webb is still on an emotional high, flush with confidence. "You think I can run another lap?" he asks.

I throw the question right back at him. "What do you think?"

"Hell, yeah! I know I can!"

THE FINAL RUN BEFORE MT. SAC

A few days later, Webb completes a final tune-up for Mt. SAC. It's a workout that leaves even him with a detached sense of awe about his own abilities.

He whoops with joy after effortlessly running 1000 meters in 2:26. "Did you see how chilling that was?" he says in astonishment afterward. He then runs four business-like 43-second 300s one after the other, and finally, after a quarter jog, puts the exclamation point on his session with a 53-second quarter *into* a swirling wind.

Warhurst squints into the sun and shifts his jaw from side to side, crunching numbers in his head as he reassesses Webb's fitness. He can't help chuckling incredulously, "53 is totally hot at the end of that. That's an old Sully workout."

Warhurst knows that Webb's fitter than he was in April a year ago. Yet the coach also knows that he ran his race a month later at the Prefontaine in ideal conditions. That's why, in a phone conversation late yesterday evening, he told Webb not to worry about running a personal best at Mt. SAC. "Just win the race and qualify. That's all you gotta do." Given Webb's fitness, he knows he's capable of a 3:37 or 3:38, but he couldn't care less as long as he hits the NCAA automatic qualifying time of 3:41.5. "Anything else," he told Webb, "is icing on the cake."

A 3:41.5 is not likely to satisfy Webb this weekend. After blistering the quarter, he gives me the feeling that he beat more than his own expectations out there. I sense that with that quarter he also imagined demolishing his competitors and critics.

Panting heavily, his words bursting forth between breaths like machine gun fire, he says, "People say that just because I don't run as much mileage as Ritz [Dathan Ritzenhein] does . . ." and then he pauses. In the void, I know he's finishing his sentence: "I'm not as tough as them. I'm not as dedicated. I'm not as—screw that! Let's see them run that workout. They're good, but I work my ass off."

CHAPTER:09

ALAN WEBB: STAGE LEFT

Alan Webb is leaning over the sink in his hotel room at the Holiday Inn, hocking greenish-yellow loogies into the sink. Despite feeling as if a midget on methamphetamine is hammering away in his skull with a sledgehammer, Webb is bullish about his chances this evening at Mt. SAC in his long-awaited collegiate debut in the 1500 meters.

He wants to run 3:37 tonight, good enough to set a personal record, qualify automatically for the NCAA Championships, and break the track record, meet record, and American junior record in one fell swoop. If only his damn ear would pop and the hours would rush by in a wink so he could race already! He's running in the last race of the evening, at 9:45 P.M. Pacific time, long after this easterner has usually gone to bed.

Runners from universities across the land annually make the pilgrimage here in hopes of getting fast times and qualifying marks for the NCAA Championships in the famously still evening air of Walnut, California. At the track, heat after heat of distance events is going off, and, as usual, tons of athletes are getting fat personal bests on another magical Mt. SAC night. Despite his congestion, Webb hopes to be next.

THE RACE

Later, Webb watches the races from a distance, alone, high in the stands, with his headphones on. He taps his right foot nervously over and over. If only Warhurst were here, he could ease Webb's tension and have him laughing with some idle chatter. His coach, however, is back in Michigan.

It kills him not to be able to come to watch Webb run, but his baby could be born anytime now, and the 59-year-old father-to-be would not chance missing the birth of his first son. Although the baby, already named Luke, isn't officially slated to greet the world until early May, Kalli Warhurst's age, 40, makes it more likely the baby could be born early.

Webb won't dare sit any closer to the action. He learned that lesson last night when, besieged by high school and college students seeking his autograph, it took him 20-odd minutes to navigate his way from one side of the stands to the other. They had him sign everything, from scraps of paper to *Track and Field News* covers and an article about him torn from the pages of *Sports Illustrated*.

Most of the autograph hounds were polite. Some had special requests, such as "Can you sign it 'To Samantha'?" Most were content to get his standard signature: "Alan Webb, MILER." Webb offered a kind word to everyone and invariably asked their names and shook their hands—even those who rudely shoved pen and paper in his face with the command: "Sign this." I thought his composure was remarkable, especially for a 19-year-old.

At 8:20 P.M. Webb heads down to begin his warmup at a large grass athletic field next to the stadium. While he goes through his routine of drills and accelerations, groups of runners from any number of universities and running clubs circle the field.

The scene is tense, with most runners moving in silence as the stadium speakers fill the night air with the announcer's chatter. To Webb's dismay, the autograph hounds find him here, too. It takes considerable audacity to approach an athlete who is getting ready to perform, yet Webb displays admirable restraint when he beseeches them, in a tone of mild annoyance, "You mind waiting until after my race?"

Just 20 minutes before race time, Webb's feeling loose. His endless series of drills and accelerations on the lower field seems to have settled him. Sitting on the grass by the entry to the track, Webb sings along as Led Zeppelin's "Stairway to Heaven," not his usual "One Hit Wonder," plays through his headphones.

As the third section of the 1500 finishes, Webb stands, takes off his headphones, and does his best Nick Cage impression from the movie *Gone in 60 Seconds*. He holds his hands up by his chest, pauses for a second as he shakes his index fingers, and says to me, "Let's go!"

The evening air is now chilly, yet thousands have stayed to watch Webb. Spectators stand two and three deep by the start and finish areas as the announcer lists the field of 16, a who's who of collegiate milers. As the runners mill around before the start, Webb makes the rounds, shaking their hands one by one. It's puzzling behavior for someone readying for battle. The gesture reeks of insecurity. Perhaps the jitters I saw in the stands, when he was tapping his feet incessantly, have resurfaced.

The class of the field radiates out from the pole. Arkansas's Chris Mulvaney is in lane 1, Stanford's Jonathon Riley and Don Sageare are in 2 and 3, Villanova's Ryan Hayden and Adrian Blincoe are in 4 and 5, and Webb is in 6. The tension builds as the announcer goes through the list of Webb's accomplishments, and the crowd responds with a roar of applause. Shouts of "Come on, Webb!" resound across the track as they line up to go.

A false start, almost unheard of in the 1500, cuts the tension as it gives expression to the jangled nerves of the competitors. They line up again, and this time . . .

CRACK! It's a clean start. Down the first straightaway the field engulfs Webb, and by the turn, he's surprisingly been spit out the back of the pack. But the pace is slow. They pass the 200 mark in 30 seconds, and Webb moves out to get into better position. Down the homestretch he moves in lane 3. He continues to make his way to the front, where he takes the lead only 300 meters into the race.

There's no need to take the lead so early in a race of this caliber unless the pace is so slow you want to just hammer it. Given Webb's goals and his 300 split of 45 seconds (a 3:45 1500 pace), I assume he's taking the lead to put the hurt on the rest of the field. Yet he does nothing to increase the pace, and as they hit the quarter in 60 seconds, the others are tightly bunched behind him.

I watch expectantly for Webb to move on the second quarter, but with each hundred, his cadence never varies. He's running as if it's an interval workout at Ferry Field, each hundred the same as the last, yet now he's got a pack of hungry milers nipping at his heels. Webb passes through 800 in 2-flat, unaware that Eric Garner, the University of Washington's lanky miler, has torn past seven or eight guys to move up on his outside shoulder in the last 100 meters.

Without hesitation, Garner blows by Webb down the backstretch, and in an instant, Webb's aura of invincibility pierced, *five* other milers, led by Blincoe, rush past.

Down the homestretch it's Garner, Mulvaney, and Blincoe, followed closely by Hayden and a little-known miler from the University of Montana, Scott McGowen, then a slight gap before Webb in sixth.

As Garner hits the final lap in 2:44, Webb finally breaks loose from his malaise and reacts. He bursts to close the gap and in a few strides has attached himself to the back of the pack of five runners who had passed him. His move to the back of the pack coincides with a strong move by Villanova's Blincoe. Approaching the 1200-meter mark, with only 300 to go, Blincoe has moved past Garner into the lead and begins ratcheting up the pace. He looks great as he hits the 1200-meter mark in 2:59, but Webb's in good position. Furthermore, the quickness with which he latched onto the front pack on the bend indicates that Webb has a lot of fuel in the tank.

Into the final backstretch, Blincoe drives his arms, launching his kick for home, putting some ground between himself and the field. All eyes in the stadium are now fixed on Webb, waiting for him to unleash his kick.

Down the backstretch, to the crowd's delight, Webb obliges, moving from fifth to fourth and right to Mulvaney's shoulder in third with 200 meters to go. Blincoe is still within reach.

And then Webb stalls, just as Villanova's Hayden flies by his outside shoulder into the turn. He doesn't respond to Hayden's move. Worse, as he runs through the turn, he tightens visibly. A group of runners passes him in a feeding frenzy down the home-stretch.

In front, Blincoe grits his teeth and pumps his arms furiously, not once turning his head to see what's developing behind him. His head tilts ever backward as he approaches the line, muscles flooded with lactic acid, but it's too late for Montana's McGowen, in second, to overtake him. Blincoe wins in 3:41.85, and when Webb finally crosses the line, he is buried in ninth place with a time of 3:44.74.

The air is filled with silence. One by one the milers walk toward the starting area to gather T-shirts they discarded prior to the race. Webb walks with them, then continues past, walking alone down the backstretch toward the far end of the track.

No one says anything as he walks past on the track, his face an expressionless mask. Though he never publicly stated his objectives, not a soul in the stadium is oblivious to his profound sense of embarrassment as he makes his way toward the exit. For Webb, those seconds as he walks down the backstretch feel infinitely longer than the hours he waited to race.

Exiting the gate on the far end of the track, Webb spies a mass of reporters jogging his way, eager for him to put words to his shame. He runs away from them as Michigan's sports information representative, David Crabtree, an affable young graduate of the University of Texas, rushes past, anxious to cut off the herd. "Oh, no," he says as he runs across the field to hold the reporters at bay, "here we go."

With Crabtree's aid, Webb is given some time to collect himself. He heads off to the outskirts of the athletic field, where he sits alone, too distraught to cool down. There, the realization hits home that as of right now, he is nothing more than a guy in the race—at the collegiate level.

Back in the stadium, Michigan assistant coach Fred LaPlante waits with Wiz and quarter-miler Kevin Lamb for Webb to emerge. With the exception of those few coaches waiting for their milers to finish jogging, the place is empty. LaPlante frets over what he can possibly say to Webb. He has been a collegiate coach for 25 years, but he could coach 25 more, and it still wouldn't matter. Moments like this are invariably difficult to handle.

While waiting for Webb, I think back to Sully's words after Webb's 1200 time trial a week ago. Sully ran a 4:01 mile after his 2:53 time trial. Webb's 1500 time of 3:44 converts to a 4:01 mile, so Webb's on a par with what Sully was able to do his freshman year after a cross country season. And Sully certainly ended up okay. He finished third at the NCAA Indoor Championships in the mile later that winter. Lamb, who solidified his status as the quarter-miler for Michigan's distance medley relay at Penn next weekend with a 47-second performance today, understands as much. He says, "I'm no distance runner, but I know enough to know that 3:44's not bad. He's still my [relay] anchor anytime."

At last, Webb walks into the stadium and up the steps toward the Michigan crew. All eyes are on him as he slowly climbs toward LaPlante. Everyone scrutinizes his facial expression for clues to the depth of his disappointment. To the relief of all, as Webb reaches LaPlante, he manages a smile and a resigned sigh. At that, LaPlante wraps his arm around Webb's shoulder.

The rest of the Michigan guys quickly close in on Webb to give him a reassuring hug or a pat on the back. To no one in particular, Webb says, "The way I figure it, I'm about 109 meters away."

Despite the setback, Webb's as ambitious as ever. In his eyes, a 3:44 would have been a great time for the mile (1609 meters).

CHAPTER: 10

THE GATHERING STORM

It's late morning in late April on another windy and gray Ann Arbor day. Alan Webb is at the track for a short speed workout, his last before he runs at the Penn Relays this weekend. He has his last exam this afternoon, so he's here by himself.

The shock of his performance in California is starting to wear off. As bad as it was, Webb feels grateful that he got such a bad showing out of the way at Mt. SAC, where the crowds were relatively smaller than at Penn; more than 40,000 will watch the relays in Philadelphia.

Still, the feeling he had when he was sitting off by himself after the race is not one he's likely to forget—or want to forget, for that matter. As he stretches, Webb recalls how frustrated he was after the race. "I finally got a little light," he tells me, "and I fell flat on my face. The whole time I was thinking that the whole winter would just go away once I got a good race in. I talk about track a lot, you know. After the race, I was like, Oh, my God, I'm *that* guy. I'm the guy that choked. Oh, man, this sucks!"

He laughs resignedly and adds, "You know, that's the lowest I've ever finished in a race since my first race. I just wasn't ready for all those people."

As Webb finishes his strides, legs churning pistonlike beneath him, Coach Warhurst arrives at the track, clucking and humming like an excitable kid. He's philosophical about Webb's performance. While his workouts indicate to Warhurst that he is capable of at least an NCAA qualifying time of 3:41, he knows Webb must learn to race at the collegiate level.

On this morning, Webb runs a typically spectacular workout, reassuring Warhurst that he's okay. After Webb runs the last quarter of the first set in a restrained 56 seconds, Warhurst asks him to imagine what it's like to run four of them in succession. Webb replies, "Let's not get ahead of ourselves," to which the coach exults, "He's learning! He's learning!"

One step at a time.

"You got a bull's-eye on your back," Warhurst tells Webb after he blisters his last quarter in 53 seconds to finish the workout. "Everyone wants a piece of your ass, and they got a good piece of it this weekend." He thinks Webb was intimidated at Mt. SAC and masked it by being outgoing. Webb admits as much, telling Warhurst that he was running on pins and needles, afraid to hold his turf with some well-timed elbows, fearing that "they'd get me" if he was aggressive.

So Warhurst spends a good while talking with Webb after his workout, teaching him about tactics, positioning, and the mental aspects of collegiate racing. And they discuss this weekend's distance medley relay at Penn, in which they expect Webb will most likely be chasing guys down from behind but where tactics may still come into play. To Warhurst's delight, Webb listens attentively throughout. Warhurst concludes Track 101 with the most sage advice of all: "Just go race and have *fun* this weekend," he says, "and redeem your damn self."

"Damn right," Webb says emphatically.

MEDIA ATTENTION

Heading back to his office, Warhurst can't contain his glee at what just transpired. "What a breakthrough," he says. "The boy is learning. I love it. He's smart enough to know that what he needs to do now is work on his racing skills. That's why the college system is so cool. . . . It's a bridge to the pro level. He may have had thoughts that he was ready to go pro earlier, but now the kid knows better."

In his office, Warhurst settles into his chair to prepare for the rest of the afternoon. The phone rings. It's Dick Patrick from *USA Today*. Warhurst swivels his chair away from the computer.

Warhurst and Webb have received an avalanche of media requests heading into Penn. Mindful of the fact that Webb is a student and has a social life, Warhurst does his best to limit requests for his time, but he makes an exception for Patrick, one of the nation's most recognized track reporters, and for the *Washington Post*, which is Webb's hometown paper.

Warhurst converses freely with Patrick and gives him an honest assessment of Webb's status. "A 3:44 for most mortals in their first race in 9 months is tremendous," Warhurst tells him. "But because he's Alan Webb, it's a disaster. You've gotta get some WD40 on his wheels, that's all. He's a little rusty, but he's gonna be just fine." Warhurst feels great about their conversation when it ends, but he has no way of knowing that when Patrick's story is published in a few days, it will turn his life upside-down.

BRANNEN'S COMEBACK

One day later, Warhurst is back at Ferry Field presiding over Nate Brannen's workout. Brannen began running again last week after 6 weeks off to repair the stress fracture in his left foot. Amazingly, he looks none the worse after his hiatus. If I didn't already know about the injury, I'd have no idea Brannen was staging a comeback. Raw talent like his shines as bright as the lights in Times Square.

Warhurst watches him intently to see if he's putting more weight on his healthy foot than on the injured one, and Brannen checks out. There's no hitch in his step. The coach is left to marvel at the quickness with which Brannen pulls through each stride. That quickness is what enables him to hit top speed in a matter of steps, an ability that can make Brannen great. The other milers here, Webb included, may have a slight chance at besting Brannen in a quarter; all of them can run the quarter in 48 seconds or better. But no one can hang with him through an acceleration drill. He'll separate himself from the pack every time.

Women's distance coach Mike McGuire walks by Warhurst as Brannen's wrapping up his run. "Who's running the 1200 [at Penn]?" he asks.

It's a fair question. The relay includes legs of 1200, 800, 400, and 1600 meters. In his first workout, run while Webb was in California, Brannen drilled all of the candidates for the 1200 leg at Penn. Brannen's form has made Warhurst contemplate using him, but he won't let himself be tempted. "It's not fair [to Brannen]," he says, "I'm not gonna put him in there to run 2:58 when I know he could run 2:51." That a 2:58 in a 1200 leg is the best that Michigan has to offer is frightening when I consider that the leaders will be running around 2:50.

Warhurst scans assistant coach Fred LaPlante's group of half-milers, all of whom are struggling through a workout, and informs McGuire of his choice for the 1200: Dave Cook, referred to by all as "Cookie." McGuire's eyes bug out of his head when he hears it. "Cookie?" he says incredulously. "Holy shit! Webb's gonna throw the stick in the stands he's gonna be so far down!"

Suffice it to say that Cookie doesn't imbue the staff with confidence. A fourth-year junior out of Portage, Michigan, Cookie is an enigma. He oozes talent. He's a lean 5'10" with shaggy hair and willowy legs, and his light, loose stride is the envy of many on the team. Last spring, he ran a very respectable 3:47 for 1500 meters, but Cookie is more known for what he doesn't do.

Cookie always comes to practice with a smile, he does what he's told, and the guys love to have him around. He just never gets out of his comfort zone. He never suffers in practice, and he never goes the extra mile like Webb. He's simply content to skate by and enjoy the ride. At this point in his career, the coaching staff doubts they will ever turn the key to his ambition.

That's not to say Warhurst won't try. He decided on Cookie a week ago, and ever since, he's been trying to get him keyed up to run leadoff at Penn. Over and over, he's been delivering the message as only Warhurst can: "Don't fuck it up!"

Cookie's doing his best not to let his nerves get to him. The pressure, he insists, is not on him but on the other leadoff legs, who don't have an elephant like Webb on anchor. "They gotta gap me," he says. He knows he can hang for at least two of the three laps. The third lap will be a matter of will, and now, in the locker room after his last hard run before Penn, he's confident he can get it done.

Unfortunately for Webb, Cookie's not the only shaky leg. Warhurst and LaPlante aren't worried about their quarter-miler, Kevin Lamb, who can run a 47-second quarter and should be able to get the stick around without losing more than a second. They are concerned, however, about their half-miler, Jeremy Schneider, a soft-spoken computer engineering major from Bloomfield Hills, Michigan. At about 6'3", the aptly nicknamed "Big J" has a long, loping stride. He has a reputation for stepping it up on relays, and Warhurst and LaPlante figure if he catches fire, he could run a 1:48 at Penn. Unfortunately, he looks awful today at practice.

As LaPlante watches, Schneider bails out of a workout with the other half-milers and sits on a bench in the middle of the infield with his head down. LaPlante has seen Schneider cut his workouts short before, so it doesn't overly concern him. Frankly, he says, "He doesn't have many good workouts in the first place. He's done this before. He's gutless. If Cook doesn't run well, I'll guarantee you

Schneider won't run well. If the first two guys run halfway decent, and there's somebody to run with, Schneider might run well."

LaPlante figures that at best Michigan will be 6 seconds down on the first exchange, 7 by the second, and 10 by the third, "and that's if we run pretty good." Webb's not around to hear this, and that's probably a good thing, because if Michigan is that far behind when he gets the baton, he just might be tempted to hurl it into the stands.

CHAPTER:11

THE PENN RELAYS

I t's 8:30 on Thursday morning, April 25. Some of the Michigan runners competing this evening at the Penn Relays distance carnival, including Sean Moore, Tarn Leach, and Wiz, are trickling into the locker room to get their spikes and uniforms before boarding the bus to the airport. Alan Webb is taking a later flight to Philadelphia.

Warhurst, fresh from a run, is sitting on a bench in the locker room when they arrive. He looks haggard. Perspiration is dripping down the salt-and-pepper stubble on his face, his hair is unkempt, and sweat has soaked through his long-sleeved T-shirt. I get the impression he's been sitting here for a while, too beat to move.

Moore walks in and pauses. "Jeez," he says, looking at me with a mischievous smile, "do we have to help that man?"

"Shit," Warhurst replies, "that wind was so stiff, it was blowing me backward!"

Unfortunately, Warhurst won't be joining them at Penn. He's still awaiting the birth of his baby boy, Luke. Everyone wants to meet the little guy, the product of what Warhurst describes under a picture of him and his pregnant wife on the University of Michigan Hospital Web page as "the shot heard round the world." He'll have to settle for Sully giving him a blow-by-blow account of the races from the stands.

Warhurst boards the bus before it departs. "There's gonna be 40,000 people there, so you might be nervous. Now, I remember when the first bullet whizzed by my head in Vietnam. My ass puckered right up. That's nervous." He has a special message for Dave Cook: "Don't fuck it up!" Warhurst knows how to keep 'em loose.

TRAVEL NIGHTMARES

This is Sully's first trip as the bossman. As such, Murphy's Law dictates that everything that can go wrong, will go wrong. Here then, is a partial list of the mishaps Sully endured over the first 8 hours of the trip.

1. The flight is delayed due to a security breach at Detroit Metro Airport.
2. Four of the guys' luggage doesn't make it, including Wiz's. A fifth-year senior, Wiz has had it drilled into him by now that you always carry your spikes and uniform in your carry-on. Of course, he put his backpack with his uniform into his luggage during check-in.
3. After making arrangements for the luggage to be delivered to the hotel, Sully and the guys head outside to board their

shuttle. It is summarily swiped by another party. They wait 30-odd minutes in the rain for another to arrive.

4. Checking in at the Pennsylvania Inn, Sully is informed that the Michigan group's rooms have been given to another party.

5. Sully then heads over to meet headquarters to pick up the race packet. The packet is devoid of race numbers and competitors' passes. He's sent through the bowels of Franklin Field to find the "problem desk." When he's given another packet, he opens it to discover it's completely empty. "I was ready to kill somebody," he says.

Number snafu fixed, Sully enters his hotel room at 3:20 P.M., in a daze and completely famished. He hasn't eaten since breakfast. He feels as if someone out there is playing a twisted joke on him to see if he really wants to be a coach, a job that he's quickly finding out goes way beyond holding a stopwatch. Warhurst laughs when Sully calls looking for some moral support, saying, "Welcome to the world of coaching, Sully!"

The kicker, however, had come when he was dealing with the hotel mix-up at the front desk of the Pennsylvania Inn. The guys were loitering a good distance behind him, waiting for their room keys, when Sully's cell phone rang. It was his agent, Mark Wetmore. Sully turned to the team and, in an uncharacteristically loud and angry voice, pointed to a stack of *USA Todays* sitting on a shelf. "Grab me a copy of the paper!" he ordered.

The guys quickly opened the paper and started rifling through the sports section. On the eighth page, they saw an article by Dick Patrick entitled, "Pro Possibilities: Michigan's Alan Webb Might Not Return to School."

In the article, Patrick quoted Webb discussing the travails of his winter: "A lot of stuff went on that people don't know about and won't know about. I was missing all these races I wanted to run. I was missing training I really needed. It wasn't good." Moreover, the article opened a can of worms that will dog Warhurst and Webb throughout the remainder of the season. "For now, I'm coming back," Webb is quoted, "but there's a possibility to do something else."

"Webb," Patrick wrote, "could command a lucrative shoe-company contract, continue running on his own, and run professionally."

In the lobby, Sully refrained from engaging the guys' speculation over Webb's future, but once in his hotel room, he doesn't mince his words. "It frustrates me to see that he's kind of playing Ron," he tells me. "You can see Ron's so excited about what Alan's doing. It's frustrating to see what's going on behind the scenes. Ron's got blinders on somewhat. He sees it but he doesn't want to fully believe it."

Sully and Warhurst both know that Webb has continued to maintain a strong relationship with his high school coach, Scott Raczko, since the fall. But after that closed-door meeting with Warhurst earlier in the season, Webb appeared to fully buy into the Michigan program. His comments in Patrick's article come as a shock to Sully, who feels as if Raczko is undermining their program.

When I reach Raczko later in the weekend, he denies Sully's charge. Dick Patrick spoke to him after speaking to Webb, and right then Raczko knew the story would cause a stir. He thought, Oh, God, here we go. Although he adamantly states that he'll always offer Webb his advice if asked, he denies trying to influence his decisions.

"Alan is old enough to make his own decisions. He went to Michigan, his decision. Going to college, his decision. Whether he stays at Michigan or doesn't, that will be his decision," he says. "He's smart enough. He'll take advice from different people and lay it on the table and make the best decision for himself. I'll support him no matter what he does and be confident no matter what he does that things will work out well for him."

But Raczko is also an outspoken critic of the American collegiate system's ability to develop top talent. For 99.9 percent of runners, he thinks it works great. It helps pay for college and offers them tremendous competitive opportunities. But for that 0.1 percent good enough to take it to a professional level, he says, "It's different. And it's different for a distance runner than for a sprinter. With distance runners you have the three-season thing, plus there's the possibility you may go over to Europe. You're talking about quite a few seasons, and on the international level typically you won't see that."

He points out that many top high school runners go to college and "stagnate." He asks, "How many on the national level get out of college and make big surges after that?" The answer, unfortunately, is "not many." And for those high school stars who stagnate in college, the future is grim. It is a financial and athletic struggle to succeed as a professional runner.

Of course, there are exceptions, and Warhurst coaches two of them, Tim Broe and Sully. In the end, though, Raczko concludes, "Everybody is freaking different. That's why Alan has to do the Alan Webb thing, regardless of what people tell him."

LAST-MINUTE DISTRACTIONS

In his hotel room, Sully doesn't want to engage in any more speculation. He's here to see to it that Webb and the others run to the best of their ability at one of the season's marquee meets. Patrick's story serves as nothing more than an unwelcome distraction. Yet, as someone who bleeds maize and blue, he views Webb's waffling with distaste. "I don't want him to be here if he doesn't want to be here. It just causes friction. If he wants to go, we'll just wish him the best and move on."

Sadly, Webb is virtually lost in the debate over what he should do, just a pawn in the game. When Raczko asks Webb about the story later in the weekend, Webb tells him, "I really wish he wouldn't have printed that. I just wanted to be honest."

Webb arrived late Thursday night and went right to bed. On Friday, in the early afternoon, the Michigan distance medley relay team meets in the lobby to make the short walk from their hotel to the stadium. Webb sits in a chair, hair gelled, headphones on, calm and collected. The same can't be said for Cookie. He has a serious case of bed head, and he's wearing the kind of thick rope necklace you see hippies selling in the parking lots of Grateful Dead shows and Phish concerts. He nervously asks Sully if he has some last-minute advice. "Yeah," Sully tells him, "don't fuck it up."

Sully knows what it takes. While Michigan has a rich history at Penn, having won more championships than any other institution except Villanova, Arkansas, and Penn, it's a dated one. The plaques hanging in the locker room in the track building are relics of another era. In Warhurst's 28 years at Michigan, his men have won but one Penn Relays championship. Sully anchored the Wolverines to victory in the relays' flagship event, the distance medley relay, in 1998.

As the runners walk toward Franklin Field on a gorgeous afternoon, strangers wish Webb luck. He thanks them and keeps moving. He displays none of the nervous energy he did a week ago.

The same can't be said for Schneider. He's a bundle of nerves, but he takes solace from the fact that he felt the same way when he ran on Michigan's mile relay team here as a freshman. He was so nervous then that he threw up his pre-race PowerBar before he even hit the line. He went on to run a career-best 46-second split, however. "Which gives me an idea," he says jokingly.

Michigan's quarter-miler, Kevin Lamb, is the coolest of the quartet, in part because he knows that his leg will not make or break the race for the team.

Lamb, Schneider, Cookie, and Webb head to a secluded area on a grassy knoll on Penn's campus to warm up away from the madness. To Webb's relief, he's allowed to warm up in peace. (Earlier this morning, a young man asked for an autograph while Webb was relieving himself in a hotel restroom.) And to everyone's relief, Cookie feels fast and strong in his warmup. The bounce in his stride eases his nerves.

About 20 minutes before race time, the Michigan team heads to the paddock inside the stadium, the first holding area where the distance medley relay teams will check in. They're one of the first quartets to arrive. Webb puts on his headphones and sits against the wall. Soon after, the other teams, from schools such as Wake Forest, Tennessee, Connecticut, Georgetown, Villanova, and Arkansas, file in. While the runners put on their jerseys and spikes, an official outfitted in a Penn Relays blue blazer and red-and-blue striped tie sits on a giant lifeguard stand and starts barking out the names of the schools. Cookie raises his hand to check in Michigan when it's called.

Several minutes later, they're shuttled to the holding pen by the start line on the track. It was relatively quiet in the paddock, but here next to the start, the atmosphere is charged. The stands by the finish line are a sea of green and black. Jamaica's top talent annually makes a pilgrimage to Penn, and their loyal following always sits there, raucously cheering and waving Jamaican flags. The noise, the pageantry—it all adds up to the most electric atmosphere in all of track and field.

The officials line Webb and the other milers up against the wall, and unlike at Mt. SAC, Webb keeps to himself. Soon, the runners are gone, flying down the homestretch on some last-second strides. As they do, announcer Bob Hersh's concussive baritone voice fills the stadium: "On the track now is the distance medley championship of America, the greatest event in the greatest track meet in America."

One by one, he announces the teams with such gravity, pausing after each name—ARKANSAS . . . MICHIGAN . . . VILLANOVA— that it feels as if this is the most coveted prize in track.

Arkansas is undoubtedly the co-favorite today with Villanova. While Villanova won the distance medley in a remarkable 16 consecutive years, from 1969 to 1981, Arkansas subsequently dominated the event, winning 13 of the next 20. With superb steeplechaser Daniel Lincoln on leadoff and South African star Alistair Cragg on the back end, Arkansas has the horses to take back the crown Villanova wore a year ago. Like Villanova, they expect to win—nothing less.

THE RELAY

CRACK!—and they're off. The 1200-meter runners bang into one another like pinballs off the start, jockeying for position into the curve.

Within seconds, as Sully watches from the east stands on the backstretch, he hears a loud gasp emanate from the fans on the homestretch. On the track, Lincoln, Arkansas's leadoff man, hears a loud "Shit!" moments before he hears the sound of a baton hitting the ground. He turns his head to see Villanova's Ryan Hayden turning in the opposite direction to retrieve it.

Hayden had been gripping the baton at the very top, not in the middle, and his arm swung backward just as Abilene Christian's Jean-Marie Ndikumana came tumbling into him. As Ndikumana braced himself, his arm flew into Hayden's baton, popping it loose from his hand.

A year ago, Villanova won the event for the first time in 20 years. And they validated that title by winning the distance medley at this year's NCAA Indoor Championships. Now, seeing Hayden lurching backward to retrieve the stick, Lincoln has a single thought: Go! He doesn't want to lead, but given the circumstances, he's more than happy to hammer to squash any hope Villanova may harbor of getting back into contention.

The development is a bad omen for Michigan. Sully was hoping the leadoff leg would be a tactical "sit and kick" affair. In such a race, Cookie would at least have a chance of getting the stick across in contention. The hot pace spells trouble for him.

Yet, for 800 meters, Cookie hangs gamely onto the back of the pack. He comes through the half at the back in 1:55, but 100 meters later, as he heads into the backstretch, he starts to slowly lose contact. With 200 meters to go, his gait slows to a painful crawl. As Cookie tells me later, "That's when the fat kid from the slow heat jumped on my back."

Back in Ann Arbor, Brannen watches the race on his computer monitor via a live Internet broadcast. He stares wordlessly at the screen as he watches Cookie fall out of contention. All year, he'd looked forward to this moment. Now, to watch the race go up in smoke when he should have had the stick is too much. Before Cookie can even finish his leg, Brannen abruptly turns off the monitor.

Even Villanova's Hayden, who had stopped dead and run backward to retrieve the baton after his initial gaffe, catches Cookie in the final homestretch. Cookie is still running as the clock ticks over 3 minutes. Sully wordlessly shakes his head in disgust. Michigan is buried in last place, 10 seconds off the lead, when

Lamb sets off on his quarter. Like Villanova, their day is done, and three men have yet to run.

Lamb runs a superb quarter, recording his first-ever sub-47-second split, and passes even Villanova when their quarter-miler, Paul Moser, trips before he can pass the stick to Jason Jabaut for the 800-meter leg.

Schneider follows up with an awful 1:55 leg.

Then Webb and Blincoe, the two most heralded milers in the field, battle it out in the back of the pack on their anchor legs, with little more than pride at stake. Blincoe sits on Webb for three laps before Webb starts gapping him on the backstretch of the final circuit. Blincoe rallies and passes Webb down the final homestretch. Both take little consolation in recording the two fastest splits (3:59.1 and 3:59.82) of the day.

Sully has mixed emotions about the race. He's extremely disappointed with Schneider and Cookie. "What do you say?" he asks. "You can't get up for the Penn Relays? That just doesn't make sense."

But he has high praise for Webb. While he lacked the gear to hold off Blincoe down the stretch, Sully's confident that will come. He notes that his own great performances here were always off an extensive indoor season. Webb, he says, is just "3 or 4 weeks behind what he needs to be really competitive. And that's just a lack of training from indoors, but it's gonna come. He's in much better shape than what he's raced."

After a long cooldown, a visibly frustrated Webb comes and sits in the stands with his father and younger brother Chris. "I just don't have that extra gear yet. I don't have that last little bit yet." More troubling for Webb is that he doesn't feel engaged when he's racing. "I'm just not *in* it," he says. His eyes widen as he plaintively holds out his hands. "What do I have to do?" he asks. "Do I just have to go out really hard and hold on? Do I sit back? I don't know. I guess I'm running scared or something."

That he may be running scared is a startling admission. The pressure he feels, coupled with his lack of finishing speed, is admittedly taking a toll. Here again, however, Webb displays the desire that separates him from so many. He vows to avenge two consecutive defeats at the hands of Blincoe tomorrow in the 4 by 800 relay. "I want to go out in 51 or 52 and just blast it. And if I die, fine, I don't care." No matter how he runs it, though, Webb knows the tonic for his bruised psyche. Contemplating tomorrow's race, he says, "I just need to run fast."

On Saturday, Webb does just that. Running the second leg on Michigan's 4 by 800 relay, he splits a 50-second first quarter before fighting home to valiantly complete his second leg in 1:49.6, proving that while his extra gear may not be here yet, it's inching ever closer. Moreover, the Michigan quartet acquits itself splendidly. Schneider, in particular, runs a solid anchor leg in 1:51.1 to bring Michigan home in fifth. Not so gutless after all.

CHAPTER:12

HOMEWARD BOUND

On the van ride back to the airport from Penn, a weary Alan Webb turned to Sean Moore and said, "I just want to go home." While his weekend was a step forward, his performances failed to meet his expectations.

Worse, they failed to meet the expectations of the unforgiving media. Take, for instance, the write-up in the *Ann Arbor News*: "Webb was unimpressive at the Penn Relays on Friday. He ran a disappointing 3:59.82 for 1600 meters to anchor Michigan to a ninth-place finish in the distance medley relay . . . He ran a disappointing ninth in the 1500 meters at the Mt. SAC Relays last weekend." The headline reads, "Webb Might Leave U-M."

The analysis lacks perspective and is typical of a hypercritical media that expects Webb to run nothing less than a personal best every time out.

So now, just a few days removed from Penn, Webb is going home to get away from it all. Nate Brannen wonders if Webb will ever return to Ann Arbor. Last night, Brannen asked him whether he planned to return from this trip, and Webb was noncommittal.

Before he leaves for home, however. Webb must meet with Coach Warhurst, and Warhurst is pissed. He felt completely blindsided by Webb's comments in *USA Today*. He can handle Webb deciding to turn pro, but he sure as hell doesn't want to be the last to know. Awaiting Webb in his office, Warhurst tells me he's "ready to blow up at him."

When Webb arrives, Warhurst shows him the coverage in the *Ann Arbor News*, and Webb defuses the situation by sincerely apologizing for the way the news of his contemplating his future was released. He promises that Warhurst will be the first to know of his plans when the season is over. The meeting ends with their relationship once more on solid ground. It's clear to all in the Michigan camp, however, that major fault lines lie just beneath the surface.

A HOST OF INJURIES

Warhurst can't afford to dwell on the Webb situation. He has other athletes to attend to, with Brannen foremost among them. Over the weekend, Warhurst met Brannen out at Ferry Field for a session of 3 by 2-K. It did not go well. Battling fierce winds, Brannen quickly fell off the pace, and when he fell further off on the second 2-K repeat, Warhurst pulled the plug.

Warhurst wanted to test Brannen's strength in that session, and he didn't like what he saw. Now he must decide whether it's in Brannen's best interest to compete this season or to redshirt and save a year of eligibility. As of now, Warhurst plans to race him un-attached in the 800 meters at Ohio State this weekend, meaning that Brannen will compete, but not in a Michigan jersey. That will allow him to retain the option to redshirt the season. In one day's time, however, Brannen will emphatically change those plans.

And then there is Sully. This morning, while Webb met with Warhurst, Sully was back in the office of his physiotherapist, Pete Kitto. By now, Sully knows the office all too well. Over the last 2 months, Kitto has performed every imaginable type of therapy on Sully, including the option of last resort, cortisone shots. For Kitto, Sully's lack of response to all the therapy pointed in one insidious direction: a stress fracture in his lower back, in his sacrum. To check that out, Sully was left with no alternative other than to drop a thousand bucks and get an MRI.

The test showed activity in precisely the area where Sully has been ailing. A bone scan is needed to further clarify what that means, but Kitto has seen enough. "Sully," he says, "it looks like you got an occult [hidden] fracture in your sacrum." He speculates that it will be another 3 or 4 weeks before Sully can resume run-ning.

Sully takes the news in stride. After all, in the past 8 weeks, he's cross-trained diligently, day in and day out, determined not to re-peat his mistake of 1996, when he ballooned by 20-some pounds and struggled to return to form. More than anything, he's relieved to finally have a diagnosis. At the same time, he's incredulous that the shove he received in a 1500 in Manchester this winter jarred him violently enough to crack the bone.

After a year of intensive work with McMullen, Broe, and Sul-livan, Kitto isn't nearly as surprised. "These guys," he says to me, "just pound the hell out of themselves. They're professional bone crackers." If anything, Kitto is disappointed that he didn't order the MRI earlier. "My gut told me something was up with Sully after a couple of weeks. But I'm learning more and more about runners, and if I get another guy like Sully who doesn't respond to treat-ment, I'm always gonna want to rule out a crack, I don't care what it is."

"If it doesn't respond in 2 weeks, you gotta pull off all the stresses right away," he continues. "The healing time would probably have been the same with Sully, but maybe we'd be 2 weeks ahead. We wouldn't have tested him on the road so much."

Kitto knows Sully won't cry over spilled milk. "Sully's a vet," he says, "and he's practical. He's not highly emotional. He won't go nuts." He will just keep on plugging away to get back. Sully has been in touch with former Michigan standout Brian Diemer, and together they've discussed what Diemer did in 1992 to come back from the same injury to make the U.S. Olympic team. If Diemer can do it, Sully figures, so can he.

This year is not an Olympic year, but nonetheless, as Sully leaves Kitto's office, he vows to be back, even if it means he's not racing until the last meet of the summer.

"It's hard," he concedes, "to be here [at Kitto's rehab], to be in the pool and on the bike, but I'm motivated to show I can come back from this. We'll see, maybe it will only last a week, but I'm motivated now at least."

This afternoon at practice, since school is now out, Warhurst distributes cash to the guys who are still running, to cover their living expenses. "The eagle shits today, lads," he says using an old army expression for payday as he hands out the money. It's not lost on the guys that should Webb turn pro, the eagle's gonna shit a hell of a lot bigger than this.

"HE'LL GET EATEN ALIVE"

When he arrives home that evening, Warhurst calls Webb's parents to talk about their son's possible desire to go pro. In an hour-long conversation, he reminds them that Webb was only ranked 78th in the world last year in the 1500 and states emphatically that should Webb go pro, "he'll get eaten alive." And he furthers his case for Webb to stay at Michigan by reminding them of what he's done with Sully and how he took Paul McMullen from 3:48 to 3:33 last summer. Warhurst's wife, Kalli, cheers him from the sidelines as he talks. She later says that she has never seen him so persuasive.

Warhurst is pleased when he hangs up. He feels that Webb's father, Steve, listened and agreed with what he had to say. I ask Warhurst why he's so keen to have Webb remain at Michigan. He answers, "I don't need the money; I don't need the notoriety. I think I've got a good enough reputation." Still, Warhurst's human, and deep down he believes he can get the most out of Webb. And he wants that responsibility. "I want him to stay here for selfish reasons, too," he says. "I want to coach the next great American miler."

Warhurst knows that he's not alone in that regard. He feels that when Webb goes home tomorrow, Scott Raczko will be singing an altogether different tune from what Warhurst told Webb's father. What will Webb do? Five weeks from now, Warhurst will have his answer.

3 MAY

CHAPTER:13

FROM ROOMMATES
TO COMPETITORS

I t's now Wednesday, May 1, and this morning, Alan Webb is departing for the airport with several duffel bags jammed full of his belongings. He is still weary after returning from Penn on Monday and shuttling nonstop until 9:00 P.M. to move out of his dorm and into a new room in Fletcher Hall. He'll stay there for the month of May and part of June to continue training while school is out.

Because of his fatigue, he postponed yesterday's scheduled workout. He'll do it at home in Virginia this afternoon under the supervision of his high school coach, Scott Raczko.

I wonder whether this is the beginning of the end of his stay in Ann Arbor. Webb is torn between staying at Michigan and going home, attending classes at George Mason University, and running professionally. But, he stresses to me, if he goes pro, it won't be for the money. He would do it so he could train under Raczko again. Unlike many collegiate athletes who turn pro early, Webb comes from a well-to-do family. Since his father is an economist with the World Bank, money, Webb says, is not an issue. And, he stresses, it has nothing to do with Coach Warhurst personally. Like his teammates, he is fond of Warhurst. So I ask, "What's the issue?"

"It's all about the running for me," he says. "Where am I gonna do best? The whole situation here [at Michigan] is not what I thought it would be."

In particular, Webb tells me he's frustrated with his lack of training partners and with Warhurst's coaching. When he enrolled at Michigan, he expected to train regularly with Sully, Brannen, McMullen, and Broe, but, due to injuries, all have suffered. He's trained with Brannen and company just a handful of times this year.

"I can train by myself at home," he says. "I've been doing that my whole career." And despite Warhurst's appeals to have faith in the Michigan program, Webb still feels that the "technical" aspect of running—meaning all the drills and strength exercises he does outside of his track training—is both crucial to his success and neglected by Warhurst.

Furthermore, he's concerned about how much time Warhurst will be able to devote to his training in the future. The Warhursts' baby is expected any day now, and Webb feels that fatherhood will just add another huge time commitment to Warhurst's already full schedule. Something will have to give, but what?

And then he considers Raczko, who is young, single and, in Webb's opinion, better positioned to fully devote his energies to Webb's training, despite his responsibilities as head cross country and track coach at South Lakes High School. Should Webb desire to do a stint of altitude training or to race overseas, he feels Raczko would be in a better position to accompany him on those excursions.

When I ask who will fund this, Webb answers that he is confident that he will be able to get an endorsement contract to pay for the remainder of his college studies, cover his training expenses, and compensate him enough to "live reasonably." I wonder if he'll be able to secure such a contract, so I seek out those in the know, the now-ubiquitous sports agents.

THE BUSINESS OF TRACK AND FIELD

Between them, Mark Wetmore and Ray Flynn represent many of America's greatest middle-distance and distance runners. Wetmore represents Tim Broe and Kevin Sullivan, among others. Former world-class miler Ray Flynn represents star milers such as Paul McMullen and Bryan Berryhill. Each has seen Dick Patrick's story in *USA Today* and knows that Webb is considering turning pro. I ask them, "What's Webb worth?"

Flynn acknowledges that, given Webb's notoriety, the amount would be "significant; his upside is huge." Wetmore thinks Webb would command "well into six figures," something only a handful of professionals, generally athletes with world championship medals and U.S. or world records to their names, can command.

Both are quick to stress, however, that they believe Webb's development would be best served by racing collegiately. Says Wetmore, "To throw him to the wolves with milers such as El Guerrouj would be very destructive for him. It's a race of attrition [on the Grand Prix circuit]; you just hang on and run fast. Simply running fast there is not going make him a star. What makes a guy a star is his ability to win races. And to win, you have to have a killer instinct, that confidence that when it's time to put it down, you can put it down on anybody. Some of the European races kill those instincts. You just get in a line and run 3:30, 3:32 [for 1500], and that's not teaching the proper things."

Should he stay at Michigan, Webb may run only a 3:37 in the 1500, but he'll learn the skills that it takes to win. He has the talent, but he needs to acquire racing skills in order to be a great championship runner, and championship races such as the Olympics will ultimately be the crucible within which Webb is judged and his long-term value determined.

Flynn concurs with Wetmore. When he was learning the ropes as a young professional miler in the early 1980s, he says, "there were a lot of softer races to grow into [in Europe]." Those days are long gone. Now, he says, "every promoter wants a record in his race." Runners who aren't up to that level end up suffering loss after loss, which can psychically and physically destroy a young athlete who lacks the maturity to cope with defeat.

Flynn believes Webb's deliberations may be a result of some frustration on his part with his early-season results. He emphasizes the need for patience. "You need time to grow," he says, "to mature and learn new methods or new training. Running never goes in a straight line up. You go to plateaus, sometimes you slip, and then you go to the next level. It would be helpful for him to grow at the level he's reached because there are a lot of expectations and demands from sponsors when one goes open and races out of college."

Nevertheless, Flynn knows that should Webb go pro, companies such as Nike will be willing to pay him handsomely. There won't be a shortage of agents seeking to represent him. Flynn knows the business, and, as a sub-3:50 miler, he has an athletic pedigree that should appeal to Webb's sensibilities. In the end, Flynn's misgivings about Webb going pro wouldn't prevent him from signing him. "If he does decide to go that route, I think I have best credentials to guide him. I know athletically as well as commercially many of pitfalls one can run into."

THE NATURAL

Webb has now left for the airport with his head chock-full of questions and doubts. I head to practice this afternoon with Nate Brannen, who has doubts of his own.

Although Brannen has posted a few decent workouts in the week and a half since returning to the track, his most recent workout over the weekend went terribly. His shins are now throbbing so painfully that he doesn't know if he'll be able to run at all today, much less this season. He's decided that if he can't complete today's assignment, an all-out 600-meter effort followed by some 200-meter repeats, he'll scrap his plans for any type of spring or summer racing season.

He brings his racing flats and spikes to the track after completing his warmup, then does a few high knee drills and strides before taking a seat on the track. His deadpan expression provides no insight into his thoughts, so it's with a certain degree of surprise that I see him minutes later with bags of ice on his shins. He tells me his shins ache too much to run. He's done. There's an air of finality in his voice.

For 10 minutes, practice goes on without him. Only then does Coach Warhurst approach to see how he's doing. He tells Brannen that the half-milers are doing an all-out 450-meter effort in a few minutes. If Brannen's up to it, Warhurst suggests he run with them for the first quarter-mile of his 600-meter run.

By now, the ice has rendered Brannen's shins almost numb. The way he figures it, the pain can't be worse than it was earlier. He laces up his spikes and jogs to the starting line to meet the other runners.

Sully watches with keen interest as Brannen heads toward the start line. For 7 weeks, they worked out together in the pool and in the weight room. Until then, Brannen had never seriously lifted weights or cross-trained, so there was nowhere to go but up, and the strength gains he has made are now visible. The weight training has added some bulk to his arms, and the resistance running in the pool has added mass to his quads. He can feel his increased horsepower when he runs, but he worries that the strength and extra weight will adversely affect his speed over his primary race distance—800 meters.

Senior Kevin Rogan leads a trio of half-milers as they pass 200 meters between 25 and 26 seconds. Brannen comes through comfortably a few strides behind them. He maintains his position around the turn and down the homestretch until he approaches the quarter-mile mark, when, to Sully's astonishment, he suddenly moves to the outside of lane 1 and bursts past them. Despite coming through the quarter in a blazing 52 seconds, Brannen is speeding up.

The speed flows out of him through his quick, long stride around the bend. Into the backstretch, Brannen cannot comprehend how fantastic he feels. He thinks, Screw it; I'm just gonna do the whole thing. I'm gonna run an eight. He cruises down the straight before accelerating again through 600. Warhurst can't believe his eyes. "Holy shit!" he says.

Brannen continues into the bend before deciding not to waste an all-out 800 in practice. He pulls the plug and slowly comes to a halt near Sully around the far side of the bend. Calmly, he walks over to where he left his racing flats and sits down to change out of his spikes. Sully smiles at his young friend and says, "That makes me sick! You've been out of the pool for a week. Maybe you should just run in the pool and do workouts."

Warhurst walks over to Sully. They look at each other's watches as if to verify that the frozen numbers aren't the result of some freak malfunction, but the times check out. Brannen has just gone from sitting on the track with his shins cloaked in ice to running 1:18.5 for 600 meters. The run is his fastest 600 *ever*. His previous best, run toward the end of his last outdoor season, was 1:18.9.

Brannen remains impassive. He laces up his flats and hits the track for some 200s. If the 600 wiped him out, it doesn't show. He hits the first one in 25 seconds, cruising. Warhurst asks him to ease up on the effort, and he responds with two more in 28 and 26 seconds before calling it quits. He has the strength to continue scorching the track, but his performance has come at a cost: His shins are once again screaming at him, so much so that he needs immediate relief.

He doesn't stick around to gab, and he doesn't go for a jog. Instead, he walks straight from the track to the field house and into the training room, where he removes his shoes and jumps into an ice bath.

Warhurst has seen enough today to know two things: Brannen will run this Sunday at Ohio State, and he'll run for Michigan. In Columbus, Brannen will face the only freshman in America with a faster personal best in the mile than his 3:59.85: Alan Webb. Shirt off, standing in a tub full of ice, Brannen says modestly, "I wouldn't mind racing him." Try as he might, he can't stifle a smile.

CHAPTER:14

STALKING SHADOWS

O nly an hour and a half remain until Nate Brannen and Alan
Webb face off at the newly christened Jesse Owens track at
Ohio State University. It's a bright, sunny day, and Brannen
takes refuge from the sun with several of his teammates in the
concourse beneath the stadium stands.

Webb was here, too, until a middle-aged man emerged from the
stadium with a camcorder and stood 10 feet from him, recording
him in the mundane act of doing nothing. Feeling creeped-out,

Webb went and hid in the can for 5 minutes. As Webb exited the restroom, the man emerged from the shadows and again silently filmed him from uncomfortably close proximity. Webb took off for parts unknown and successfully shook the guy, returning safely to join his teammates 20 minutes later. Despite himself, he is a man apart.

Webb's feeling confident. He hit a couple of great track workouts at home in Reston this past week, even modifying the meat of Friday's session, a hard 1000-meter run, to a hard 600 in order to have more snap today. It was the work he did off the track, however, that really caught his attention.

He ran a 10-miler through the streets of Reston yesterday morning (and subsequently drove his new ride, a Mitsubishi Eclipse, to Columbus, arriving late last night), on a route he ran frequently in high school. He struggled to run slower than 6-minute miles. He checked his watch at the first mile: 6:10. Slow down, he thought. Next mile: 5:58. Slow down. Next mile: 6:01. When he finally did manage a 6:20 mile, it felt as if he were walking. "Last year I couldn't do that," he says. "I had to put effort into it to run a 6-minute pace."

No matter how well Webb runs, however, he continues to be plagued with doubt. Last fall, he prided himself on making strength gains without sacrificing any of his explosiveness. Now, stronger than ever, he wonders if the strength gains he's made have come at the expense of his speed. He questions whether he could run a 47-second quarter as he did a year ago.

Still, warming up now, he feels phenomenal, especially since his stalker has vanished. But can he find his former form?

"STEP ON THE STARTER, STEP ON THE GAS . . ."

Warhurst is as anxious as Webb to know the answer. If only he were here to witness the event. Alas, the Luke watch is now officially in overtime. Warhurst boarded the bus before it departed yesterday and waited until the yip-yapping stopped and he had everyone's attention. "I got certain numbers for the Luke alerts," he said. "If it doesn't happen this weekend, I'm gonna drive out here to a country road somewhere and bounce her around, just to get the juices flowing."

When the laughter subsided, he continued. "No excuses. You got nice weather this weekend, so go do it. And remember: Step on the starter, step on the gas, don't let the floor fall out, or you'll fall on your ass."

In Warhurst's absence, Sully is here, and in the minutes before the race, he stands at the end of the backstretch with Webb and Brannen. Neither appears unduly nervous, although Brannen's steely exterior belies considerable anxiety. He felt sluggish and heavy-legged during his warmup. He reminds himself that this is a good thing. He feels sluggish before every big race, so it means he's ready. He asks Sully if he has any final advice. Sully laughs. "You know how to run the 800 better than I do. I don't have to tell you anything." And Webb? Sully smiles and says to me, "I don't think he'd want to hear anything from me anyway."

They make their way to the start. Lining up with them are Michigan runners Dan Cooke and Jeremy Schneider. In addition, there's Oregon's Simon Kimata, a gangly 6'3" flier from Nyeri, Kenya, who's the current class of the field. He boasts a best time of 1:47.92 from last spring and finished fifth in the 800 at the indoor NCAAs.

Despite Kimata's stellar credentials, he merits next to no introduction from the announcer, who breezes through the competitors until he arrives at Alan Webb. As at Mt. SAC, Webb is given the lengthiest introduction of all. A group of high school students, who have traveled from all around Ohio to watch him race, cheer wildly as he's introduced.

Fittingly, Webb and Brannen are aligned next to each another in lanes 4 and 5 for the start. Minutes earlier, they shook hands with their heads bowed in concentration, avoiding each other's gaze. The nature of the silent gesture served first to acknowledge the bond they share as boys in blue and second to serve notice that just the same, they would soon be locked in no-holds-barred competition.

With the crack of the starter's gun, the runners bolt from the start. Only 100 meters in, Kimata is already clear of the field. Brannen wastes no time as he heads off in pursuit. His legs still feel sluggish, but he goes to the front of the first chase pack. He comes through 200 meters in a quick 23.3 seconds. Webb comes through in the rear of the field several seconds later. He can't believe how fast it feels.

Though the pace slows considerably over the next 200 meters, Kimata still enters the last lap with a 2-second lead on the field. Brannen comes through the quarter looking comfortable in fourth position. Webb, however, languishes next to last.

Again, the pace accelerates through the curve. And on the backstretch, Brannen bursts from the chase pack in hot pursuit of Kimata. With each stride, he cuts into the real estate that separates him from the Kenyan. He rolls through 600 meters in 1:18, the same mark he ran in practice earlier this week, but he's still a good 20 meters behind.

Webb also makes his move on the backstretch, passing runners until he reaches the 600-meter mark, when he stalls. It's eerily reminiscent of the move he made on the backstretch at Mt. SAC.

Kimata's early effort hits him in the last hundred, and his body tightens and slows. Brannen fails to respond; he, too, is suffering. Don't tie up, he thinks. Relax. Don't tie up.

Webb is now foremost among the contenders in the chase pack. He moves out to lane 3 to get some running room. He tries to burst and run away from the field. He drives his arms and implores his legs to get on it, but they simply won't respond.

Kimata hits the tape in an impressive 1:47.25. Brannen just eludes a wave of runners that threatens to crash on him and finishes second in 1:48.92. Half a second later, Webb hits the finish in 1:49.46. His mark is good for fifth place. Michigan State's Andy Lixey finishes sixth in 1:49.98. He is shocked to finish so close to Webb. He's heard so much about Webb's wheels that he figured he was done for when Webb passed him. To his amazement, Webb didn't accelerate as much as Brannen had. "Webb didn't seem to be very sharp," Lixey says afterward. "He doesn't seem to have the foot speed I've heard about."

LESSONS TO LEARN

In a rush, Webb grabs some belongings and storms from the track. Gathering his sweats on the far bend near Sully, Brannen is ticked at Webb's indignant manner. He says to Sully, "What does he think, he's just gonna kill us? I'm a 1:46 guy. [Kimata] is a 1:46 guy. He can't come in here and just walk away with the race."

Plus, the half-mile is Brannen's race: He specializes in that first and the mile second. For Webb, it's the other way around. He's a miler first and a half-miler second.

"That's what he's got to learn," Sully tells Brannen. "You didn't think you were just gonna go out and kill everybody. As we've been saying, he's not racing high school guys anymore."

In Sully's mind, Webb's hubristic strategy doomed him. "Webb was second to last at the bell," he tells me. "You're talking about guys who run 1:47, 1:48 [half-miles]. When you're trying to make up a second, a second and a half on them, that's tough to do. Brannen was always in the mix. He was never farther back than fourth the whole race."

Webb needn't be so hard on himself. Given the hole he dug for himself on the first lap, he ran quite creditably, especially considering that most of his competitors, like Brannen, are true half-milers. The race was also a considerable improvement from Mt. SAC. While he didn't finish his move today, he didn't fold, either. Moreover, he put himself in a position to pass a lot of guys in the homestretch by moving out to lane 3 for an open lane.

He just lacks that fifth gear right now, which, given his training, is no surprise. Warhurst has yet to focus on Webb's finishing speed because they're aiming to extend his season until the World Junior Championships in mid-July. The series of workouts the coach has planned for Webb is designed to allow him to peak in July, not now. That speed will come; it's just a matter of time. Webb understands this, yet the loss rankles him. "I still want to race well now," he says. I realize that patience may be one of the hardest lessons he'll ever grow to learn.

Driving back to Ann Arbor with Brannen and me in his new

Eclipse, Webb is still not ready to accept today's result. He wasn't trying to play it cool on the first lap. He wanted to go out quicker, but even his 26-second 200 felt hard. "I don't know what is up with me. I'm running like shit lately. I just have no speed. I can run all the workouts I need to, I just can't turn it on in the end. I hit all my times in my workouts, so I get pumped up, and then I get in a race and everything just feels so fast."

He had hoped that running quick times in his recent workouts would make running fast from the gun today feel easy, but it didn't. Worse, though he wanted to get up and run with Brannen with 300 meters to go, he couldn't. He physically could not do more than pass the few people he did. Exasperated, he adds, "I just didn't have anywhere to go."

He then dwells on the extensive pre-race introduction he received, which only adds to his sense of disappointment.

Webb continues driving north on Highway 23, straight past bucolic farms and red barns. He excitedly recounts that this is where "my coach," Scott Raczko, was raised. Raczko ran 100-mile weeks here as a high school freshman, he tells us, and he ran a creditable 4:17 mile as a sophomore. Despite that early success, Raczko now promotes a decidedly low-mileage program. "That shows he learned something along the way," Webb says.

Webb pulls off the highway to grab a bite to eat at one of those ubiquitous strips that has nothing but filling stations and fast-food joints. Driving stick shift is new to him. He's learning on the fly. As we head for home, he guns the motor, shifts gears, and accelerates, and his eyes widen as he feels the horsepower beneath him. I white-knuckle the armrest. He drives ahead undaunted, and all the while I feel as if he's struggling to keep it all under control.

A few hours later, we arrive at Ferry Field. Brannen and Webb grab a set of clubs and a couple of golf balls and head to the infield to lazily knock around a few. Before long, Webb tires of the exercise and starts circling the outer lanes. He goes on for miles. Daylight turns to dusk. Brannen returns to his dorm.

Alone in the shadows of the field, Webb lines up some hurdles for some speed development drills. Whether it takes all night or all year, he won't quit until he finds the shades of his former self.

CHAPTER:15

QUALIFYING FOR
THE NCAAS

Pride was on the line. Granted, they were all hackers, but
Alan Webb was damned if his team was going to finish the
worst of the lot. Three guys went for it—the last putt of the
Michigan track team annual best-ball golf tournament—and fal-
tered. Webb stepped up to the 8-footer on the 18th hole with his
team's pride at stake. He banged it home. Jubilation ensued as his
foursome was spared the indignity of a last-place showing.

Hours later, as the guys dress for track practice, everyone— sprinters, distance guys, and jumpers—is reliving the highs and lows of the golf tournament. This is exactly what Warhurst wanted. Less than 2 weeks out from the Big Ten Outdoor Track and Field Championships, the golf tournament is a way to develop some cohesion among the guys. Mission accomplished.

It's funny that as practice begins and the guys joke and carry on as a team for what seems like the first time all spring, the clouds actually scatter and sunshine welcomes the Michigan men. It feels like a rebirth, a new beginning, and in many ways, that's exactly what today is. On this May afternoon, incredible as it may seem, Webb and Brannen are training together for the first time all year. Warhurst, Brannen, and Webb have waited 9 months for this.

It's fitting then, that they put on quite a show.

The levity of the moment dissipates and the air becomes pregnant with ambition once Webb and Brannen lace up their spikes at Ferry Field and prepare to go through their paces together for the first time all season in their toughest assignment of the year so far. They start with quarter-mile repeats. First Brannen tows Webb through a quarter in 53 seconds, then Webb matches it. Brannen takes the helm for the third quarter and hits it in 53, with Webb again in lockstep with him.

They've blitzed through the quarters with such synchronicity at such an awesome speed that it seems as if they've been doing this for years. At the same time, the competitive tension crackling between them is so palpable that I wonder if either could run this well alone. I figure that they probably could, but a little something extra seems to come out of each man as he hears the other's footsteps and feels the other runner breathing down the back of his neck, ready to pounce at the slightest falter in pace. As Brannen later tells me succinctly, "It's easier when I know that if I slow down, Webb's gonna pass me."

Webb has a longer session on tap today. He approaches Warhurst for a solo quarter while Brannen waltzes through two 24-second 200s. In contrast, Webb suffers through the quarter, dying to just over 56 seconds. He rests his hands on a hurdle and lowers his head as soon as he finishes. He wants to quit. It feels as if there's a pool of lactic acid forming right behind his forehead.

Here's where Warhurst tests him. He's done it to all his guys, taking them beyond where they think they can go, pushing the limits, prodding for more. Brannen is dying, too, but he has learned to live with the discomfort in his legs. He thinks back to last year when his coach would ask him for 600-meter repeats and he'd come through the first 400 meters in 54 seconds, pick it up on the next 100, and blast the final homestretch in 12 seconds. Over and over he did that, working on his end-of-race turnover, teaching himself to suppress the urge to scratch the acute lactic acid itch by tightening his body, and just letting the speed flow. And he saw the results.

So they set off on another 300, this time with Tim Broe. Down the backstretch, it's Broe, Brannen, and Webb. Around the bend, Brannen switches gears, blasting by Broe as if he were an arthritic jogger. By the time Webb sees the move, processes it, and responds, Brannen is 10 meters in the clear. Webb works one, two, three strides, and he passes Broe entering the homestretch. But just as he closes, Brannen hits fifth gear and puts more ground between them. The invisible tether between the two stretches once more, and then Webb goes after him. With each stride, Webb gains. Brannen hits the finish in 37 seconds, and Webb follows a second later. Broe comes around and keeps going, hitting a quarter around the bend in 54.

DON'T FIGHT IT

Brannen's done. Webb's not. He walks around the bend, hands on his hips, head down, lactic acid piling up. One more, Warhurst tells him. "Whatever is comfortable," he orders. "Do it." Webb sets off down the backstretch of his final 300 meters, letting the lactic acid crawl through his legs. He thinks, Don't fight it, don't fight it; let it flow.

Down the homestretch he comes, concealing his agony. Bang. He crosses in 40 seconds, triumphant. The lactic acid now feels like a

100-pound brick in his forehead. He obligingly lowers his head and rests his hands on his knees. He's hurting now, but down the homestretch, he never let the pain contort him to the point where his wrists flicked uncontrollably and his head snapped back. He controlled it. Webb owned his pain.

Brannen goes over to him, and they slap hands. "Man," Webb says to Brannen, "I wanted to stop after the quarters."

"I wanted to stop, too," Brannen replies, "but your body can take it. I always feel better when I stop and then I do two more. Hell, just get it done. It benefits you so much. In a race, when you hurt, you just say, 'I've been there before.'"

Webb's legs feel heavy. He's still not where he wants to be. But he's getting there. Warhurst approaches the pair and exults, "You got through it with your teammates, *that's* the key. They're gonna help you get through this. Nice! Good job," and he shakes Webb's hand.

Sully, still recovering from his back injury and fresh from another pool workout, catches this, and he's green with envy. "How's the pool?" I ask.

"It's wet. It sucks."

One day later, Sully and Brannen are walking to the Ferry Field parking lot after a pool run. Warhurst informs them that he's received word that New Zealand miler Nick Willis, just 18 and already the owner of a 4:01 mile best, will be sporting the block M on his vest next fall. Brannen and Webb's workout yesterday is still fresh in the coach's mind. He wonders whether Webb will be in Ann Arbor next fall to scorch the turns with Brannen and Willis.

NOW OR NEVER

It's Thursday, May 9, and tomorrow evening Webb will line up at the Len Paddock Invitational at Michigan in what realistically is his last shot to qualify for the NCAA Championships in Baton Rouge, Louisiana. Only the Big Ten Championships remain after this, and conference meets, tactical in nature as they are, are notoriously poor settings for qualifying for the national championships. Theoretically, if Webb misses this chance, he could go for it at the Big Tens, but neither he nor anyone else hoping to qualify this weekend is entertaining that possibility.

Brannen will do his part to aid Webb tomorrow evening by rabbiting for him and Broe in the 1500 meters. He'll lead the first 1000 meters of the race, breaking the wind and setting the pace, before he drops out. It's an especially unselfish gesture, as Brannen doesn't have a qualifying time either, and his opportunity to qualify for the NCAAs in the 800 meters won't come until Saturday afternoon. No doubt he'd rather go into that effort fresh. That's what teammates are for, though, and on Saturday, Webb will return the favor by towing Brannen through the first 600 meters of his 800-meter race. There is no margin for error this weekend.

Most of the guys have gone out for a 4- to 6-mile shakeout this afternoon. Webb, however, is on his own program. He'll do 2 miles, then a "mini-workout" of 4 by 150 meters, just to get his legs feeling a little peppier for tomorrow night. He did this in high school, and now, searching as he is for that winning feeling, he'll do it again.

His 2-mile warmup takes him past 801 Granger, a quaint Victorian house just ½ mile from the track. It's his early childhood home. Passing it doesn't inspire much sentiment; he was too young to remember much. About the only thing he does remember from those years is getting a chocolate dip cone from the local Dairy Queen on the way out of town when his family moved to Virginia.

A half-hour later, back at the track, Warhurst watches as Webb switches gears through some 19-second 150-meter repeats. "Relax up top," the coach says, "you look good." On each repeat, Webb glances over at him. "You see that look?" Warhurst says. "He needs a lot of help. He needs to see that someone is watching him." That he's run 3:53 is irrelevant. Just like any other 19-year-old, Webb has his insecurities—except that his doubts are compounded by the fact that a nation's hungry eyes will be watching tomorrow night. It isn't easy being Alan Webb.

The next evening, I find Webb in the track building an hour before the 1500 meters. He is all business on the indoor track, meticulously going back and forth down the straightaway as he goes through his drills. A relaxed Broe emerges from the locker room as Webb starts on a high-knee version of a carioca. Broe yells "AY-AY-AYA!" and takes off over one hurdle, then another, set up willy-nilly on the track. The contrast between the two is striking.

Both know the drill. Brannen has agreed to pace them through the first 1000 meters, then he'll drop out of the race to save his legs for his own race—the 800 meters. After the 1,000-meter mark, Broe will take over, staying on NCAA qualifying pace. If Webb feels good, Warhurst has given him the green light to go after Broe in the final 200 meters.

Broe has no intention of letting that happen. A year ago, he was the rabbit for Paul McMullen at this meet. Passing the 1000-meter mark in 2:30, McMullen was nowhere in sight, and neither was anyone else. Warhurst told him to soldier on. He kept the pace and won the race in 3:44, while McMullen trudged home 4 seconds later. He wants to go quicker tonight—with or without Webb in tow.

CHASING BROE

More than 500 fans pack the Ferry Field bleachers on the homestretch as the runners do final strides on the backstretch. Nights can be as magical here as at Mt. SAC, with flags lying still against their poles. Unfortunately, the weather is not cooperating tonight. It's not terribly blustery, but the swirling winds that wreak havoc every afternoon on the field's backstretch are still fitfully unleashing old miserly coughs.

At the starter's *CRACK!* Brannen sets off. Just 100 meters in, he looks over his shoulder and sees Broe 5 meters back. Webb is a couple more meters behind Broe, and the rest of the field follows him.

By 300 meters, Brannen is 10 meters up on Broe, and another 10 separate him from Webb. Webb had hoped to draft off Broe, but the pace is so hot that it's each man for himself. Brannen hits the quarter-mile in 54 seconds. It's way too fast. Broe fearlessly follows in 56, with Webb cautiously following another 2 seconds back.

Brannen settles into pace on the second lap and comes through in 1:54. He looks over his shoulder in wonderment every 10 seconds or so. He can't believe that he's all alone, and that it feels so easy.

Down the backstretch, Brannen ponders running away with it. Around the turn, reason gets the best of him, and he drops off the track. Broe is now alone in first. He passes 1000 meters in 2:26, with Webb still 10 meters back.

In the homestretch, Webb's rhythm picks up visibly, and he closes the gap on Broe. Broe presses on through 3/4 mile in 2:56. He had wanted to run under 3:40 tonight, and it's now well within his reach.

Broe fights a blustery wind down the final backstretch, with Webb in hot pursuit. Webb's long strides and forward-leaning torso cut through the wind with little effort. Around the bend, the crowd comes to life, and ripples of noise fill the night at the sight of Broe's lead vanishing under the assault of Webb's pistonlike stride.

Broe reacts to the crowd's exhortations with a burst of his own, yet down the final homestretch, Webb still closes on him with every stride. Into the race's final 50 meters, only 2 meters separate Webb from Broe. Everyone's on their feet, waiting for Webb to roar past Broe for the win.

But Broe's saved a little, too. He charges toward the line, never letting Webb climb onto his shoulder. The crowd turns silent as Broe crosses the finish and Webb follows a few steps later. University of Virginia graduate Ray Weeden crosses in third some 5 seconds after that.

Broe assertively nods his head up and down after he finishes and the mass of spectators quietly scurry toward their cars. Webb walks toward the backstretch, irritated at having lost again to one of his training mates. Some little kids rush onto the track after Webb, in search of autographs. No one approaches Broe.

It doesn't take Webb long to smile. He's just run 3:41.46, a precious 0.04 second under the automatic qualifying time for the NCAAs. He's guaranteed his spot at collegiate track's Big Dance.

Broe's another story. He's just run 3:40.67. It's his best time ever, worth about a 3:58 mile. "Damn!" he says angrily. "3:39 just sounds so much cooler." Make no mistake, though, he's pleased with the effort. He ran a long, hard workout 2 days ago. He's ready now. He'll take it easy this week, then, on May 18 at the Adidas Oregon Track Classic in Portland, he'll take a shot at Henry Marsh's 20-year-old American record in the steeplechase—and the $50,000 bonus offered to the winner.

Steve Webb, sporting a Michigan cap, joins Alan on the backstretch. He's all smiles. He knows the weight that has just been lifted from his son's shoulders.

BRANNEN ON DECK

Moments later, Brannen, Webb, and Broe are together on the backstretch, chit-chatting about the race as they change into their sweats. It's the first time the three of them have run together this spring, and it couldn't have turned out any better. Working together, Broe earned a coveted personal best, and Webb secured his qualifier for the NCAAs.

Also for the first time this spring, Webb betrays neither bitterness nor frustration after his loss. He tells Broe, "I tried to go with you, but I just couldn't go at all." His tone of voice suggests he knows it won't be long until his legs are once again under his control. When Broe reassuringly replies, "Hey, man, it'll come," Webb nods in agreement.

"Finally," he says a short while later as he slips on his Nikes. "Going in the right direction."

One down. Brannen's on deck.

The ease of his effort while rabbiting Webb did nothing to soothe his nerves. He tosses and turns for the duration of Friday night, nervously fretting about his race early the following afternoon, his last good opportunity to qualify for the NCAAs. Finally, at 7:00 A.M., he gets up and heads out for a short jog to ease his nerves. It works. The run soothes and emboldens him. All night, he worried that his legs would lack some zip after rabbiting Webb, but he finds them feeling full of juice. Better yet, the sun is out and the air is still—perfect conditions for a qualifying assault.

Throughout the morning, however, Brannen's spirits sour along with the weather. The sky turns a soul-sucking slate gray, and the wind resumes. He can sense the wind bouncing around on the backstretch of Ferry Field and fears it will affect his race, slowing him down. Thank God he's got Webb to rabbit for him. He'll need his help to break the wind. "Mentally, I'm here," Brannen tells me as he prepares to go. "I'm in the right place. Physically, I'm not there yet."

Webb isn't taking his rabbiting chore lightly. He deeply appreciated Brannen's assistance last night and is eager to return the favor. He goes to the start line for one last 100 from a standing start minutes before the race, then clicks his watch at its conclusion: 12.5 seconds. Right on pace. He's not about to let Brannen down.

They line up for the race. *BANG!* Webb bolts off the start from his position in lane 8 and, by the bend, Brannen is right on his heels in second. No more than a foot separates him from Webb down the backstretch. The crosswind hits them as they charge down the straightaway, but that's the least of Brannen's worries. He knows he'll have Webb to shield him through the first 600. What's worse is the steady headwind that's kicked up down the homestretch. He'll battle that alone.

Down the homestretch for the first time, Brannen tucks even closer to Webb to shield himself from the wind, accidentally clipping Webb's heels as he seeks refuge behind him.

Together they pass the quarter-mile mark on pace in 52 seconds, but they're not alone. Running just out of Brannen's slipstream is a tall, sinewy runner from Central Michigan with a loping, almost languid stride that suggests there's much more in store. His name is Ian Searcy.

Halfway down the backstretch, Brannen hears Searcy's footstrike quicken behind him just as Webb drifts out toward lane 2. The hairs on the back of his neck stiffen at the threat. Without a moment's hesitation or a glance back, he bolts. He flies past Webb into the curve and gaps Searcy by 10 meters. There's nothing left now, he realizes, but an all-out drive for the line.

For the third time in the last 2 weeks, he hits the 600-meter mark in 1:18. He continues around the bend and into the homestretch. Cranking down the homestretch, he feels his legs becoming leaden, and he glances back repeatedly to ensure that he's checked Searcy's challenge. While Searcy has done nothing to close the gap Brannen opened on his burst into the final curve, he also shows no signs of wilting. It's evident to all that should Brannen falter, Searcy will continue right past him.

Brannen's shoulders start to ache with the burn of lactic acid. Only 50 meters remain. Warhurst's counsel loops over and over in his brain: Don't muscle it, just swing 'em. Just swing the arms.

Brannen slows a bit with each stride, but his form never becomes robotic. At last he crosses the line. One second later Searcy follows, completing a fine run of his own. Brannen buries his head in his hands as the acute throbbing in his quads and shoulders starts to dissipate. He closed as best he could into the wind, but he has no idea if it was fast enough to earn his ticket to Baton Rouge. His heart flutters as he awaits the results.

Then, the word: 1:47.62. Off to the side of the track, Warhurst grins unabashedly. While Brannen's just missed the automatic qualifying time of 1:47.5, only a handful of runners will meet that standard, and the field will be filled by those with the next fastest times. Brannen's time will certainly place him high enough on the list to get the invite to the NCAAs.

All year, Warhurst has awaited the sight of Webb and Brannen working together to raise themselves to new heights. In the past week, they did it in practice, and now, each has incalculably assisted the other to punch their tickets to the NCAAs. That they did so at home in Ann Arbor in a low-key meet with but a few local schools makes their performances all the more impressive. Says Brannen defiantly, "Who says you have to go to Stanford to qualify [for the NCAAs]?"

Jogging around the streets of Ann Arbor soon after his race, Brannen can't contain his excitement. "I don't understand how I'm running so fast on no training," he says. "I got 3 weeks until NCAAs. If I get 3 weeks of training, what can I do?" Doing so well now with just 3 weeks of running makes Brannen think he could have run 1:45 last year had he gotten into the right race. Better yet, he thinks he it may be possible in just a few more weeks.

Webb shares Brannen's optimism. His 600 today in 1:18 proves to him that at last his speed is coming around. With the disappointments he has endured, however, Webb is decidedly more cautious in his optimism. Sitting on the track with Brannen before a low-key 4 by 400 meters, Webb says confidently, "After everything that's happened, we're not gonna go backward from here. We may not have run world records, but we're gonna get better and better, and then we're talking some real-deal stuff."

He talks of minute improvements in his times from 3:41 to 3:39 to 3:37. No longer is he anxious to post world-beating times right now. If Warhurst could hear Webb now, he'd smile.

The afternoon ends with Brannen and Webb running legs on the Michigan freshman 4 by 400-meter quartet. They run freely, oblivious to their times. They laugh and exult before and afterward, jawing all the while with the upperclassmen that they're gonna paste 'em. For Webb especially, it's a throwback to an earlier time, when joyous, carefree running, absent any consequence, was the only goal there was.

CHAPTER:16

SHADES OF GREATNESS

Nate Brannen should be excited. In a few minutes, he and Alan Webb will be hitting their hardest track session yet. This workout on the afternoon of May 14 is their last hard session before the Big Tens at the University of Wisconsin this weekend. But he can't get over the pain in his shins. They're aching, and the ibuprofen isn't cutting it anymore.

He learned that painful lesson 2 days ago on the morning after his 1:47 in the 800 meters. Five miles into a 7-miler in the rain, the muscles along his shins spasmed violently, stopping him dead in his tracks. There he stood in the pouring rain, clenching and releasing his fists and doing all he could not to scream as the muscles refused to release. So much for ibuprofen.

Jogging was futile. The rain accelerated, adding insult to injury. Twenty-odd minutes later. he walked into the locker room, shivering and miserable. If only he'd been like Webb and taken the day off, he'd have avoided the trauma. Not even a couple of doughnuts from Washtenaw Dairy, Warhurst's traditional Sunday treat for the guys, could cheer him.

Back from his own 14-mile run, Mike "Wiz" Wisniewski spoke for Brannen as well as himself when he told Warhurst he needed to make a trip to the hardware store to buy a fresh set of legs. "You'd better go to the welders and get a pair of brass balls while you're at it," came Warhurst's reply.

Webb, on the other hand, feels refreshed after having slept a whopping 22 hours the last couple of nights. And despite the firestorm raging in the media over his future, he seems mentally at ease as well. Hours ago, sitting at his desk in his cramped temporary dorm room in Fletcher Hall, he read an interview on runners world.com with former mile world record holder Peter Snell in which Snell stated that Webb should forgo collegiate running and go pro.

"That's interesting that he said that," Webb commented. He said it assuredly, as if he had come to a decision regarding his future yet was being careful not to tip his hand. Brannen watched as he read it, and true to form, didn't ask him to elaborate. While Webb's future is a matter of considerable speculation elsewhere, it's a topic no one here addresses directly with Webb, and it will remain that way for the rest of the season.

COUNTDOWN TO THE BIG TENS

On the track, Webb and Brannen quickly set off on a hot 600. Webb sets the pace, and through the first 300 meters, Brannen hangs 15 meters behind him. Brannen closes the gap down the homestretch and hits the quarter right on Webb's heels. He cruises behind Webb through the next 100. With Warhurst yelling at him to "stay right there," Brannen keeps his engine in third gear down the backstretch as well and finishes right off Webb's shoulder in a crisp 1:21. Tim Broe wouldn't have been so kind. "Brannen should've blasted him over the last 100," Broe says from the sidelines. "Webb's mentally fragile now. Brannen needs to get in his head while he can."

Webb won't let that happen. Not today. He runs with an unburdened gallop and clarity of focus, as if a colony of bees had been buzzing incessantly around his head and has suddenly vanished. He strides commandingly beside a straining Brannen through a pair of 54-second quarters before unflinchingly blasting away from him on the turn of a subsequent 300. *C'est la guerre.*

Webb holds his hands in the air and shrugs as he sets off on a jog before another 300-meter effort. It seems as if he's saying, "I don't know or care to know how or why, but I'm in the zone." For the first time since late fall, the speed is effortlessly pouring out of him.

He's not the only one who's relishing this. Warhurst has waited all spring for this moment, which at once validates Webb's effort and Warhurst's methods. "He's feeling his oats now," Warhurst says. "See, if they're just patient, I can get 'em where they need to be."

Brannen doesn't share in Webb's glory. He can't. The pain in his shins is as piercing as a dagger. He kneels broken on the track with his toes extended behind him, trying to stretch the muscles and release whatever it is in his shins that feels like marbles to the touch.

Webb cruises through a solo 39-second 300, and with only one remaining, Warhurst cuts the reins. "You want to run fast, you can run fast," he shouts. All eyes are on Webb as he sets off down the backstretch. Approaching the turn, he knows he's going to roll. The ease of speed is there. Passing the steeple barrier 150 meters in, Webb explodes for home. He's not running on the track as much as skimming effortlessly over it. In a flash, he's done—in just over 38 seconds, his fastest practice 300 to date at the tail end of his best run of the spring. "I'm finally feeling good," he says.

SULLY ON THE MEND

Two days later, on Thursday afternoon, the team piles aboard a chartered bus for Madison, Wisconsin. Once more, Warhurst is landlocked in Ann Arbor; Luke is still stubbornly refusing to make his debut. Sully is traveling again in his stead, and he's jacked, not because he's going on a road trip but because he's just been cleared to do something he's waited 10 torturous weeks to do: run.

Last night he went to physical therapist Peter Kitto's office for the results of his $1,000 bone scan. It was agonizingly inconclusive. He expected to see a photo of his bone with a crack in it. What he got instead was a three-paragraph diagnosis that suggested that he had a small crack in his sacrum. He read and reread the document, searching for something, anything. In the end, those three good-for-nothing paragraphs looked just as amorphous as his injury.

Kitto came in and discussed the options with Sully. Gone was his usual smart-ass attitude, and that in itself was a bad omen. They finally settled on Sully taking another couple of weeks off his feet before resuming running. Sully couldn't hide his disappointment. Those 2 weeks could mean the difference between racing in September in Rieti, Italy, or playing Bond on his PlayStation at home in Ypsilanti.

Sully wanted another opinion, so Kitto sent him across the hall to check with his partner, Dr. John Anderson. Like Kitto, Dr. Anderson understands Sully's predicament and knows that he needs to race this season in order to secure a contract for next year. Moreover, his digital watch reveals what his middle-aged doctor's physique does not: He's a runner. He understands the stresses Sully will inflict on his body on the road to fitness.

"I would try it out," he advised. "You know your body better than anybody. Lace 'em up, take it for a test, and see what happens. If it [the fracture] still shows up, you're recovering, you're not healed. You're smart enough and have enough experience to know what your body is about. So be patient and let me see you in a few weeks."

Sully grinned unabashedly with a wild look in his eyes and gave a thumbs-up. "Sweet dude!" he said. He decided to start his come-back Friday in Madison with a short 2-miler. He has no idea where this will lead. Right now, he's overjoyed just to have a chance.

Unlike Webb, whose road to fitness was an often lonely, solo en-deavor, Sully will have company. On Tuesday afternoon, Paul Mc-Mullen also decided to make a comeback, albeit with legs as Herculean as his 3:33 and 1:45 times for 1500 and 800 meters in summer a year ago. At the end of the fall, after a long and well-de-served layoff, he had rejoined Warhurst and started training again. Once again carrying the 25 or 30 pounds he had shed the previous summer through a diet of twigs and berries, he lasted but a short while before injuring the piriformis muscle in his upper glute.

MCMULLEN'S INDECISIVE PAST

While recuperating from his injury, McMullen turned to the bike to stay fit. And unlike most runners, he actually liked it. Then, in February, he went to Southern California for "Camp Saucony," a week-long camp where Saucony's select few elite triathletes and runners under contract, of whom McMullen is one, gather to go over the new product line, do some training, and have some fun.

His first day there, McMullen tagged along with Ryan Bolton, a 2000 U.S. triathlon Olympian and former All-American cross country runner at Wyoming, to a bike shop called Nitro that caters to top-shelf triathletes. They were fitting Bolton with a bike to borrow for the duration of his stay. Without a bike of his own, Mc-Mullen asked Bolton if they would consider lending him one as well. Bolton explained to the storeowners that McMullen was a 1996 Olympian as well as the top-ranked U.S. miler in 2001 and got him a bike for the weekend.

For the next several days, McMullen rode and swam with Bolton and Ironman triathlon legend Dave Scott. But it was his first ride with Bolton that left an indelible impression. It felt natural to him. The next day, he went riding with Bolton and Scott again, and again it went really well. Through it all, Scott was geeking him up, telling him he was made to be a cyclist.

That was all McMullen needed to hear. Fed up with the awesome lengths he had to go to in order to shed weight and get into prime shape, and figuring that in 2001 he ran as well as he possibly could, Paul McMullen, runner, became Paul McMullen, cyclist. And in his typical fashion, he launched himself into it full-throttle, riding as much as 400 miles a week while running a couple of miles every other day to remind his muscles of running's demands.

On Tuesday afternoon, I asked McMullen why, after months away from the track, he had showed up to run under Warhurst once more. He explained that 10 days earlier, he had finished 11th out of 30 guys in a race in Ohio against good regional cyclists. More important, he raced as a lieutenant for his team captain (the race's eventual winner), chasing down every breakaway and "sucking 'em dry" until the cyclists were swallowed up by the peloton (a densely packed group of riders). Still, he finished just a minute off the win. That race answered a question that had been burning within him for 8 weeks: Could he be a good cyclist? The answer: Yes, he could be really good.

He told me, "Once I answered that, I decided to finish up my running career and just say goodbye to it. I felt I had to force cycling this year, to establish myself. It didn't take that long to beat good people and do well in a good race. It took me 8 weeks, from March 1 to May 4, to find out that I could do it. Now that I know, I'm gonna take a break for 6 weeks, come back [to track], say goodbye to my sport, and then get back to [cycling]."

McMullen began his comeback on Tuesday afternoon with a light session of 2 by 400 meters. Out on the track, he looked huge, even next to Webb, who's built like an Ivy League free safety. Watching him thunder around the track in 57 seconds elicited plenty of oohs and aahs from Warhurst and the gang. Fortunately, McMullen has a sense of humor. Laughing, he said afterward, "I felt like a circus animal out there."

But who'll be laughing in 6 weeks? Kitto, for one, is skeptical that McMullen can get into shape in that time. While he did go from 3:50 to 3:33 in 6 weeks last summer, when he came to Warhurst then, he had been running for months on his own and had started to diet as well. Now, he's trying to cram everything into the same short time. Even Warhurst, who learned never to doubt

McMullen after his immaculate progression last summer, admits the cards are severely stacked against him.

By August of last year, McMullen was down to 172 pounds. Now, he reckons he weighs "in the upper 190s." He concedes that he'll be lucky to get down to 180 in 6 weeks. Percentage-wise, 8 pounds may not seem like much, but try strapping 8 pounds to your back and sprinting around the track. You'll quickly feel otherwise.

As awkward as his body felt out there, all he had to do was look over and see Sully standing on the sidelines to be grateful for this opportunity. And once he slipped his spikes on at the end, dug them in for a couple of 100-meter runs, and heard the familiar *flit, flit, flit* of his toes clawing the track, he felt a rush through his nervous system at the visceral memory of what it felt like to tear around the track.

He's counting on that muscle memory to get him to the line in Palo Alto in 6 weeks' time with more than a chance to succeed. He looks to guys like American 800-meter record man Johnny Gray, who raced at a world-class level into his late thirties, for inspiration. Athletes like Gray, he says, "have this depth of muscle memory left, and they can call on it to get to a certain level and extend their career. But they don't have to work as hard as everybody else because once their body reaches that height, it's not that hard to help remind it to do it fast again. That's what I'm doing right now. You never know if it'll work twice, but it sure as hell worked last year. We'll give it a whirl."

Today is a starting point.

THE COUNTDOWN CONTINUES

On Thursday afternoon, the Michigan team disembarks near Wisconsin's Dan McClimon track for practice. Webb and Brannen aren't racing until the trials of the 1500 and 800 on Saturday, so Warhurst's assigned them three sets of 3 by 200 meters.

Athletes from Wisconsin, Minnesota, and Iowa also circle the track, all doing different runs at varying speeds, creating an atmosphere of controlled chaos. And still, as fast as Brannnen and Webb sprint around the extremely wide turns on the unforgiving, sandpaper-like brown track, they can't be missed. Heads snap to and fro to watch them zoom past.

With cool efficiency, they smoke through the first two sets in an average of 26 seconds, then 25. Such is their pace that Sully has to run across the infield to clock each one. He keeps it loose and gets a rise out of Webb and Brannen when he tells them to slow it down lest the scurrying across the infield break his back again.

Brannen launches into the third set with Webb on his heels: 23 seconds and change. Webb takes the next one: 24 seconds. Both feel smooth and powerful, and Brannen's aching shins are the only impediment to blazing through the last one. Yet Sully senses the competitive tension in the air as the two alpha males line up for the final repeat. "Don't blast it!" he orders.

They ignore him. Brannen explodes from the line in lane 1 as Webb stumbles off the start in lane 2. In four steps, Brannen makes up the stagger start. As they round the turn, I wonder whether Brannen needs this one, needs to prove to Webb after Tuesday's session that he's still got it.

Neither gives an inch as they race around the curve and down the homestretch. Brannen pushes it just that little bit at the end to take it in 23.9 seconds, with Webb no more than a fraction of a second behind.

Sully smiles at the pair. "Good job guys; we are ready!" Webb turns to Brannen, "Good job, Nate. Nice work." They shake hands.

CHAPTER:17

THE BIG TENS

On May 18, at the track for the first day of the Big Ten Championships, Sully gets the long-awaited call from Coach Warhurst. For Sully, the coach's first words about his healthy newborn son, Luke, show that fatherhood hasn't changed him—yet.

Says Warhurst, "He's got big balls and big feet and he's hairy all over!" Throughout the afternoon, the coach takes congratulatory calls from the guys, and each time, he lovingly tells how Luke peed on the nurses moments after being born. "Just like his old man," Warhurst says proudly, "he comes out pissing all over the world!"

Having stood by Kalli's side for 2 days straight at the hospital, Warhurst's in dire need of some sleep, but he can't rest until he hears how his other boys are doing. On this day, they make him proud.

Alan Webb is the first to race, in the first of two preliminary heats for the 1500 meters. For an athlete of Webb's caliber, the preliminary rounds of a conference meet should be little more than a nuisance to be survived with minimal expenditure of energy. He need only run conservatively and advance to the next round.

Today, however, Webb's preliminary race means more. He hasn't tasted victory since the Big Ten Cross Country Championships last fall, and it has been almost a year since he last won a race on the track. With his run today, he wants to finally win again—and send a message to his competitors that he is the man to beat.

Minutes before his start, in the staging area just off the track, Webb absentmindedly removes his T-shirt and puts on his uniform jersey. The starter sees him and threatens to disqualify him for violating the uniform rule, which states that athletes may not remove their jerseys on the track.

Seeing the official scolding Webb minutes before his race, Sully goes berserk. He cringes at the thought of informing Warhurst that Webb was disqualified for something so innocuous. Moments later, Sully is at the start, arguing with the starter. He reminds her that she is not an official and that her responsibility is to start the races—period. She refutes him, arguing that starter or not, she is still an official authorized to enforce the rules.

Sully walks away, seething. There are moments when he hates track, when the officialdom of the sport wields its power in an ungainly way, like a dunderheaded giant recklessly swinging a club, unmindful of his tiny glass house. Walking away, he says, "And we wonder why our sport's not popular."

Sully's not alone. An opposing coach walks past him, looks disgustedly at the starter, and says, "This is ridiculous."

Webb gets off with a warning. And although a bit taken aback by the official's zeal to enforce the uniform rule when all he was doing was changing into his jersey, the incident doesn't ruffle him. He simply puts on his headphones and resumes performing some last-minute strides. He keeps the headphones on until moments before his race and approaches the line with instructions from Sully to advance to the final as comfortably as possible, nothing more.

ADVANCING COMFORTABLY?

Webb's strategy becomes evident immediately, when he loafs off the line to the rear of the field. He stays well out of harm's way, hanging well off the back of the field in dead last through the race's first two laps, harnessing his energies for one big move. When Webb runs past Sully at the half, Sully yells to him to prepare to move: "Get ready, Webb, get ready!"

As his competitors await his move, they cautiously increase the pace as they begin to jockey for position nearing the final lap. No one wants to be at the tail end of the pack when Webb goes. Approaching the bell signaling one lap to go, Webb shows his class, making a move the likes of which no one has seen since he burst after the field on the final circuit of the Prefontaine mile a year ago.

He roars past the field and within seconds puts 10 meters on the other runners, continuing his acceleration around the bend until only 300 meters remain. Then he abruptly steps off the gas and, like a cat toying with helpless mice, lets his competitors scurry back within arm's reach down the backstretch.

Around the turn into the final 200 meters, he runs only as fast as necessary to stay just clear of the field before accelerating ever so slightly down the homestretch, finishing a step ahead of the field in 3:53.35. He's closed in an effortless 45 seconds for the last 300 meters, a 4-minute-mile pace. His burst on the curve brought him around the race's third circuit in a still-quick 57 seconds.

Webb controlled the race from start to finish, and, just as important to him, he controlled his own effort and pace the whole way. He chats contentedly with Sully as he gathers his belongings by the start line afterward and then watches the second heat. His good spirits intensify when he watches John Jefferson, a freshman at Indiana who occasionally raced against but never beat Webb as a high-schooler a year ago, win the heat with an unimpressive 3:52.94. While Jefferson's time was better than Webb's, he exhibited none of Webb's control and restraint. This suggests that he doesn't have the reserves of strength and speed to handle an all-out Webb.

Is there a serious threat for Webb lurking in the field of contenders tomorrow? Has one of the runners today judiciously held his cards close to his vest, saving every last ounce for the final? Time will tell. As of now, Webb has seen nothing from his competitors to give him cause for concern.

BRANNEN'S TURN

Several hours later, Nate Brannen lines up for the first heat of the 800 meters with a more arduous task. Webb had only to finish in the top four in his heat to guarantee his spot in the final. Brannen must win or suffer the possibility of missing the final should runners in the three subsequent heats run fast enough to bump him out. While 12 men will advance to the final of the 1500, only 8 will advance to the 800-meter final. His instructions: Win as easy as possible.

Unlike Webb, Brannen lines up with a good idea of what may unfold. In his heat is five-time Big Ten 800-meter champion Jason van Swol of Illinois. A year ago, the lanky 6'5" runner won the title in a creditable 1:47.88. This spring, however, Van Swol has failed to find his form. He's entering this meet in the very predicament Brannen narrowly escaped a week ago: He must qualify here for the national championships. To do it, he'll have to run close to his personal best of 1:47.24. With a seasonal best is of 1:50.7, he'll need a mighty effort. And assuredly, his competitors won't make his quest any easier by sharing pacing chores. Like the others, Brannen lines up planning to take a ride on the V-train.

At least Van Swol's muscles will be loose. All day, the sun has intermittently served as a welcome salve for the cool, crisp lakeside air. It is shining on Van Swol as the race goes off; he faithfully follows the script and plays the role of leading man.

Almost a foot shorter than Van Swol, Brannen hides behind his human shield as Van Swol cuts through the first quarter-mile in 54 seconds. Around the bend and into the backstretch, the fatigue of towing the field quickly envelops the leader like a leaden cloak. On the backstretch, Brannen feels the pace lose its bite. Then he senses commotion behind him as Minnesota freshman Ryan Ford starts to move on his outside. Brannen had wanted to wait longer before gunning for home but now is forced to do otherwise, not wanting to risk getting boxed behind a tiring Van Swol. He bolts around both runners and into the lead.

He quickly gaps the field. Comfortable with his 5-meter cushion, he cruises into the final turn. The Michigan team is situated here on the bend, on a set of bleachers 150 meters from the finish. His teammates scream for him, "Go, Blue! Go, Blue! Go, Blue!" as he runs past. Brannen rides their enthusiasm around the turn for home while glancing over his shoulder again and again to check his turf. One by one, his competitors crack under the pace.

None crack more than Van Swol. With his hopes of capturing the race and advancing to Baton Rouge shattered, he slows to a crawl. Five seconds after Brannen has inched across the line in a pedestrian 1:51.41, Van Swol mercifully stops the clock in last place in 1:56.75, the sun having set on his collegiate career.

Moments later, Brannen is sitting on the grass in front of the Michigan bleachers on the far turn, in sweats and his trainers. The experience feels oddly surreal to him, as if he never raced at all. He watches as his mates fight valiantly yet fruitlessly in the next three heats of the 800. He and Webb are the sole members of the Michigan team to advance to the finals.

RUNNING FOR PERSONAL GLORY

It's a subdued bus ride back to the hotel that evening, the air heavy with the weight of deflated dreams. For most, the end today came quietly, without the roar of an appreciative populace to fill the void. Brannen and Webb are now the Maize and Blue's only hopes in their respective events, and in the overall team competition, Michigan is buried in ninth, one lone rung above cellar-dweller Illinois and without hope of climbing much higher. "It's dropped from a team championship to an individual one now," Brannen, the precocious freshman, says flatly, wanting in his heart for it to have been so much more. "My team is out of it, so I'm just running for myself now." Alone.

Ultimately, in track as in life, we all are.

Webb and Brannen awaken the next morning feeling hungry, like a couple of lions after their prey. Analyzing the field the morning of the race, Sully sees a couple of young bucks who could potentially threaten Webb: Wisconsin's Josh Spiker and Indiana's John Jefferson. Both have run about 4 minutes in the mile: Spiker set his 1500 personal best of 3:43.11 last year in his redshirt season as a freshman at Wisconsin, and Jefferson ran 4:02.68 this past winter. Like Webb, Jefferson is a true freshman. Spiker redshirted indoors, but he also claimed a top-10 NCAA finish when he beat Webb and finished eighth at the NCAA Cross Country Championships in the fall. Although living in colder climates, Spiker's and Jefferson's running is just as hot.

Brannen's situation is murkier. Van Swol was the big gun in this event, and now he's out. Brannen doesn't know much about the competition and pays no mind to anyone in particular. Heading to the track this morning, he tells me that while his 1:47.62 at the Len Paddock Invitational will definitely be fast enough to advance him to the NCAAs, he's looking for an automatic qualifying time today—1:47.5 or faster. He's aware that such a time would also beat the track record of 1:48.41, but he sees that as irrelevant. He'd like to go out aggressively in 51 seconds for the first quarter-mile, but he won't lead so early in the race. Above all, his primary objective is to win.

He knows that won't be easy. Listening to Brannen discuss his strategy, Sully says guardedly, "They're gonna give you a good run. They're not gonna give it to you, that's for sure." Brannen listens, then asks Sully how he would run the final. Sully advises him to surge 250 meters from the wire. Not many of his competitors will be ready for a move at that time, and if they hesitate, Brannen may quickly gain an insurmountable lead of 3 to 5 meters on the field. Brannen wordlessly takes in Sully's counsel as the bus pulls up to

McClimon track. In front, Michigan assistant coach Fred LaPlante rises and turns to his men: "Okay, guys, give 'em hell!"

Webb's race is first. Like Brannen, his primary objective is to win. All he wants is the hardware, and he's ready to run what it takes, be it 3:40 or 4:10, to win. Unlike yesterday, Warhurst has given him explicit instructions. He wants Webb to move three times, with 300, 200, and 100 meters to go, each time saving a little something for the final sprint.

This strategy presents Webb with a considerable risk, however, in that it opens the gates for everyone in the field to win the race in a kick. Off a fast pace, Webb is the clear favorite, but a slow race is an equalizer for the rest of the field unless Webb truly has the best kick. Thinking of his 200s a few days ago, he believes he does.

But is he the savviest racer? Readying for the start, Webb betrays no nerves. In part it's due to the fact that the field, while strong, is no better than any other he has faced thus far. More important is that he's also free to compete as he seldom has since his sophomore year in high school, without concern for his time. That, too, liberates him, and his loose demeanor reflects this.

Lining up for the race, many of the other competitors make their way over to shake Webb's hand and offer him luck. He politely shakes their hands but goes no further to ingratiate himself with them. He's here to beat them.

As the starter calls them to set, Webb crouches down with one arm up and one touching the track, like an old-school sprinter. With the shot, they're off. Webb's out well, but it's Wisconsin's Spiker who takes the lead. Earlier in the season, Spiker harbored big ambitions of doing well here today, but an ankle injury suffered playing football 5 weeks ago has seriously curtailed his training. He hopes to slow the pace enough to give himself a shot against Webb because he knows he can't win a flat-out footrace.

A hundred meters in, Spiker drastically slows the pace, hoping someone will pass him and take over the pacing chores. With no takers, he thinks, Okay, I'm just gonna run as easy as I can and wait for the real racing to begin. He lopes through a gentle first quarter-mile in 66 seconds.

Webb also crosses the quarter trying to stay relaxed, but he's in a precarious spot. Minnesota's oak-like junior miler, Andrew McKessock, and his even more mammoth teammate, Martin Robeck, have boxed him in against the track's rail on the inside of lane 1, in fourth place. Webb tells himself to run as if he's alone, with a long, loose stride, and he moves to the middle of lane 1, arms wide and taut, ready to deliver a crushing blow to maintain his space. Indiana's Jefferson sits right behind him, ready to respond to any early move Webb may make.

Although the pace picks up a bit through the second quarter-mile, it doesn't alleviate the congestion. Webb passes the half-mile mark in 2:08, hemmed in to the rail. Sully yells to him to be patient and relax as Webb continues to do just that, waiting for a break so he can move out and away from the riffraff. Around the track they go, with McKessock still firmly trapping Webb on the rail in fourth.

Down the homestretch approaching the bell lap, things begin to open up. Webb senses McKessock losing his balance, and in an instant he's down. Webb safely hurdles him as Robeck bolts from Webb's right shoulder after Jefferson, who's just made the first big move, accelerating into the lead and pushing the pace through the race's last curve.

McKessock's pain was his teammate's gain, and approaching 300 meters to go, Jefferson leads, with Robeck cranking beside him and Spiker hugging the rail behind him. Webb runs in the middle of lane 1 on Spiker's outside shoulder, just as Warhurst taught him, and here the break is clear: One of these four will win the race.

Webb feels it's time to move up on Jefferson. The plan was to go with 300, 200, and 100 meters to go, and with 300 to go, he moves to the outside of lane 2 to get by Robeck, only he's not doing it because it was preprogrammed—the kid is racing on instinct.

Webb flies past Robeck and Spiker on the backstretch. Into the final turn, he moves up and onto Jefferson's outside shoulder. Jefferson reacts to Webb's move, blasting for home. Webb feels the surge and figures Jefferson is going for all he's worth. Webb feels like he's got more in the tank, so he tucks in right behind him.

Midway through the turn, however, he can feel Spiker moving behind him and closing the gap. Not wanting to get boxed in lane 1 by Spiker, Webb reacts, swinging wide enough in lane 1 to force Spiker to go wide into lane 2 should he want to pass now.

Webb's move works, and into the homestretch, Spiker is at bay. Webb's got another gear, and he waits, eager to use it. Finally, 80 meters from home, with the homestretch crowd screaming, Webb blasts into his final gear. Twenty meters later he's past Jefferson, but Spiker is actually closing on him. Across the track, Sully watches wordlessly, not believing his eyes and dreading the thought of another devastating loss for Webb.

Just 50 meters from the tape, Spiker is sprinting fastest of the three, gaining on Webb, pumping his arms furiously and begging his legs to follow. But by now he's starting to sense that maybe it's too late. Despite closing fast, Spiker realizes he's out of control. Lacking speed training over the last 5 weeks because of his injury, he doesn't have his usual sprinting ability. His arms are doing their part, but his legs are not responding. He leans forward more with each stride, still gaining on Webb but powerless to stop his momentum. He knows he can win, if only he can stay upright.

For the next 20 meters, the crowd watches feverishly. Jefferson cracks ever so slightly but decisively, unable to keep up with Webb. Then, 30 meters from the tape, Spiker realizes he can't will his legs to do what he has not trained them to do. He goes down in a rush, chest first, as if he's been shot in the back. He slaps the track, his momentum curling his legs up toward his head like a scorpion's tail. Lying on the track, title squandered, his rage boils as he considers that this gaffe may have also cost his school the team title. He scrambles to his feet, desperate for any point he can salvage.

Webb feels a rush of emotion as he breaks the tape unimpeded, and he thrusts his arms into the sky in celebration before bringing them together in prayer and gazing heavenward. He thanks God for the victory, which once and for all lays to rest all the anguish and frustration he's endured since injuring himself this winter. He's flush with victory, overcome at having finally, finally ended a race to joyous cheers instead of funereal silence. He'll savor this moment for the rest of the afternoon.

ONE TO GO

An hour after Webb's run, it's Brannen's turn. For him, it feels as if he's been following Webb's lead in some way for 2 years now. It adds to his pre-race anxiety. Warming up, he does nothing out of character, keeping to himself and doing his usual pre-race strides, high knees, and butt kicks, but his face is tight with anxiety and concentration. Last night, while Webb slept like a log in the bed beside his, Brannen tossed and turned, fretting endlessly about today.

At the gun, Brannen gets a clean start. He breaks even with the pack as each runner in the field hits the backstretch and sets his eyes on being in good position entering the second turn. Brannen slithers through the maze of spikes and elbows down the backstretch and hits the 200-meter mark directly off the shoulder of the leader, stocky Minnesota senior Toby Henkels. Pale-skinned, with short-cropped brown hair, Henkels has the thick-chested, broad-shouldered physique and the slightly bowlegged, compact gait of a hockey player. He bulls his way around the corner with none of Brannen's finesse but with every bit of the grit.

Brannen sits on Henkels's shoulder through the quarter-mile in 53 seconds and rounds the bend. Approaching 250 meters to go, the pack is bunched tightly behind him, but he feels good. He readies to make his move and then, right in the middle of the backstretch, moves past Henkels into first.

To Brannen's bemusement, his move into the lead does nothing to separate him from the field. He hits 200 meters to go with Henkels on him like a sock. Brannen can feel his suffocating presence and battles him around the turn as he moves to Brannen's outside shoulder and tries to bull his way past. Brannen doesn't dare even turn his head to look. He doesn't have to.

It stays like that, a two-man race, into the homestretch, where Brannen desperately tries to summon his kick one more time. He calls for it and nothing happens. He can't understand it. His legs feel fine, he's not tying up, and his respiration is normal. He just can't shift gears. His mind races for an answer: Why won't my legs just *GO*?

So immersed in their locked-at-the-hip slugfest for the tape are Brannen and Henkels that they are completely unaware of Wisconsin freshman Dan Murray's homestretch rush in lane 2. Henkels ekes past Brannen in the race's final meters, but by then, Murray has flown by both of them. He claims the Big Ten title and a new track record time of 1:48.20. Brannen's time is 1:48.39.

Brannen quickly makes his way back to the Michigan contingent, brow furrowed, lips tight, and blowing smoke. He removes his spikes and sits on the grass in front of the Michigan bleachers. For minutes he sits wordlessly, his face frozen in hot confusion, working through the race in his head, his inability to switch gears an unsolvable riddle.

Warhurst is just as baffled. When Sully calls after the race and tells him that Brannen finished third, the coach is silent. It's a first: Warhurst at a loss for words. Sully approaches Brannen, who, though he sits just feet from his teammates, is isolated in his anguish and duly left alone. Sully doesn't try to cheer him up with any "but you ran so good!" comments. Instead, he tells Brannen the truth: He ran a great race. Tactically, it was perfect. He just didn't have what it took. He may have lost, but he didn't beat himself.

Several minutes later, Brannen is still there, picking at blades of grass between his feet. Already he's come to terms with the loss. He won't flog himself over his inability to change gears. He's processed the internal anger. Now all that remains is the ache of having lost. He can hear the commotion behind the Michigan bleachers as a gaggle of high school girls get Webb's autograph. "I'm Anne," one of them says coyly. "Anne Available." Brannen continues to pluck at the grass, head hung low, his once-defiant posture now the slouch of the beaten athlete. He can let go of the anger. The disappointment, though, is rooted deeper.

When he boards the bus bound for Michigan late that afternoon, Brannen has the sparkle in his eye once more, thanks to a 400-meter split of 47.5 in the 4 by 400-meter relay. I ask him what he learned this weekend. He looks me dead in the eye and says emphatically, "Never to shave my legs again."

A few days ago, Brannen and Webb showed up at practice with

freshly shaven legs and a distinctly orange sheen. Earlier that afternoon, after shaving their legs, they had both paid a visit to a local tanning salon. "Holy shit!" Tim Broe said when he saw the pair. "I'm embarrassed to be affiliated with this program at the moment."

At the time, Brannen laughed at Broe's old-school way of thinking that holds that shaving your legs or tanning is a less than manly thing to do. But now he realizes that shaving his legs for the race—to gain a psychological advantage—may have backfired. No longer will he search outside himself for the edge he needs to win. The confidence he has now, after having redeemed himself in the 4 by 400-meter relay, comes from within.

When he tells me he'll let his leg hair grow back, I can tell that he now has the confidence he needs to win.

For a long while, the stench of defeat hangs in the dank air. Then a few bottles of water start making their way toward the back of the bus. Soon clutches of them are heading back and a gang of guys is converging toward the belly of the bus with watches out, clocking water-chugging duels that have broken out en masse. The guys erupt when Webb breaks the chugging record and laugh just as hard when Brannen flaunts his recompense for repeated failures to get the record: a grossly distended belly. When the water's gone, there's a hunt for more ammo, until someone sees crates of it at the front of the bus: bananas! Soon there's a battle for the dubious title of banana-scarfing champion.

Only a stop at a rest station halts the action. Once again on the bus, gestalt of the moment gone, the team settles in for the rest of the ride to Ann Arbor. Some play cards, some sleep, some read, and others watch *The Fast and the Furious* on the overhead video monitors. Tomorrow, with the exception of Brannen, Webb, and Wiz, every Michigan trackman on the bus will be moving out of Fletcher Hall, their season done.

CHAPTER:18

A MATTER OF HEART

Two nights ago, the guys returned from the Big Ten Championships in darkness and sleepily filed off the bus to Fletcher Hall and their respective off-campus homes. Now, less than 2 days later, it's as if they had never been here. The locker room is barren. With the exception of Wiz's, Brannen's, and Webb's, the lockers are devoid of a year's worth of detritus. The unseen, however, lingers: the reek of sweat.

Webb and Brannen are waiting for Coach Warhurst to arrive so they can get started on their hardest workout yet. They'll start with an 800-meter run, follow it with two 600s, and finish with another 800. Sully did this indoors once in 1:55, 1:25, 1:25, 1:54, and he barfed afterward—the only time in a decade that Warhurst has literally brought the workhorse to his knees. That's legend in these parts, and for Brannen and Webb it adds a competitive edge to the workout that Warhurst's looking for right now.

While it's past 3:00 P.M. and Warhurst's still not here, neither Webb nor Brannen is in a hurry to get started. Although the Michigan men finished ninth at the Big Tens, the Wolverine women won their championship, and last evening they threw a late-night end-of-season bash. Webb and Brannen were out until the wee hours, partying one last time with their friends.

While fatigued from his late night, Brannen is glad he went out. At first, in an odd way, it lessens his anxiety about the workout today. Going in tired, he expects to hurt at the end of the intervals, and when that happens, he'll attribute it to lack of sleep rather than to the effort itself. Webb also rationalizes his late night.

As they continue talking, though, Brannen begins to change his mind. Rather than going into the workout expecting to do poorly, he's now ready to tackle it head-on. He figures that whether they went out or not is irrelevant. "It's all mental," he says. "If you think you'll run shitty because you went out, you probably will." He's not about to let last night's fun stop him today.

Warhurst pulls up to the indoor track building looking totally bedraggled. A clean shave an hour ago does nothing to disguise the bags under his eyes or his unkempt hair. But after 5 days and nights in the hospital, and his wife's arduous 46 hours of labor that culminated in a cesarean section, they have their little boy. And that makes him smile. "I'll tell you," he says proudly of his 8-pound, 12-ounce son, "he's a big son of a bitch."

Brannen and Webb understand how fried Warhurst is right now, and they see the fatigue in his eyes. They've both decided to propose to the coach what they'd like to do in the few workouts that remain prior to the NCAAs after today's session. Webb tells Warhurst he wants to do seven 400-meter repeats, as he did before the Prefontaine Classic last year, and Brannen says he'd like to do some of the acceleration workouts that helped him peak a year ago. Warhurst listens to each of them in turn and grants their requests before sending them on their way to warm up.

As they depart, Warhurst heads into his office to tie up some loose ends. While shaving earlier, he remembered that a recruit is coming in tomorrow, and he has to take care of that. He's also preoccupied about the Big Tens. He's disgusted by what he perceives as a lack of fight in his guys. For a moment he considers that if he could have attended the meet, he might have given them the spark they needed. He quickly dismisses the notion. "Shit, you gotta have the fight inside you," he tells me.

Before he can reach his office, one of the assistant athletic directors intercepts him. They meet for 15 minutes, during which Warhurst learns that some of the track guys trashed Fletcher Hall last night. This eats at him even more. "Rest assured, we're having a staff meeting, and there are gonna be some changes around here," he says, steaming.

And then there's Kalli's condition to consider. Although she exercised throughout her pregnancy, the c-section "really beat her up." In 5 days, he's due to leave for Baton Rouge, and right now Kalli needs help performing the most basic tasks, such as getting up from a chair. In his office, he adds the task of hiring a nurse to a to-do list he keeps on a scrap of paper.

At last he heads back to Ferry Field, where Webb and Brannen are raring to go. But before he meets them, he shoots off in his Montero to the Washtenaw Dairy for some deep-fried goodness and a cup of joe. He's way beyond the capacity to function on adrenaline alone right now. While there, he plays Luke's numbers (time of birth, date of birth, etc.) in the lotto. He's a superstitious sort, and he figures these numbers have to be as good as Sully's numbers during the Olympic Games. He played those to the tune of $500, just a digit away from eight large.

"WEBB, GO!"

Today, it's Webb's and Brannen's numbers that count most, and with his performance, Webb puts himself atop the list of greats who've completed this workout. The two trade leads through the first three intervals in 1:55.5, 1:26.7, and 1:25.9. Knowing Brannen's still an ounce shy on conditioning, Warhurst yells across the track, telling him to bow out after 600 meters of the last 800.

Both struggle on the last one. Brannen agrees to tow Webb through the quarter-mile, but 300 meters in, he doubts he can make it even that far on pace. He turns and says, "Webb, go." Nothing. "Webb, go!" Nothing. Webb tries to pass him into the turn, but he can't summon the strength. Together they charge on, and on the backstretch Brannen moves out to lane 2 to let Webb pass him on the inside if he dies.

Seeing the finish line is the only thing that keeps him going. He finally staggers to a relieved stop after hitting it a tick or two under 1:30. Webb passes him on his inside right at the 600 with another half-lap to go. Into the final homestretch, Webb checks his watch and sees he has to pick it up if he wants to hit his split. He quickens his arms, his legs respond, and he consciously resists the urge to muscle it. He can't prevent his arms from flying out, though. It's the telltale sign of his fatigue. Webb controls his effort right through the line, then reaches for his left wrist. Watches click: 1:56.1.

Webb's jacked to have run so fine after two races over the weekend, with little sleep and only a day of rest. A short while later, he'll marvel at the tension in his legs. Not even this session could turn his taut steel springs into Jell-O. Add his fitness to his Big Ten win, and it becomes clear why he prays for a fast pace at the NCAAs. Webb plays out an ideal scenario in his mind. He wants it hot: 1:55 at the half and 2:54 at ¾ mile to drop the pretenders. "It'll be me versus two guys," he tells me. "That last 200, it'll hurt here [he slaps his legs] and here [he beats his heart]. If anyone wants to play around with me on *that*, go ahead."

Brannen and Webb laugh their way through the cooldown, reminiscing about the wild times they had last night. Now that they've nailed the workout, the memories are that much sweeter. And for Brannen, it's one more step toward putting his Big Ten race out of sight of the rearview mirror.

But Brannen's not looking back. In the locker room afterward, sitting with Webb and Warhurst, he asks the coach if they'll be going to Europe to race the big dogs this summer. Warhurst is non-committal. He tells them the trip, something they often discussed in early March, is now on a wait-and-see basis. It's quiet after that. Webb knows the trip hinges in large part on whether he stays at Michigan or goes pro. Ever unspoken, the issue of Webb's future still cannot be ignored.

THE NEW WEBB

Three days later, on Friday, May 25, Webb sets out to perform the only workout that will satisfactorily rid his conscience of the daunting vestiges of his former self and prove that Webb circa 2002 can trump Webb circa 2001. For him, the success—or failure—of the exercise is fraught with profound psychological ramifications. At the Big Tens, for the first time all season, Webb demonstrated the looseness, the air of nonchalance of one at the height of his powers that he exhibited at the end of his glorious 2001 campaign. For the first time, I saw the look that Scott Raczko describes as "a positive nervousness." A confident Webb, Raczko says, "gets excited; he can't wait to go. That's a real key."

But now, with only a week remaining until the NCAAs, Webb remains skeptical that he's climbed his way back to the top. He needs something special to reassure himself that after all he's been through this spring, he's got his mojo back. He needs a magical workout on a par with what he did almost exactly a year earlier as his final tune-up for the Prefontaine mile. Webb did six quarter-mile repeats in 54 seconds that day—and then a seventh in 52. That workout, more than any other, amazed the public. More important, it proved to Webb that he was ready to take on the world.

Now, on a sunny day in Ann Arbor, 3 days from the 1-year anniversary of his 3:53.43 mile at the Prefontaine Classic, Webb takes on his biggest competitor: himself. He's repeating his defining workout of one year ago: 7 by 400 meters.

After two intervals, Webb 2002 is looking good. He runs his first quarter-mile in 54 seconds. After a quarter-mile jog, he blitzes the second ahead of pace, in 53.6. As he jogs into the third one, he's hopeful he can run under 54 seconds for the next four and then blast Webb 2001 into oblivion with the last one.

A hundred meters into his third 400, however, he hits a road-block. All spring, he has battled Ferry Field's wicked winds. Now, out of nowhere, they make another unwelcome visit. Webb strains down the backstretch as the wind bounces off the Intramural Building and batters him, alternately sideswiping him and hitting him head-on. It's an unjust reality that at Ferry Field the swirling winds can impede you on the backstretch and then again on the homestretch. Down the homestretch, Webb battles again. It's as if he's running into the wind all the way around the track. He finishes, discouraged, in 55 seconds.

On his jog between the third and fourth intervals, he starts be-rating himself for going out last night. The guys rolled back into Ann Arbor at 1:30 A.M. He can't believe he was so cavalier as to stay out that late on the eve of the year's most important workout. If he hadn't gone out, maybe he would have that little extra juice to keep on pace. He vows to get adequate rest from here on, then re-focuses on the task at hand.

He grinds out the fourth 400 meters in 54.4, but the wind is un-relenting. Try as he might, he slows incrementally on the fifth and sixth quarters, to 54.7 and 54.9.

A year ago, he ran his last one in 52 seconds. He wasn't battling a significant wind then, so even though he's running a couple of tenths slower now, he's content to call it a draw so far. But he needs this last one. God, does he need it.

He takes an extra 200-meter jog, gathering all his courage for an all-out assault on Webb 2001. As he makes his final prepara-tions, Warhurst asks him to ditch his watch. He wants Webb to *feel* it.

In Webb's race against time, he has developed a dependence on his watch, often checking his splits in hundred-meter increments, and this has maddened Warhurst, who'd like to see him run more according to feel. Winning requires moving on instinct, feeling when the time is right and reacting with reckless abandon. Work-outs, Warhurst stresses, are designed to prepare you physically and mentally for the rigors of racing; he wants Webb's effort to dictate his pace instead of his watch dictating his effort. Racing the mile, especially in a championship like the NCAAs, is the furthest thing from the controlled environment Webb seeks in his workouts.

Webb grudgingly relents and launches himself into the last 400, blindly racing his former self. He squeezes every last ounce of energy out of himself on the last one and staggers to the locker room. His entire body throbs in pain, and it feels as if a pool of cement is hardening in his forehead. He lies on the floor for 5 minutes, head pounding. He'll take the pain now.

He just ran his last 400 in 52.8 seconds.

That evening, in a journal he keeps for the postseason, Webb's verdict—the only one of consequence—on the battle he waged today with his omnipotent past is inconclusive. He writes: "Now I am excited, for a weird reason, though. I am excited because I felt shitty in my workout today. I did this exact same workout last year in about the same times. I probably averaged a few tenths slower today, but I felt terrible after the second one. Plus, today the wind was killer . . . I am way stronger than last year, just a little less focused. Let's fix that!"

Despite his intentions and the similar results to a year ago, I wonder if this session was the tonic that his fractured ego still desperately needs.

CHAPTER:19

THE NCAAS

Three days before his heat at the NCAA Championships, Alan Webb stands at the mouth of Louisiana State University's Bernie Moore track stadium for the first time and takes in the scene before him.

The track is already humming with some of the finest collegiate athletes in the land. Music blares over the stadium loudspeakers, and although the damp Louisiana air feels like a sticky glove against his skin, it's not nearly as suffocating as he imagined it would be.

He laughs aloud when he thinks of the announcer at Ohio State who declared their track "the greatest facility . . . in the world." That was nice, but LSU's magnificent facility is unlike any other he's ever seen. Every inch of the track is covered in rubber tartan, and a distinct eight-lane yellow swath of tartan, accented by the giant purple letters *LSU*, cuts right through the heart of the in-field—a showcase for the brilliant speedsters of the bayou.

By the 1500-meter start line, Webb sees a gigantic billboard that says NATIONAL CHAMPIONS. It lists the years the LSU women have won the national championship in track and field. Webb counts them one by one, from 1987 through 1997. "Wow," he says, "11 straight."

Webb's eyes move farther west and settle on Tiger Stadium. From here the steep upper tier of seats that cascades over the stadium looms large and imposing. Built to accommodate the Louisiana fans' unquenchable appetite for Tiger football (and LSU's desire for their greenbacks), the stands are a testament to the fact that sports are big time in the bayou, and the jewel of a track facility before Webb proves that track is not lost among them.

Webb gets a feel for the tartan when he spikes up for his final pre-race workout. It feels great: soft enough to be forgiving on the shins yet firm enough to propel him from stride to stride. He glides through a couple of 200s in 26 seconds before Warhurst convinces him to ditch his watch.

Freed from his digital governor, Webb consciously plays with his gears on his last 200-meter run, much like a racecar driver fine-tuning his engine. He flies through the finish in a swift 24.3. For Webb, all systems are Go.

"STAY OFF THE RAIL"

Two days later, Nate Brannen sits on the sofa in his room at the Residence Inn, hair gelled, in sweats. He's mindlessly watching the tube. All day he's been thinking back to indoor NCAAs and the anguish and embarrassment he felt at not making the final. Come hell or high water, he wants a spot in this one.

One to go

Nate Brannen sprints through the 400-meter mark of the NCAA
800-meter final on May 31. Florida's Moise Joseph (right) and
Tennessee's Marc Sylvester are in hot pursuit.

Just did it

Brannen looks heavenward in relief after setting a
new personal record and University of Michigan record in
the NCAA 800-meter final.

Too close to call
Alan Webb (far left) lunges across the line in a blanket finish
in his preliminary heat in the 1500 meters
at the NCAA Championships on June 1.

Chris Lear

One last time

Michigan coach Ron Warhurst discusses the game plan with
Webb prior to the NCAA 1500-meter final.

Off and running
With the field strung out behind him, Webb rolls through the
400-meter mark of the NCAA 1500-meter final in 58 seconds.

The Sage Expressway

In the NCAA 1500-meter final,
Webb (far right) sees Stanford's Donald Sage (center) sprint
past him and into the lead down the final homestretch.

The veterans
Coach Warhurst clocks Kevin Sullivan (left) and
Paul McMullen as they finish a gut-wrenching 60-second
quarter at Ferry Field in June.

Chris Lear

Still their guy
Weeks after Webb's departure, the team stands together
(from left, Tim Broe, Kevin Sullivan, Coach Warhurst,
Nate Brannen, and Paul McMullen).

Stuck in traffic on the bus ride over to the stadium, Warhurst looks at Brannen, his well-groomed freshman, and offers some words of wisdom: "You better make the final, or you'll look like a stooge with the 'do."

"I know," Brannen says, grinning. "All the time I spent fixing it won't have been worth it." Arriving at the stadium, Warhurst offers more substantive advice: "Stay off the rail and make that final!"

That's all the advice Brannen needs to hear, for he knows just how the race will run. In his section, the first of three heats, is defending NCAA champion and Botswana native Otukile Lekote of South Carolina University. Lekote won the NCAA 800-meter race a year ago in 1:46.68 with his patented front-running style, and he's primed to repeat that performance here.

Brannen expects Lekote, the fastest collegian of the season by more than 1 second with a mark of 1:45.27, to take it right from the gun. Usually everyone just lets him go unchallenged, but Brannen thinks he has it in him to latch onto his coattails and go for the ride. If he doesn't hold on for second, the last automatic qualifying spot in his heat, he figures he'll still run 1:47, a time that should earn him a spot in the final. The top two finishers in each heat plus the runners with the next three fastest times will advance to the final.

Warhurst climbs out of the competitors' stands by the 200-meter mark when he sees Brannen walking down the yellow tartan aisle in the middle of the infield toward the start. He's lingering behind the field, hoping to get another stride in before the race, but that's not going to happen.

In Brannen's heat are Dan Murray of Wisconsin and Toby Henkels of Minnesota, Big Ten foes who bested him in Madison at the Big Ten Championships a week ago. They don't concern him. They went out in 54 seconds for their first quarter-mile at the Big Tens, and Brannen believes they'll struggle to beat him off Lekote's fast pace.

Brannen lines up in lane 3, with Lekote in his line of vision in lane 5. With the exception of the World Track and Field Championships, this is Brannen's biggest race ever, and his nerves are consuming him as the starter calls him to the set position.

BOOM! Brannen jogs off the line. Brigham Young's Mao Tjiroze has jumped early. At that, a rush of adrenaline pours out of Brannen, quieting his body and mind. Settled, he endures another false start when the starter's pistol fires a blank. Then at last the gun sounds, and they go.

Breaking at 100 meters, Lekote already has the lead. Down the backstretch, the runners fight for position. Lekote leads a tightly bunched pack through 200 meters in 24 seconds. Brannen settles into fifth on the outside of lane 1 with Minnesota's Henkels on his inside. While he planned to be right on Lekote going in, he's still within striking distance, and more important, he's not trapped. He maintains his position through 400 meters in a quick 51 seconds. He feels faster than he ever has now. The pace causes him no distress.

Brannen maintains his position through 600 meters, which he hits for the umpteenth time this season in 1:18. Such is his speed that he's itching to move, but he hesitates, not sure if he can sustain a surge for the finish from this far out. He moves into third and lopes around the bend on the outside shoulder of Kansas State's Joseph Lee, now the only obstacle between him and the finals.

With 150 meters to go, Brannen shifts gears and glides smoothly past Lee into second. He sets his sights on Lekote. Adrenaline surges as he closes on the leader, who's a good 5 meters up. Brannen's instincts scream to get him. He looks over his shoulder and finds that he's clear of a struggling Lee. No other challengers appear. Brannen again considers going for Lekote, glances back, and thinks better of it, deciding to save his juice for the final. It's Lekote, 1:46.49; Brannen, 1:47.00.

Warhurst loves it. Brannen ran perfectly, never getting caught on the rail on the inside of lane 1. He ran his fastest race of the season, and he made the final. Webb's just as excited. Seeing his roommate run so fast in a trial reassures him that he's capable of running as fast as necessary to qualify for his own final in his 1500-meter heat tomorrow. At the Big Tens, it was Webb who set the goal for Brannen to match. Now the roles are reversed.

"A GOOD TEAM WITHOUT HIM"

The following morning, Brannen and Wiz head down to catch some breakfast in the Residence Inn with just minutes to spare before closing time. Brannen lazily grabs a *USA Today* from the counter. He flips to the sports section and sees Webb's photo atop the page, along with the headline "Webb May Run as Pro."

He reads Dick Patrick's article in silence until he reaches a quote from John Cook, a former coach at George Mason University and a mentor to Webb's high school coach, Scott Raczko, in the third column. "This kid is a huge, bright light in American distance running. If he gets the right agent, right coach, and the right logistical support, he could blossom." In the article, Raczko maintains that he hasn't really spoken to Webb about turning pro but that he'll support him no matter what he decides to do.

Brannen looks up from the story, disgusted. "I'm sick of it. We don't need this and Warhurst doesn't need this. Too many guys have been overlooked this year because of Webb. We'll be a good team without him. I hope he stays another year. Imagine what teams we could put together at Penn [Relays] next year in the 4 by 1 mile and distance medley relay. But if he's gonna go pro, he should just say it and leave."

But if Webb does leave, Brannen feels he will be making a poor choice. "How can he get a better deal than what we have here? We get our education for free, we get all the equipment we need, and we travel to whatever meets we want."

What's unfortunate is that Webb has said nothing to Patrick to further fan the flames. The speculation is building despite him. His remarks to Patrick were, "I'm not thinking about it that much. I'm running in a Michigan uniform this week. As for now, I'm coming back. If anything happens, everybody will find out. My focus is on the prelim and getting to the final."

By the time Brannen sees the story, Warhurst is already out on the links playing in a coaches' tournament with other members of the Michigan staff. He knows Cook is a mentor to Raczko, and he bristles at Cook's comments. He tells me, "In my mind, there's no doubt [Cook's] involved in it now. Webb's a 19-year-old kid, and he should be told what to do in a situation like this. And Raczko's saying he will support whatever Webb decides to do? He's involved and Cook's involved. And what the hell does that mean, 'if he gets the right coach, the right agent, he'll blossom?' What the hell's that supposed to mean?"

Cook, who retired from George Mason in 1997 and now sells tracks from his home in Florida, is in Baton Rouge for the NCAAs. I decide to find him and get his perspective.

At George Mason, a tiny commuter school in northern Virginia, he won—big and often. And he wasn't afraid to bend the rules if it was in the best interest of his athletes. "When we won the NCAAs [indoors, 1996], I took the kids to Albuquerque for 6 weeks during Christmas break—legally or illegally, I don't care; they [the NCAA] can do whatever the hell they want to me. That's the year [Ugandan miler Julius] Achon ran 3 miles under 4 minutes at the NCAA meet. I had four guys running 1:46 indoors. We pushed everybody off the track."

Despite his success coaching collegians, Cook tells me he believes that if Webb is ever to make it to the top of the world, he'll have to leave Michigan. That's because, more often than not, success in college doesn't translate into success on the world stage. In 1987, Cook coached Abdi Bile to the world championship in the mile. But that achievement came at a cost. "When I coached Abdi Bile, I had the worst teams at George Mason that I ever had. You know why? I gave Abdi every second. If there are 60 minutes in hour, I coached him 50. I had terrible teams, but I also had the world champion in the mile. That's the commitment I made," he tells me.

Cook thinks Webb is a talent on a par with Bile. And while he says he has great respect for Warhurst—the last American coach to lead an American middle-distance or distance runner to an Olympic medal (Brian Diemer, steeplechase, 1984)—he believes Warhurst is trapped within the constraints of the collegiate system. That system requires him to field competitive teams in cross country, indoor track, and outdoor track, leaving little time, in Cook's estimation, for sustained training.

Says Cook, "The schedule is predicated: I gotta go here, gotta go there, Penn, conference—on and on and on."

Cook prepared Bile differently than his other athletes. He didn't let him run the NCAA Cross Country Championships his junior year. Indoors, he ran only two races, a 1000 and a mile. Again he skipped the NCAAs. In the spring he focused all his training on the World Championships in Rome, once more at the expense of NCAAs, where he ran only one 1500. In Rome, Bile crushed the field, winning the world 1500-meter title in 3:31 with a devastating 1.47 in the last 800 meters.

Cook leans in conspiratorially after I silently ponder Bile's staggering feat and says, "Now how the fuck you gonna compete with that?"

Cook maintains that his collegiate stars who earned Mason the 1996 NCAA title could not have risen to Bile's heights—but not because they lacked the talent. Worn out from the collegiate schedule, he says, "they were all done for the summer."

Cook places a heavy emphasis on what he calls "alactic training," or non-running work. His system involves everything from ballistic hill work and hurdle drills to sandbag drills and shot put tosses (something he learned from the Cubans and Ana Quirot), all with a particular ratio for a specific purpose at a specific point in the training. Cook counts every single hurdle—so many thousand this year, so many thousand the next. "It's not just helter-skelter like, 'Oh, go do drills.' Certain times of year we do speed hurdles, certain times of year we do strength hurdles, and then we mix and match," he says.

The premise of all this is to take advantage of all of the body's "energy systems." Cook likens it to plugging holes in a dike: Once all the holes are plugged, you're ready to rock. But you can't do the system halfway. Cook requires his athletes to follow his training recipes meticulously. Anything less won't bring success, and worse, can lead to injury. The problem is, Webb believes in this system more than he does in Warhurst's, and for the last year he has been caught between the two.

Raczko, who studied under Cook for 2 years at George Mason, had Webb on the system in high school, where Webb had his greatest success. But Warhurst's approach is entirely different, with no emphasis on alactic training. So Webb has been trying to squeeze in Cook-style workouts around those he's done for Warhurst all year, something Cook sees as a colossal mistake.

Earlier this week, Cook ran into Webb doing crossover drills in the parking lot outside the Residence Inn. Webb complained to Cook that his ankle was a bit sore, and Cook told him to stop immediately. "When you do drills like that," he says, "you can't do them by yourself; you need supervision constantly. Here's a guy 2 days from a damn qualifying race and he's gonna go do drills someone didn't prescribe?"

Cook likens it to drilling your own teeth. "The worst thing for Webb to do is just a little of this system, not knowing why it fits in or why it doesn't. For that kid to think that he understands the system is ridiculous."

According to Cook, Webb should make a choice: Bite big-time into Warhurst's program and cut all ties with what he did in high school at South Lakes, or leave Ann Arbor and return to his roots. It's not an option for Warhurst to adapt to Cook's system. He says, "You can't expect Ron Warhurst to jump up and embrace this thing. He's been successful all his life without this and he's gonna change his philosophy because of one kid?"

He leaves little doubt as to what Webb should choose. He tells me that if he felt comfortable intervening and giving Webb advice, he would tell him to "get out of there. Go to school 9 hours a semester, get somebody to pay for school, get a good agent, go back to what made you great, be in a good medical environment, have a great massage therapist, have a great place to train, and be willing to go to altitude at least three times a year at different phases. Be a big-time athlete now. *Now.*"

Cook insists he has never given this advice to Webb directly. "I don't mess around with other people's kids," he says. He also claims he has no interest in coaching Webb. But he has told Raczko that should Webb go pro, he'd be happy to advise Raczko and help with matters such as altitude training or navigating the European circuit.

Later that afternoon, I catch up with Warhurst, now back from the golf course at the Residence Inn. A round on the links has done nothing to soothe his ire. He alludes to a small plastic knife that he long ago taped to the outside of his office door in Ann Arbor, "for all the administrators who stab me in the back." His gut tells him that someone's knifing him now. He flatly reiterates his assertion from earlier in the morning: "Cook's involved, and Raczko's involved."

Regardless, it's a dilemma that has been roiling in the media since April, and now, on the eve of Webb's first race at the NCAAs, it's come to a boil. Is it distracting Webb from the task at hand? His competitors couldn't be happier.

DAMAGE CONTROL

Webb pops into Brannen's room hours before heading to the track for his qualifying round of the 1500 meters. On a desk, he spots an open laptop with an icon that reads "mtsac.mov." It's a digital film clip of the final laps of Webb's race at Mt. SAC. Webb and Wiz hunch over and watch Webb's nightmare unfold again before them. Webb stares blankly at the screen, as expressionless as when it first happened. It's the first time he's seen this video. He pulls away as if waking from a bad dream. "Man," he says, slowly shaking his head, "if that happened tonight . . ." He pauses in thought, then says, "I don't know what would happen."

Back from the links, Sully gets on the Internet in Warhurst's room. When Brannen asks what he's doing, he says, "trying to find that article." An Internet junkie, Sully's checking to see if the running message boards are once again crackling with Webb speculation.

Warhurst takes it a step further. Steve Webb arrived late the night before; Warhurst sees him at the hotel and asks whether he knows what's happening behind the scenes. Steve says he doesn't. Both agree it's best if Alan doesn't see the *USA Today* story before he races this evening. Despite the "news," Warhurst is still fiercely protective of his guy.

Webb hasn't seen the story. In his hotel room, he watches the Weather Channel for the forecast and scribbles in his journal. He's excited to see his family, who have traveled here to see him run, and he can't wait to toe the line. "You make it happen," he writes. "DESTINY IS CRAP!"

One hour prior to his prelim, Webb heads into the LSU Field House beside the track, the staging area for the race. Security guards stand behind a table, checking those coming in to see if they're properly credentialed. As Webb walks in, he glances down at the table and sees his picture atop the sports page of *USA Today*. Warhurst spots this a moment too late, but he moves quickly to cut between Webb and the paper to block his view. He breathes a sigh of relief as Webb walks right past into the staging area, but he's powerless to stop him a short while later when he heads back past the table to use the washroom. "Oh, well," the coach says, "he's gonna see it sooner or later."

Webb returns and nonchalantly slips his headphones on, humming along to Jamiroquai's "Virtual Insanity." Warhurst wastes no time getting Webb's attention for a pre-race strategy session. They sit alone on the field house bleachers and Webb listens intently as Warhurst shares his thoughts.

He's in the second of two heats with guys who have all run within a second of one another this season. The top four in each heat plus those with the next four fastest times will advance to Saturday's final. His heat includes Stanford's 2000 Olympian Gabe Jennings, but he's not in top form, rebounding from a hiatus this winter. No one in Webb's heat has run well enough of late to be deemed the favorite. Because the field seems so evenly matched, Warhurst focuses on Webb's tactics. He urges Webb not to get trapped on the rail, to give himself a clear lane to the finish. "Don't be afraid to run out in lane 3," he says. "You can be there if you have to be to do what you gotta do, which is get to the final." Now it's up to Webb. Warhurst leaves the gym 40 minutes prior to race time "to walk around and bite my knuckles." Laughing, he adds, "Maybe I'll hold a press conference."

Webb doesn't deviate from his pre-race routine. He goes through his drills and strides. All business, he keeps to himself as he cautiously goes through the motions, his anxiety visible on his face.

His expression changes from concentration to doubt. There is none of the conscious swagger you'd expect if you knew about Webb only from reading the papers. Brannen was just as nervous a day ago. In this way, Webb is no different from any of his competitors. If anything, the combined force of stinging losses, inner turmoil, and the media circus have accumulated like bricks one atop the other beneath him, leaving him alone on a high and precarious perch.

Wiz and Brannen come into the field house to lend some support. "I love prelims and I hate prelims," Webb tells them as he changes into his Michigan jersey and prepares to go to the staging area. "I love them because they work the kinks out, but I hate them because they're another race. What happens if something happens?"

Warhurst watches the first heat from the athletes' area around the 200-meter mark to see how fast it goes. For three laps, Villanova's Adrian Blincoe tows the field around at an honest 4-minute-mile clip before Connecticut's Dan Wilson explodes from the field down the final backstretch. Surprisingly, no one challenges him, and he coasts to the win in 3:40.27, looking every bit a favorite for Saturday's final. Six guys stream past in the next 2 seconds, meaning that seven are across in 3:42 or faster, with eighth-place Rob Vermillion of Colorado State way back at 3:48. Should the second heat be slow, only the top four finishers will be guaranteed a spot in the final.

Unlike any meet thus far, the announcer gives Webb no elaborate introduction. He's announced as the Big Ten champion, and he takes his spot on the starting line in lane 5 next to James Bowler of Nebraska and Big East champion Tom Parlipiano of Villanova. The list leader in heat two at 3:41.08, Charlie Gruber of Kansas, is in lane 8. Not much is expected of Gruber after his disastrous seventh-place performance at the Big 12 Championships a week and a half ago, but Gruber harbors other thoughts. He entered that race fatigued from exams and graduation. He gathered himself after that performance, reminded himself that he'd still put in all the work and was still fit, and left for the NCAAs keeping all options open.

At the gun, Gruber shoots off the line. Like every other runner in the field, he hopes for a fast pace but doesn't care to do any of the work to ensure that pace himself. But after a slow first 100 meters, he senses a crawl of a first lap coming, so he grudgingly decides to take over the pacing chores "to keep it honest." He picks up the pace, and the rest of the field follows him through an opening lap in 60 seconds. Gruber slows on the next lap, and the tightly bunched field passes 800 meters in 2:04. The slow pace virtually ensures that only four or five men from this heat will advance.

Webb comes through the half-mile mark in about sixth place, content to play kicker's roulette and take his chances at the end. Warhurst watches as the pack runs three abreast into the far turn and toward the 1000-meter mark. He watches closely, waiting for Stanford's Jennings to begin a long drive for the tape. He continues to wait as they round the bend.

Finally, approaching the bell lap, Jennings and his teammate Grant Robison move up to Gruber's shoulder, but still no one challenges his lead. Gruber has run slowly to conserve his energy for just this situation. He feels ready to respond to any threat on a moment's notice. Around the last turn, he watches the field out of the corner of his eye. Behind him, the milers jockey for position, and Webb follows suit, running wide in lane 2 to have freedom to move.

Rounding past 1200 meters in 3:04, with only 300 meters remaining, Gruber senses Jennings coming on his outside shoulder and reacts instantly, kicking into high gear for home. Sully, in the stands by the start, sees Webb running comfortably and in good position in lane 2 in mid-pack as the action heats up. He knows what he would do in this situation. He'd gun it all-out to have the pole into the final 200 meters and let them chase him home. He waits for Webb to react similarly, but before Webb can blink, a slew of runners flies past him on his outside shoulder, just as they did on the final backstretch at Mt. SAC.

Into the final turn with only 200 meters remaining, Warhurst starts fearing the worst. Only five will make it, and Webb moves by him buried in eighth place. Around the turn into the final bend, American University's Sean O'Brien challenges Gruber for the lead and takes it. Behind him, Webb dashes furiously over a 30-meter stretch and passes a gaggle of runners, bringing himself in contention with the leaders as he enters the final straightaway. But he doesn't finish the move, and he settles right there.

In the stands, Sully holds his breath, thoughts coming in rapid succession: What's gonna be in the paper tomorrow? What are they gonna say about Ron? What are they gonna say about the kid? He's already got so much pressure on him.

Webb moves out even farther down the homestretch to get a clear run for the finish and amazingly, the entire field—10 strong— is moving abreast as if this were a 100-meter dash. Webb charges toward the tape—in lane 5! He's thinking of nothing but getting there first. Then, in the final meters, he capriciously decides to ease his effort and save a little something for the final.

In lane 1, O'Brien desperately throws himself into the lean; one step later, he sees the track coming up at him before smashing into it.

It's done, and too close to call. Webb's confident he made it, but he can't be sure until he sees the scoreboard. The names flash on the board and Webb's eyes search down from the top for his name. He can't believe his eyes. "What? Oh, God, no!" But he knows the scoreboard doesn't lie. He sees "7 Webb Mich."

For a second, he's numb. Then the names start shuffling on the board like Ping-Pong balls in a lottery drawing. They stop shuffling and Webb sighs deeply when he sees his name in third. The difference between the winner, Stanford's Grant Robison, and the 10th and last-place finisher, Brendon Mahoney of Georgia Tech, is a scant 0.5 second. The difference between Webb and Jennings, the sixth-place finisher and first nonqualifier, is 0.06 second.

As at the Big Tens, Webb ran his final 300 meters in 40 seconds. And if he's learned anything tonight, it's that, while he's as strong as an ox, he is no faster than the other milers in the field off a slow pace. He thought of moving in the middle of the race to take advantage of his strength but decided against it. The final, he tells me, will be different. "Before [the race] I worried if I went too soon I'd hurt myself, but if I feel good [in Saturday's final], I'm gonna go and take the lead."

Despite the fact that Webb left his final kick until the last second, Warhurst sees the race as a big move forward for him. "He stayed outside, he didn't get trapped, and he ran smart. That's another learning experience for him."

LOOKING AHEAD TO THE FINALS

With the heat less than an hour old, Sully and Warhurst are already strategizing for the final. "The biggest thing," Sully says, "is that you have to be very realistic with yourself, and you have to know what's your best strength and your worst weakness. The last thing you want is to have the race set up so that it's playing into other people's hands. You want to avoid a race geared toward your worst weakness—at all costs. If that means you have to go 100 meters earlier than you'd like or you have to take a lap, so be it."

An awful lot of guys looked good out there today. Dan Wilson looked superb in the first heat, and no one in heat two eliminated themselves from title contention. Given Webb's less-than-explosive finishes in past races, Sully and Warhurst decide that his chances are best with a fast pace—something around 2:56 or 2:57 at three-quarters. As this evening demonstrated, if it comes down to a kick, it's anybody's race. It's possible that Webb can rise to the challenge and run a 38-second final 300 meters, but it's not as likely as closing in 40 seconds off a fast pace.

Webb breathes a sigh of relief and smiles widely when he sees Warhurst. It was close, but he got the job done. They survived to fight another day. An air of weary relief permeates the Michigan crew on the ride back to the hotel, the virtual insanity of the morning hours long since past, but not forgotten.

CHAPTER:20

THE FINAL SHOW

At the track for a shakeout this morning before his evening race, Nate Brannen sees that he's drawn lane 3 for the final. Coach Warhurst tells him that South Carolina's Otukile Lekote and Texas Tech's stellar freshman Jonathan Johnson are likely to go like hell from the gun.

"So," Brannen asks, "should I just get up on [Johnson's] shoulder?"

"Yeah," Warhurst responds, "get on his outside trail leg." He hits Brannen on the shoulder for emphasis. Just like that, the plan is in place. Brannen only hopes his shins are okay. He forgot to take ibuprofen before his run this morning, forcing him to cut it short after just 1 mile.

In what seems like the blink of an eye, it's 7:45 P.M., and the finals of the 800 meters will go off in 30 minutes. The sound system is pumping an audio feed of the meet into the LSU Field House. Brannen can't hear it. He walks around the track with headphones that cover his ears like earmuffs, his face never varying from its stern expression.

Coaches and support staff linger behind a temporary railing that separates them from the athletes on the indoor track. It's tense in here. Other than the audio feed of the meet, I hear nothing but muffled conversations and the *pftt, pftt, pftt* of warmup pants as athletes scream down the straightaway during some last-minute strides.

Warhurst walks into the building to offer Brannen some last-minute instructions. "Okay, Gaylord," he says. Brannen doesn't crack a smile. He listens intently as Warhurst tells him what to do out there. "Whatever you do, save something for the final straightaway . . . and get on the outside of lane 1 so that if someone comes past you, you can roll with him."

Warhurst thinks Lekote and Johnson will take it out in a blistering 50 seconds, and he wants Brannen right on them. Tennessee's talented freshman, Marc Sylvester, is likely to make a strong move in the last 200 meters, but Warhurst doubts he'll be with the leaders through the first quarter-mile. Those are the three guys Warhurst and Brannen figure will be in it.

Brannen's not a grudge racer. He doesn't line up intent on beating anyone in particular. Sylvester is an exception. Darren Adams, one of Brannen's teammates, was a high school teammate of Sylvester at Cleveland's St. Ignatius High School. All year, he's been boasting to Brannen about Sylvester's accomplishments, and Brannen's tired of hearing it.

Sylvester also rubbed him the wrong way at the NCAA Indoor Championships in early March, when he strutted around the track like a proud peacock before and after his third-place performance. Contrast that with Brannen's demeanor here. Moments after crossing the finish to qualify for the final, he clapped his hands together twice in a gesture of relief. That's as much celebrating as he cares to see out of anyone. Sylvester was way over that line at the indoor NCAAs, and Brannen hopes to serve him some humble pie tonight.

After watching Brannen perform a couple of strides, Warhurst decides that he's seen enough. Brannen's never looked faster. The coach meets Brannen's gaze and motions him over. "Okay, you little shithead, get down here. You're moving so fast you're making me nervous." Warhurst smiles at Brannen and does an excited little hop before turning away. "Go get 'em, I'll see you after the race."

Brannen has one last visitor before he hits the track. At the indoor nationals, Carol Henry, a close friend and fellow Canadian now running for the University of North Carolina, consoled him in the athletes' staging area after he failed to make the final. Now she comes to give him a pre-race pep talk. "Are you ready?" she asks timidly. Standing close to her, Brannen stares nervously at the ground. His answer is quiet but unwavering: "Yes."

For his final, Brannen lines up in lane 3, with Lekote and Johnson in lanes 5 and 6. There were only eight in the holding pen when Brannen got there, and for a moment he delighted in the thought that he could finish last and still get one of the coveted NCAA plaques awarded to the top eight finishers. Then Moise Joseph, Florida's silky-smooth sophomore, entered the room. Brannen thought, Shit, I gotta beat someone.

The capacity crowd quiets as the runners take their marks. On the backstretch, Warhurst's phone rings. It's Tim Broe, checking on Brannen's race, which would have already been over if rain earlier in the day hadn't delayed the meet for an hour.

"He's on the line!" Warhurst says.

"I'll call you back!"

"No, no, no. Hang on, I'll give you the play-by-play."

BRANNEN'S GLORY

The runners take off. Only 50 meters in, Brannen can feel Sylvester on his inside and Lekote in lane 5 pulling away from him.

He reacts, kicking into a higher gear. The last thing he wants is to be buried at the quarter-mile mark and have to work his way up.

Down the backstretch, the runners funnel together toward the 200-meter mark. As expected, Lekote leads and Johnson's right on his heels. Around the bend they fly, with Southern Methodist's Roman Oravec in third and Brannen right on his heels in fourth. "Go, you sonofabitch, go!" Warhurst yells as Brannen flies past.

Down the homestretch, Lekote continues to pour on the pace, the pack strung out behind him. Brannen fights to stay loose as he approaches the quarter-mile. He sees the clock tick as he approaches: 47 seconds . . . 48 . . . 49. Before the race, he worried about beating one guy for a plaque, but his insecurity took flight as soon as he did. Now, as he comes through 400 meters faster than he ever has, he wants a shot at the win. He needs to be in it with 150 meters to go.

Down the backstretch, Lekote and Johnson put a few steps between themselves and Oravec. Brannen moves out in lane 1, poised to move past Oravec and after the leaders. He can hear what sounds like a stampede behind him. He knows there is no margin for error; the entire field is still in the race.

Moise Joseph shoots past Brannen's outside shoulder down the backstretch. Brannen lets him go and immediately follows in pursuit, passing Oravec to reclaim fourth place. He clings to Joseph as he passes the 600-meter mark. Warhurst's doing a jig, hopping up and down with the phone at his ear. "He can win it!" he yells into the phone. And then "Relax! Relax!" as Brannen churns past.

Brannen doesn't hear him. He's absorbed in the moment, focusing all his energies on the task at hand. With 150 meters to go, he runs flat-out with no thought other than getting to the homestretch.

Into the homestretch, Brannen moves again to his right for a clear lane to the finish. He can see Lekote several body lengths ahead of him. He imagines passing the leader, and his body tries to respond, searching within for a final gear with which to chase him down. Nothing flows forth.

In lane 2 outside of Brannen, Penn junior Sam Burley is running the race of his life. The diminutive Ivy Leaguer had been running 1:48s and 1:49s all spring. He came into the final thinking that while he wasn't quite as fast as his competitors, he'd have a shot if he ran a conservative first lap and the favorites dulled their finishing kicks by tearing past the quarter at an unsustainable pace. That's precisely what happened. In the homestretch, Burley starts high-stepping his way past a tiring field.

Brannen looks over his shoulder and sees Burley rolling toward him with a full head of steam some 30-odd meters from the tape. He's tying up now and powerless to respond as Burley shoots past. Then, out of the corner of his eye, he sees Marc Sylvester's bright orange uniform approaching. He runs for the wire, desperately trying to preserve his spot, and hits it moments before Sylvester.

He's done it. He's earned his plaque with a fifth-place finish in a time of 1:46.00. In just his sixth 800 of the year, he's set a life-time personal best by 0.6 second. It's also a new school record.

A short while later, he approaches Warhurst on the backstretch, clutching his plaque under his arm. Warhurst spots him and shouts, "Very nice!" They chat for a few minutes, and the normally stoic Brannen is powerless to suppress a grin. "I've never been as proud to wear the M as I was today," he says.

Already Warhurst is thinking about Webb's race tomorrow. He could also set a personal record, but if he finishes fifth like Brannen, the press will roast him. Warhurst prays now that Webb's race is a knockdown, drag-out affair like Brannen's that showcases the ability of the athletes. "But if it's a tactical situation . . ." Warhurst says, and his voice trails off. I can see the anxiety in his face as he plays a scenario through in his mind. "You let people in a race and they get excited, they can run."

JUNE

CHAPTER:21

WEBB'S LAST STAND

At 3:45 P.M. on June 1, Alan Webb walks down the hall and into Ron Warhurst's room at the hotel. He left the meet promptly after Nate Brannen's race last night so he could get to bed by 10:00 P.M. Instead, he got wrapped up in the Lakers game and didn't fall asleep until midnight. Still, he slept for 10 hours, which is plenty. And he killed the tedious afternoon hours catching up with his sister and his young nephew. He's dressed smartly in a polo shirt and tan cargo shorts. And then there are his clean-shaven legs. No stubble there. It worked at the Big Tens.

As Warhurst sits casually on his bed, Webb plops onto a sofa, facing him. "So, Ron," Webb says nonchalantly, cutting to the chase, "what's the deal with the race tonight?"

As they start mapping out the plan, their excitement mounts. Warhurst sits up straight. Before long he's up and sitting on the edge of the bed. Webb sits upright and clasps his hands across his knees.

"I want it to be 1:56 [at the half]. Come by in 2:56, 2:57, and you're gone," Warhurst says.

"If somebody takes it out in 1:56, hell, I'll take it for the third lap, then I'll go," Webb answers.

"That's exactly right!" Warhurst says. "You don't want it to come down to the [final] straightaway. I tell you what, take it with 500 to go. Get yourself in position between the 800 and the next 200 meters. Then, when you come off the turn into the straight-away with 500 to go, start cranking it. You don't have to sprint to accelerate, just change the pace and get it going fast. That way those guys can't go off a 63 [third quarter] to an immediate explosion.

"That's what they'll try to do," he continues. "You don't have to go into an all-out sprint, but make it a dramatic change in pace, and keep going and going. That will start stringing them out. Then you gotta pin those ears back that you got on that head of yours."

Webb laughs, and Warhurst goes on. "I don't want to see it—and I don't think you want to see it—where you get caught up in the last 110 when there's six guys there and you gotta start looking around. I want you to get a fair run at 500 meters out. I think you're much better off with a faster pace from there when you can get yourself going. I know you can sprint, but I think it takes you a while to get it going. Once you do, you'll feel a lot more comfortable."

Webb likes what he hears. "It's gotta be guts," he says, evoking the spirit of the great Steve Prefontaine, the charismatic American who grabbed the public's attention by the throat with his coura-geous front-running. "When it's one on one," he continues, "if it comes down to me and Dan Wilson [the winner of the first heat of the prelim], just me and him or even three guys, you can tell what's going on with them, and you can play. But if there's 10 of them, then I gotta go out to like lane 20 just to make the pass!"

On they go, talking about the trials and how Olympian Gabe Jennings is sitting on the sidelines because he played kicker's roulette. Warhurst gets back to tonight's race and says authoritatively, "I really do think, Webbster, even if the pace is fast, that you should still get in position with 500, but not a wild explosion. I can't imagine anyone letting it go 2:04 or 2:05 again. But if that's the case, when you get to 500, you explode, and you run 1:05 for that last 500.

"Visualize coming down the backstretch after a half in 1:58, 1:59. Now, you gotta understand, there may be other guys with a similar plan. When you get off the curve by the water-jump pit, start drifting out [toward lane 2] so you can start rolling down the straightaway. Don't look for an opening halfway down the straightaway and wait for the bell to go. You want to get it going with 500 to go. I think you're much fitter than anybody else in the field off a fast pace."

Webb nods in agreement. "I think so, too. I think I can finish in 55 even if the pace is 2:55. I don't think anybody else can."

Warhurst nods and tells Webb, "You want to make sure that when those bastards start thinking they gotta go, they say, 'I'm hurting. I can't go with these guys.' I think that's the best way to do it."

With the plan in place, Warhurst reminds his runner that while this is the best strategy, it will not be easy to execute. It will take patience and balls. "Once you go, you're gonna feel the pressure. You gotta know that there's someone who's gonna challenge you, and then you gotta relax even more, and if they get up on you, don't panic." Warhurst starts acting it out, swinging his arms. "Look, I know they're there . . . relax. I know they're there, pump, pump, pump, faster, faster, faster.

"I'll be at the steeplechase pit," he concludes.

Although Warhurst is done, Webb doesn't move. I can see the mice spinning the wheels in his mind as he tries to figure out who will lead the field through a fast opening 800 meters. He realizes it may be up to him. "I wouldn't mind taking the lead and setting it up," he says, "even the first lap. I just don't want to lead the entire 1500 meters of the thing."

Warhurst cautions him against it. "You know, if you take the lead, you're gonna end up setting it up."

"I know," Webb answers. It's quiet. Webb's eyes take on a distant stare.

Warhurst grows testy, his gut telling him that Webb's once more obsessing about the pace through this point, that point—time, time, time. He breaks the silence in a loud, deliberate voice. "They want to fucking win it," Warhurst says. "They don't give a shit if they run 3:45. That's just the nature of the final. It's a war out there tonight. It's a fucking war. You got no friends out there tonight. You think [Villanova's Ryan] Hayden will let up for [teammate Adrian] Blincoe? They all want to be NCAA champion. They don't give a damn how fast it is."

Webb gets up, wanting to sleep on the plan until the van leaves for the stadium at 5:30.

"Okay," Warhurst says as Webb rises. "We got a plan now, okay. Visualize that. Now remember one thing: That's a long-ass straightaway."

"IT'S WAR TONIGHT"

Boom. Boom. Boom. Webb sits on the bleachers in the field house, an hour-plus before the final, patiently waiting to begin his warmup. A voice comes over the PA: "We'd like to ask whoever's playing the drums to please stop. It's annoying some of the competitors."

Webb glances in the direction of the music and sees the Stanford contingent. It has to be Gabe Jennings. Jennings was eliminated 2 days ago; now this is the day the music died. Webb can't help laughing. It's a welcome moment of levity. "It's funny," he says, "everyone was accepting of that type of thing when he was running well. Now it's like, Shut up." Moments later, Webb pounds his right fist into the palm of his left hand as one of his competitors jogs past on the track. "It's war tonight," he says, eyeing the other runner.

Warhurst and Brannen make their way back to see Webb as the race draws near, and Warhurst calls him over for some last-minute counsel. "Come here," he says. "Sit down for a second and relax." He reminds Webb one last time to "light it up" with 500 to go if the pace is slow. If it's snappier, he's just to pick it up a notch. In a blink, it's Webb's turn to go to the holding pen on top of the homestretch with the other competitors. "This is it!" Brannen tells him. "There's no turning back now."

Webb lines up in lane 5, his muscular torso in sharp contrast to the waiflike figures of Blincoe of Villanova in lane 4 and Don Sage of Stanford in lane 6. Blincoe, the NCAA indoor 3000-meter champion, ran a race nearly identical to the one Webb ran at Mt. SAC in his heat, provisionally qualifying for the final with an anxiety-inducing fifth-place finish. Sage, a slight sophomore with dark eyes, olive skin, and short, kinky black hair, finished a comfortable third in the first heat to secure his spot in the final.

Sage ran for powerhouse York High School in Elmhurst, Illinois, and 2 years ago missed immortality by a mere 0.29, running 4:00.29 for the mile at the Prefontaine Classic. At that point, it made him the fourth-fastest high school miler of all time. Had he gone just a few ticks faster, all of America would know his name. As it is, he's quietly going about his collegiate career at Stanford. A year ago, he raced in the shadow of two Stanford Olympians, Jennings and Michael Stember, and finished fifth at the outdoor NCAAs behind his more heralded teammates in 3:39.27. In that race, he pondered going for broke with 200 meters remaining but thought better of it and pulled back. When he finally did move, it was too late. He's regretted his indecision ever since, and he's determined to go for it tonight.

A false start cuts the tension. On the far curve, Warhurst sighs deeply as he watches the field wait for Webb to retake his spot on the painted line. A moment later, the gun cracks, and the runners start charging toward the first turn. Kansas's Charlie Gruber gets out well from his start position in lane 2, and approaching the turn, the field slows beside him to let him lead. He led Webb's preliminary heat, but this is the final. He wants no part of this.

He sharply puts on the brakes, and the field stalls beside him.

Webb also gets out well, leading the pack in lane 2. As Gruber slows, Webb feels a nudge in his back. He looks left and sees Gruber stalling, with no suitor to take the pace. He takes the bait.

"He's gonna go for it!" Warhurst shouts as Webb runs past. To the coach's delight, Webb presses around the curve and down the homestretch, stringing out the field like beads on a necklace. He hits the quarter in 58 seconds and keeps going down the backstretch. Good, Warhurst thinks, keep it moving. As Webb comes around the bend without a hint of strain in his stride, Warhurst leans over the fence, yelling, "Stay relaxed up top. Keep it up! Keep it up!"

Seconds later, Warhurst's expression turns panicky. He watches in dismay as the pack makes like a rubber band contracting down the homestretch, scattering runners in twos and threes like a gathering flood behind Webb. He hangs his head as Webb passes 800 in 2:02. He thinks, Oh, well, he's on his own now.

Warhurst prays that Webb's simply gathering his resources for the crucial push 500 meters from home. He yells for all he's worth as Webb lopes past, "Get ready! Get ready! Get ready! You gotta go! Here they come!" He watches, eyes wide with anticipation, as Webb hits the top of the homestretch, 500 meters from the line. With each stride he waits for Webb to move as the milers scurry like mice behind him, readying for the final tour. Nothing happens. Webb hits the bell in 2:48, and the entire stadium knows it's going to come down to that long-ass straightaway.

Webb runs on pins and needles around the curve and into the backstretch, antennas up, waiting to respond at the slightest challenge to his authority.

Blincoe moves first, bursting free like water through a levee. Webb responds instantly, racing him to get to the turn first. Neck and neck, they sprint toward the race's final turn 200 meters from home. Webb barely beats Blincoe to it, forcing him to move to his outside shoulder.

Blincoe reacts to having lost the race to the turn with anger, furiously pumping his arms around the bend while bearing down hard on Webb. His pressure squeezes Webb against the rail, hemming in his arms and restricting his stride. Webb grimaces with every stride as he passes Warhurst with only 150 meters remaining. Warhurst can't stand it. He hops in place. "Webb's holding 'em, Webb's holding 'em!"

Blincoe's furious charge withers slightly entering the final straightaway, enabling Webb to charge into the final homestretch with a slight lead and a total conviction that in 13 seconds, he will be the NCAA champion. He's unaware that behind him, Sage is sprinting around the curve fastest of all. With 125 meters to go, Sage has found another gear.

Adrenaline coursing through him, Sage gains on Webb with every stride as he chases him down the final straightaway. Fifty meters from the tape, Webb, whose energies are still focused on battling a game Blincoe, sees Sage rushing toward him out of the corner of his eye. Maxed out, he's helpless to respond as Sage triumphantly surges past him.

Webb's last 50 meters are nightmarish. The track turns to sand before him and he agonizingly struggles toward the finish as Arkansas's Chris Mulvaney takes the Sage Expressway right past him, followed moments later by Wisconsin's Josh Spiker. Webb's final 400 is a creditable 54.8, but it's not enough.

Warhurst shakes his head. He walks a few steps to his right so he can see the results as they're posted on the giant Jumbotron by the 1500-meter start. He twists his jaw and stares plaintively at the massive screen, absorbing the following numbers, speechless:

1. Donald Sage, Stanford		3:42.65
2. Chris Mulvaney, Arkansas		3:43.03
3. Josh Spiker, Wisconsin		3:43.16
4. Alan Webb, Michigan		3:43.23
5. Adrian Blincoe, Villanova		3:43.32
6. Ryan Hayden, Villanova .		3:43.82
7. Charlie Gruber, Kansas		3:43.86
8. Grant Robison, Stanford		3:44.04
9. Dan Wilson, Connecticut		3:44.46
10. Scott McGowan, Montana		3:45.40
11. Sean O'Brien, American		3:45.52
12. Brandon Strong, Arizona State		3:46.43

Webb walks alone around the curve toward the 1500-meter start, trying to piece together what just happened. An official interrupts his reverie and steers him to the podium for the awards ceremony. He grins and bears the presentation. Minutes later, he enters the interview tent, spikes in hand, and dismissively tosses them into a box holding his belongings. He sits on a bench near the box and stares wide-eyed into space while a pack of reporters waits for him to put his anguish into words. He puts his elbows on his knees and moves his hands up around his face, blinders against an unforgiving world.

In time, Webb rises, approaches the throng, and says to no one in particular, "It's the end of an incredibly terrible year."

CHAPTER:22

LEAVING ANN ARBOR

It's Monday, June 3. Now, just 48 hours after the NCAA final, Alan Webb sits on the couch in his room in Fletcher Hall.

He finished his last run in Ann Arbor a few hours ago with a few clockwise laps around the outer lanes of Ferry Field. As he finished, he watched Sully lumber past him in lane 1, chasing Paul McMullen through a 600-meter effort in 1:23. McMullen's bulbous quads and glutes already appeared smaller and fitter after several weeks of left-hand turns.

Ten months ago, Webb never would have imagined that this was as close as he would get to working out with those two after an entire year at Michigan.

His room is now nearly barren. Nate Brannen moved his possessions into his summer home up the street earlier today, and Webb has just finished packing his remaining belongings into his Eclipse. The couch and a lone poster of Swiss half-mile world champion Andre Bucher that Brannen has tellingly left behind are the only remnants of their stay in Fletcher Hall. Tomorrow morning, Webb will head home to Reston, Virginia, for a short vacation. Officially, he's to come back soon for more training—but I'm not convinced that he'll return.

As I take a seat at a desk across from him, I remark how soulless the gutted room seems compared to just a day ago. Webb scans the room, and his eyes settle on the couch. He laughingly recounts the day at the beginning of the year when he and Brannen picked the sofa up from a curb. He remembers it as if it were yesterday. So much has transpired between then and now. He tells me that he feels "like a completely different person." He flashes a smile as he remembers the highlights of the past year at Michigan: his win at the Big Tens in cross country, a race he considers his best of the year, and his Big Ten track victory.

His grin is just as broad when he considers how much fun he had going out with Brannen and the guys to parties like the one after the Big Tens and another just a few nights ago, after his race at the NCAAs. That night he was among seven guys sardined into a Pontiac Sunfire, on their way to live it up on Bourbon Street. Webb was just another college kid among the masses that night, with his recent race the furthest thing from his mind.

In his mind, however, Webb's year in Ann Arbor was defined not by the highlights but by losses, none more poignant than his loss at the outdoor NCAAs. He wishes he could run the final all over again. With that one race, he had hoped to erase a year full of disappointments and reestablish himself as a world-class miler.

He didn't want to lead the race, but when he did, he ran that first lap with conviction, in 58 seconds, according to plan. Then, he says, an unwelcome image involuntarily appeared in his mind's eye. As he launched into the second lap, he visualized himself dying on the final straight with the entire field licking their chops behind him. That image was quickly followed by one of Josh Spiker celebrating after winning in 3:37, a time faster than Webb had ever run, while he stood on the sidelines, having just towed Spiker and his other competitors to the race of their lives. Spooked, he slowed.

"I just lost my nerve," he tells me. "I should have realized, if you're gonna push, it's gonna hurt at 600 meters. I know I could have done it, but I just wussed out. I didn't have the guts."

If only he'd sustained his early pace, he knows the outcome would have been different. But that's the insidiousness of loss.

The repeated losses Webb sustained this spring robbed him of his verve and his conviction, the very assets he used to slay the giants of high school miling just a year earlier. By the NCAAs, despite his physical readiness, he was just a fragile facsimile of his former self.

For now, the immediacy of his NCAA loss still stings, although he's already trying to bury it for good—yet another lesson in a year in which, he says, "I learned a little bit too much." He laughs resignedly as he tells me, "Every time I got on the track it was like: lesson number one, lesson number two." He's quick to take solace in the knowledge that despite his result, the fitness was there. Tough lessons like these, he decides, are what will ultimately allow him to accomplish really special things down the line.

"It's hard for me to think of these races as hardships," he tells me, "when I know in reality I have it so much easier than a lot of people. I have a full scholarship, I've done some pretty cool things, so it's like, Why am I complaining?"

If only he really believed it. For him, running is not just an activity—it defines his being. It's why, despite his full scholarship at Michigan and some notable successes, he's contemplating charting another course to get his running—his life—back on track. "It's not like fourth in NCAAs is the end of the world, but it's not what I want. I want to win, and I want to run fast. That's what it's about.

And if I can't do it here, then I want to find a place where I can," he explains.

DECISIONS, DECISIONS

Webb will leave for home tomorrow to contemplate where that will be. He knows that going home to train under his former coach, Scott Raczko, won't guarantee success, and he worries about leaving Ann Arbor. "I've built a life here; all my friends are here now."

Whether he chooses to turn professional or return to Michigan, he is ready to shoulder the responsibility for his running. "The point I'm trying to make is that it's up to me. Just because I'm running under Raczko or Warhurst or just because Dathan [Ritzenhein] is running under [Colorado coach Mark] Wetmore, that doesn't mean he's gonna get better. Dathan and Jorge [Torres] got better because they trained hard."

He continues, "Pretty much everybody on this level works hard. To get that edge, you have to have the right coach who knows when to push you and tell you when to go hard. There's no right answer. Whatever I do—which I haven't decided yet, but in the next few days it's gonna come to me—from that moment on, for the rest of my career, I'm gonna stick with that coach. There's no turning back. It's sort of weird to say, but in the next few days I'm gonna be deciding what I'm doing for the next 3 years, and that is gonna be it."

Webb came to Ann Arbor to discover whether Warhurst was the man to guide him. Earlier this season, he recognized that he wasn't giving Warhurst an honest shot. "I realized that and said to myself, Right now, this is an option [turning pro] you're exploring, but this is not the time to be doing it. From then until now, I said, You need to get on his page; you need to just listen to Ron.

"I figured I might as well take everything I can from this situation right now and decide later whether I want to come back to that." To Webb's credit, he did bite into Warhurst's system. He did what his coach asked of him, and then some.

That's not to say, however, that Raczko didn't suggest that he should be doing otherwise. I ask him whether, as Warhurst contends, Raczko in any way undermined Warhurst's authority during the season. Webb tells me he continued doing his high school weight and drill routine because he felt that was a staple of his program and an important component of his continued development. Raczko, he says adamantly, "never once gave me workouts to do. I organized all that stuff. Even when I went home, he didn't give me anything. He timed me when I was home, and I did 100 percent Ron's workouts. Not once did Raczko say, 'This is a bad workout and you should do [otherwise].' He knows the benefit of any workout is not instantaneous, so even if he did suggest another workout, it wouldn't make a difference."

He continues, "At its peak, I didn't have confidence in Ron at some points. People could have thought that I was getting workouts from elsewhere, but that just had to do with me being frustrated with myself. Raczko never said anything; there was no foul play involved.

"Now," he says, "the collegiate season's over. I've fulfilled my commitment for this year to the University of Michigan. Now is an appropriate time to explore this decision."

In early March, Webb had decided to evaluate the situation—whether to go pro or stay at Michigan—after the culmination of his year at the World Junior Championships in July. Now, after his lackluster performance at the NCAAs, that race is no longer part of the equation. Although, for now, he doesn't discount the possibility of competing at the World Juniors, he'll drive back to Virginia tomorrow morning to contemplate an issue that has taken precedence over any disruption in training his leaving may cause: his future. His decision to go home now, the finality of his language, and his effusiveness about the synergy he and Raczko have all make the decision appear to be an open-and-shut case. I'm certain he won't return to Michigan in the fall. I don't need him to tell me.

Says Webb, "I've always felt like Raczko could take me to the next level time and time again, because he did. Every year, it was simple for me. All I had to do was show up. I know I'm gonna work hard when I show up. All I had to do was show up at three o'clock, get enough rest, eat well, sleep well, and improve. I feel confident if I went back I would get better every year for the rest of my career. I just don't know if that's the case here. I just don't know, and that is what it's all about."

Webb's actions say more about his decision than his words. As he and Brannen cleared their lockers this afternoon, Brannen watched Webb remove his nameplate from his locker and pack it away with his belongings.

Said Brannen afterward, "He ain't coming back."

EPILOGUE

Ⅰn late May, as Alan Webb pondered his future, I sought out the two fastest 1500-meter runners in history, Hicham el Guerrouj and Bernard Lagat, and asked them what advice they would offer Webb about whether he should remain at Michigan and run collegiately or turn professional.

I met first with Lagat, the 1500-meter silver medalist at the 2001 World Track and Field Championships and the second-fastest 1500-meter runner of all time (3:26.34). We talked on the eve of the

2002 Prefontaine Classic in the lobby of the meet headquarters on the banks of the Willamette River in Oregon. As he stretched his legs out before him, I noticed a fresh spike wound running down one of his shins. He revealed that it had come courtesy of American miler Seneca Lassiter a week earlier during training in Pullman, Washington.

The wound didn't faze him. Long, jet-black scars, reminders of the razor sharpness of his competition—and their spikes—course up and down both his shins. Lagat excitedly pointed to each one, explaining with the pride of a blue-collar worker injured while performing his trade: "This one's from Mt. SAC, the 5000. That one's from a pacemaker in Paris last year." The pain from the Paris injury didn't abate until season's end. He smiled as he said, "Out there [in Europe], it's not easy."

For Lagat, a 1999 graduate of Washington State University, collegiate running had been much more forgiving. Yet, the most lasting lessons he learned there came quite painfully. For example, he entered the 1500 meters at the 1998 NCAA Outdoor Track and Field Championships in Buffalo in fantastic condition, with hopes of capturing his first NCAA title. In the final, he ran close to the rail and was tripped. He got up but finished a heartbreaking eighth. He later blamed himself for the fall, telling me that in college, he often got boxed in by other runners. No longer. Adamantly, he said, "Every time I run in Europe now, I am out of the box. You can't find me in the box unless something drastic happens and I can't move out."

Had Lagat not learned such lessons as a collegian, he's confident he never would have amounted to much as a professional. So when I asked him what advice he would offer Webb, he was unequivocal. "Run in college. He'll develop in college, and he'll get experience. You can win in 3:38 in college. It's so different when you get out. You need a lot of 3:38s and 3:40s to make you ready for the big time. After 4 years, that kid, no one will stay close to him. At USA nationals, he's gonna be in a world by himself because of all the [experience] he gets.

"I look at the 4 years as a preparation. Some people will say, 'Hey, he can make a lot of money in the outside world.' It's true. He can make money. But you know what? The best thing is experience. He can run 4 years in college and still have a lot of years ahead of him because he's a young guy. That's my best advice, but he's the guy who'll make the best decision for himself."

The following morning, I met with El Guerrouj, the world record holder in both the 1500 meters and the mile, and his coach, Abdelkada Kada. I asked Coach Kada about what's necessary for an American to rise to El G's level. He replied that the American collegiate system must be dismissed as a developmental ground for world-class milers. For sprinters, he said, it's okay. But for milers, he believes the demands of racing for three seasons are too great. He feels that collegiate coaches too often compromise the training of their milers in favor of short-term gain—a conference title, an invitational title, and so on. He stressed the need for a limited racing schedule, with no more than three or four races indoors and six races outdoors.

Kada, a former Moroccan cross country champion, doesn't view cross country as a necessary developmental tool for a miler. In the fall, he told me, while American collegians are busily going about the cross country season, El Guerrouj is developing a base for the summer track season. In Morocco, he shuttles between a high-altitude training camp in Ifrane, where he focuses on developing his aerobic base, and a sea-level camp in Rabat, where he begins the first phase of a periodized, year-long strength-training program in the weight room with heavy squats and other exercises. The strength program continues in the winter and concludes in spring with very specific hill sessions with repetitions up to 400 meters.

At the Prefontaine Classic, as in Morocco, El G was constantly surrounded by an entourage to minimize distractions; it included two sub-4 milers who rabbited him through his track sessions. Their purpose was to run three-quarters of every interval with him and help him develop his rhythm and speed.

In sum, Coach Kada stressed how everything, from El Guerrouj's diet to the elevation at which he sleeps, was geared toward making him faster. Adherence to this strict, ascetic training program—a lifestyle, really—is why El Guerrouj has transformed the mile to its highest form, on the Grand Prix circuit, from a tactical affair to a long sprint, a rhythm race.

It was no surprise then that when I spoke to El G, he agreed with his coach, dismissing the collegiate system as "not good at all" for developing middle-distance talent. "Athletics is a professional sport," he told me. "Either go to school or be a professional runner. Now the best athletes run professionally, and when they finish their careers, they go to school."

THE FINAL DECISION

In the end, Alan Webb decided to end his track season following the NCAA Championships, turn pro, and begin anew. He signed with agent Ray Flynn, and Nike inked him to a contract reported to be worth $1.5 million over 6 years. According to industry sources, that contract makes him one of the 10 highest-paid professional track athletes in the world.

In the fall of 2002, Webb enrolled at George Mason University in Fairfax, Virginia, taking classes part-time while he embarked on his professional career under the guidance of Scott Raczko, his former high school coach. He trained in solitude through the fall, running nary a race, before venturing to Albuquerque with Raczko for his first-ever stint of altitude training.

On February 15, 2003, after a dismal 1:52 in his 800-meter season opener in Florida a week earlier, Webb made his much-anticipated professional mile debut in the New York Road Runners Challenge Cup at the Armory Collegiate Invitational. In the same venue where he ran his first sub-4 mile, the Armory Track and Field Center in New York City, he finished third in 3:59.42, fractions of a second faster than the 3:59.86 he ran there as a high school senior just over 2 years ago. Afterward, he told me, "It's a start. Not a good start or a bad start, but a start."

WARHURST'S OTHER CHARGES

While Webb's departure from Ann Arbor in early June 2002 marked the conclusion of his outdoor track campaign, the rest of Warhurst's milers still had races to run.

Since resuming running at the Big Ten Championships in late

May, Sully had been training in hopes of starting his season at the Canadian National Track and Field Championships in late June. Despite training relentlessly, by early June, he still hadn't found his form. For Sully, the moment of truth came on June 11, when he did a session of quarters with Paul McMullen and could manage only six in 60 seconds. He decided then and there that he would not be fit enough to compete in the Canadian championships a week and a half later.

McMullen did not follow suit. On June 21, he competed in the 800 meters at the USA Track and Field Championships, finishing last in 1:52.03. That was his final competition of the year. While his performance proved yet again that there are no miracles in track, it may have been the spark he needed to train seriously once more. He called Warhurst in October 2002 and told him not to be surprised if he showed up on the coach's doorstep in the spring of 2003 to make a run at qualifying for his third World Track and Field Championship team.

While Sully didn't go to his national championships, he bit the bullet and began his summer campaign in late June with a 3:45.37 in the 1500 meters in Montreal. He made steady if marginal improvement through July and August, running several 3:40 to 3:42 races, all the while putting in 80-mile training weeks in a desperate attempt to return to form by the end of summer.

Then, on September 8, in the final race of his European season, he ran the 1500 meters in Rieti, Italy. El Guerrouj won the race in a sparkling 3:26.96; Sully finished fourth in 3:34.99. That time once again made him the fastest Canadian miler of the year and earned him the distinction of being the second-fastest North American miler of 2002. Number one was emerging American star David Krummenacker, a New Mexico native and 1998 graduate of Georgia Tech. In his summer campaign in 2002, Krummenacker won Grand Prix races in Paris and Rome, lowered his personal bests to 1:43.92 for 800 meters and 3:31.91 for 1500 meters, and finished the season as the top American in both events.

While Sully competed in Europe, his wife, Karen Harvey, was appointed head women's cross country coach at the University of Illinois. They now live in Champaign, Illinois, and Sully plans to commute to Ann Arbor periodically to train under Ron Warhurst's supervision.

Nate Brannen finished second to Zach Whitmarsh in a slow and tactical 800 meters at the Canadian National Championships. He went on to make the semi-finals of the 800 meters at the Commonwealth Games in Manchester, England, barely missing the final. As a sophomore at Michigan, he concluded a stellar cross country campaign with a 3rd-place finish at the Big Ten Cross Country Championships and a 22nd-place finish at the NCAA Cross Country Championships.

On May 18, 2002, while the Michigan men were in Madison, Wisconsin, for the Big Ten Championships, Tim Broe was in Portland, Oregon, to run the 3000-meter steeplechase in the Adidas Oregon Track Classic. In his first steeplechase of the season, Broe went out with the world record holder, Moroccan Brahim Boulami, in hopes of capturing the $50,000 bonus the meet offered to any American who could eclipse Henry Marsh's 17-year-old American record of 8:09.17. Although he went for the record, Broe faded in the race's final stages and finished third in 8:18.86 behind what he characterized as Boulami's "superhuman" winning run of 8:04.51. Boulami subsequently tested positive for the performance-enhancing drug EPO after bettering his own world record with a run of 7:53.17 in Zurich, Switzerland, on August 17, 2002.

In early June, Broe rebounded from his disappointing run in Oregon when he returned home to Peoria, Illinois, and blasted away from Kenyan Evans Rutto to win the Steamboat Classic 4-mile road race in 17:47. That win was the beginning of the end of a long season for him. While practicing one final water jump the morning prior to his steeplechase qualifier at the USA Outdoor Track and Field Championships, Broe leapt far too soon, catching the water barrier with the tip of his left big toe. To the amusement of some javelin throwers nearby, he flew into the water pit headfirst, arms out, and arose soaked from head to toe. He laughed it off then, but hours later the severity of his injuries became apparent: He had sprained his right wrist and severely hyperextended his toe. He fought through the pain to finish a disappointing third in the steeplechase final behind 2000 Tennessee graduate Anthony Famiglietti and University of Colorado senior Steve Slattery.

Broe went on to race in Europe, but the condition of his toe only worsened, and after his second European race, a 10th-place finish in 8:22 in a steeplechase at the Gaz de France meeting in Paris, he called it a season. He has filled Sully's shoes and is now Warhurst's right-hand man in Ann Arbor.

After receiving 2001 NCAA 1500-meter champion Bryan Berryhill's fax in March, Warhurst began coaching him, sending him workouts by fax and phone. While Webb wasn't at the USA Championships in late June, Berryhill was. He followed Warhurst's counsel perfectly, waiting until the final 150 meters of the race to begin his surge for home. He raced 1999 University of Arkansas graduate and perennial national championship contender Seneca Lassiter to the wire, getting nipped by a mere tenth of a second to finish second—his best-ever finish at the championships. He went on to compete in Europe, recording his seasonal best of 3:36.53 in Stockholm in mid-July.

Warhurst continued to coach Berryhill in 2003.

POSTSCRIPT

In late October 2002, I once again visited Ron Warhurst and the Michigan men in Ann Arbor, roughly a year after I had watched Alan Webb perform Warhurst's bread-and-butter workout, the Michigan, better than any man had done before. This time, Brannen and Warhurst's newest blue-chip miler, New Zealander Nick Willis, who finished fourth in the World Junior Championships 1500 in July, completed a Michigan that Warhurst called the best team performance he'd seen in 15 years.

Everyone, from Warhurst to Brannen to team captain Nick Stanko, marveled at how tight the team had become and how much more cooperative the atmosphere seemed compared to the competitive air that existed a year earlier. While everyone was aware of what Webb would have added to the mix, Stanko said that no one had ever wondered aloud how good the team would be had Webb stayed at Michigan. When I talked to Warhurst at the Big Ten Championships a week later, he put it best: "I'm happy how it is now. He's where he needs to be, and we're where we need to be. He's with his coach where he needs to be at home, and we're here where we need to be at the Big Tens with our team."

Led by Brannen and Willis, the Wolverines went on to finish eighth at the NCAA Cross Country Championships weeks later, bettering the performance of the Webb-led team of 2001 by three spots.

Like Webb, Brannen and the Wolverines are now competing in indoor track. On February 8, 2003, a week before Webb's professional mile debut, Brannen made his seasonal debut in the mile at the Meyo Invitational at the University of Notre Dame in Indiana. He finished second in 3:57.96, a mere 0.13 second behind new Notre Dame mile record holder Luke Watson. Willis, running his second mile of the season, took fourth in 3:58.15.

In March 2002, I arrived in Ann Arbor in search of answers. Instead, I left with a host of new questions, not only about Alan Webb's future and that of Nate Brannen and the other Michigan runners but also about the effectiveness of the collegiate system. Only time will yield those answers.

Chris Lear
February 2003

AFTERWORD

THE FALL AND RESURGENCE OF ALAN WEBB

In this book's foreword, Congressman Jim Ryun noted many similarities between his disappointing 1972 season and Alan Webb's tumultuous year at the University of Michigan. While Ryun couldn't guarantee Webb wouldn't have another year like 2002, he felt Webb had tasted "necessary failure" that year, and that his struggling would eventually allow Webb to find "the reward." By that, I believe he meant the knowledge, inner peace, and determination that come after facing obstacles en route to a more lasting success.

As it turns out, Webb's reward would have to wait. In 2003, reunited once again with his high school mentor, Scott Raczko, and shouldering the burden of expectation that comes with a $1.5 million dollar Nike contract, Webb had a year like he had in 2002. Only this time, it was far worse.

When he returned to Reston, Virginia, in the summer of 2002 and sat down with Coach Raczko to plot the coming year, Webb set his mind on a single goal: He would run so spectacularly in 2003 that everyone—most important, Alan Webb—would forget the struggles he encountered in his only season of collegiate competition.

Reflecting on what had made him the fastest high school miler of all time, he remembered the specialized workouts he once ran. Everything, from his strides to his plyometric routine to his weight routine, had been explicitly designed for him. "It was technical," Webb says. By comparison, Ron Warhurst had a decidedly "basic, old school approach." In Webb's mind, therein lay the reason he had succeeded as a high schooler and struggled at Michigan. But it went beyond even this. Webb was embittered by his relative failure at Michigan in 2002. In his mind, a drastic change was necessary. "Whatever Ron would do," he thought, "I'm gonna do the opposite."

Raczko and Webb reacted by laying out a plan with a heavy emphasis on the off-track work that Webb had felt was the key to his success. And with a year to get reacclimated to Coach Razcko's program, they figured he'd slowly build up his mileage and his workouts. By the time the outdoor season came around, Webb believed, he'd be "caught up" to where he had been two years before.

But that was just the beginning. Webb took stock of his entire life and decided everything in it needed a drastic overhaul. He began to track everything meticulously: his workouts, the amount of calories he consumed, his resting pulse, and the amount of sleep he got every night. Nothing was beyond quantification, beyond his control. He'd let himself down at Michigan. He'd been too easy on himself. If Alan Webb was going to ascend to the mountaintop, he needed to be perfect. And that demanded a 24-hour-a-day commitment.

By the time Webb emerged from his cocoon and made his professional mile debut at the Armory on February 15, 2003, his metamorphosis was manifest. He was gaunt, visibly leaner, and less muscular than he'd ever been in the past. He led for most of the mile that afternoon, yet when it came time to kick, the tank was empty. He finished a haggard third, in 3:59.

To Webb, the problem was obvious: He wasn't working hard enough. He dug in deeper, kept a more zealous watch on his calories, made sure he was executing his exercises to perfection, and pushed himself to the limit in his workouts.

Yet the more he worked, the worse he ran. He considered anything less than an all-out effort "a lost day." When he was at the University of Michigan, and he blasted out at the beginning of every workout, it was as if he was convinced he had to destroy everyone in order to be a success. Only now he had no competition, no teammates he could compare himself to. His only competition was Alan Webb circa 2001 and 2002. And as the failures mounted in race after race and winter turned to spring, he increasingly found himself falling short.

Meanwhile, Webb's former roommate, Nate Brannen, and the man who usurped Webb's role as Ann Arbor's mile phenom in residence, New Zealander and Wolverine freshman Nick Willis, had banner years in 2003. At the NCAA Indoor Championships Brannen won the 800-meter crown in a school record 1:47.61, while Willis anchored their distance medley relay to a third-place finish in a school record 9:29.

At the Penn Relays, the boys in blue began to make even more noise. Willis announced his arrival to the Big Time by setting a Penn Relays record with a 2:49.7 split on the 1200-meter leg of the distance medley relay. Brannen subsequently outkicked University of Arkansas' ace Alistair Cragg on the anchor leg to bring the Championship of America back to Ann Arbor. Though Willis fell in the final of the outdoor NCAA 1500 meters and Brannen finished fifth in the 800 meters in 1:47.45, their inspired seasons had track pundits wondering how well Webb might have done if only he had given Warhurst another chance. That chatter continued through this past winter, when Brannen won his second consecutive NCAA 800-meter crown, Willis set a collegiate record of 7:44 for 3000 meters, and the two bookended a Wolverine win in the distance medley relay at the NCAA Championships in a collegiate record-setting time of 9:27.7.

Meanwhile, Webb was still floundering. He had begun to see his compulsions overcome him as he became victim to his own perfectionist bent. He was "overly nutritionally conscious," a "borderline" anorexic whose eating habits left him without the energy necessary to perform well in his marathon training sessions. He was simply "going through the motions," digging himself into an even deeper hole. Says Webb, "I was so determined that everything be perfect that unless it went perfect leading into a race, I didn't run well."

By the time of the USA Track and Field Outdoor National Championships in July 2003, Webb wanted to be anywhere but on the track, racing the 1500. He painfully struggled to tenth place, running 3:47 in a tactical race won in a modest 3:44. Though the race had gone out in a pedestrian 62 seconds for the opening 400 meters, Webb couldn't handle the pace.

It was then that a dispirited Webb realized how his mistakes had compounded themselves, one on top of the next, and left him psychologically, if not yet physically, broken. Over the previous months he'd put so much on the line in practice to run workouts equivalent to what he'd run in high school or at Michigan—and on a restricted diet no less—that when it came time to race, he would toe the line feeling physically sluggish and mentally drained.

The final sign of his collapse came a few weeks later when his body gave up on him: Webb's appendix burst, bringing his season to a merciful end.

In retrospect, it may have been the best moment of Webb's season, and the moment history will possibly view as the turning point of his career. Forced by his emergency surgery to take time off, he allowed himself to do something he hadn't done all year: He relaxed. In the weeks that followed he did what most 20-year-olds would do. He ate pizza, hung out late with friends home from college for the summer, and watched movies. And during this time, he analyzed why it had all gone so wrong.

Theories abounded as to why he had run so poorly: He wasn't race savvy, he couldn't handle the pressure. Some even speculated that at 20, he was somehow past his prime.

Webb dismissed all of those theories. Instead, he says, "I had to think more generally. What does it take to be a good runner?" What he discovered, in perhaps the ultimate irony, was that in his rush to distance himself from his time at Michigan, from the first year in his life that he had not PRed in the mile, he had omitted the

cornerstone of the Michigan—and any—successful training program: a solid foundation of strength training. Though his training
sessions often lasted in excess of four hours, they were comprised,
Webb says, "of a lot of fluff. In terms of running, it wasn't that
much."

And in the success of the Michigan runners, there was a lesson.
After all, he says, "That's the reason I went there. It's not random
why I went there. [Warhurst] is a great coach; there's no denying
that."

Now able to objectively consider his year at Michigan, he
thought of the shape he'd been in at the end of November, 2001,
the conclusion of his one and only cross-country season at
Michigan. He thought of his Big 10 Cross Country Championship.
He also thought to the awesome Michigan (Warhurst's signature
strength workout) he had run a week later, in November, 2001. He
was able to consider now what Ron Warhurst and I had wondered
then: "If I was able to run a few fast quarter workouts then and run
a mile in December? Man, who knows!" (Privately, when I discussed this with Warhurst at that time, he speculated that a mile
approaching 3:50, right then, was not out of the question.)

Webb knew he needed to get back to that point, but he was realistic: It was going to take longer this time. Whereas Webb had
needed only four months to get there in the fall of 2002, he was
now starting from scratch, and he felt he needed steady training
from August to April to get there safely.

Though Webb had left Michigan after a season that was relatively superior to the one he had just endured, he decided (though
he had his doubts, as anyone in that situation would) that he would
stick with Raczko. "I just had a feeling," he says, "from the experiences I'd had in high school, that it would just work out." Moreover, for Webb, the direction he had to take was simple: "Just go
out and run hard and don't think too much about it. (Last year) I
made it too complicated, too specific. When Raczko and I sat down

after my break from running, we both realized we just needed to run hard and not worry about things so much. It made me just want to go out and run hard."

In high school, Webb had maxed out his base mileage in the mid 60s; at Michigan, he'd run slightly more. In the fall of 2003, Webb upped the ante, stringing together 70-mile weeks one after another.

Just as significantly, over the course of his sabbatical from running, Webb acquired a newfound sense of balance. He ditched his weight log and resumed more of an active social life. Says Webb, "I used to assume great athletes were consumed by their sport. That's not true. That's a myth. In fact, it's a negative thing. As much time and energy, emotionally and physically, as you put into this sport, it's a game. There are other things to do in life. It makes it so much easier to deal with it, knowing it's not the end-all, be-all in life."

Inasmuch as he strove to adopt a new mental approach, it was one he'd seen at Michigan in his old roommate, Nate Brannen. Says Webb, "Nate's really good at taking things in stride. That's the thing I couldn't understand [while at Michigan]. I saw [Nate's placid nature] as a negative thing. I felt I had to hold myself to these higher standards. I didn't allow myself to give myself a break. But that's why he bounced back and PRed that year, and I was the one that got my ass kicked [at the NCAAs]."

On December 7, 2003, Webb got his first indication that the return to basics was paying off. He lined up that day for the USATF 10K Club Cross-Country Championships against many of the country's top distance runners. He went in thinking, "Here I am, this scrub 1500-meter runner coming off the worst year of his life." But when he left, he left with the title, having outkicked NCAA 10,000-meter champion Daniel Lincoln of Arkansas in the process.

Encouraged by his progress, Webb kept on, and in a one-week span in early February 2004, Webb quelled any lingering doubts he had about his rejuvenation when he competed in both the 4k and 12k races at the USA Cross Country Championships and then ran a mile at the Tyson Invitational in Arkansas just six days later.

After having finished a disappointing eighth in the 4K race on a snow-covered course in blustery conditions, Webb decided to enter the following afternoon's 12K race. Running against the country's top distance runners, Webb finished fourth, astonishing even himself.

The following Saturday, in Fayetteville, Arkansas, Webb ran his first mile since he'd staggered across the line in Palo Alto at the USA championships 8 months earlier. Running against an international field that included Kevin Sullivan, Webb finished fourth in 3:57, just 1 second behind Sullivan. Says Webb, "At that point, after scratching just to make the final at USAs last year, all I wanted was to be in the ballpark, and *I was in the hunt!* I remember feeling good when I was cooling down; I knew we were getting close.

"Slowly, I was getting things back together. After the cross races and the mile, I knew I was fit; things were going good, things will come around."

As much as Webb's mishaps had been compounded one year earlier, his successes were now beginning to build exponentially as well. But it wasn't until April 2004 that he truly regained his stride.

From the time they'd begun training in late summer, Raczko and Webb had taken a decidedly more tempered, long-term approach. They'd begun Webb's campaign training with local, national-class runners like Ben Cooke, a James Madison University graduate with a 4:01 mile best. While he relished once more having companions to run with, those sessions also served another purpose. Says Webb, "I had to let go and not always hammer into the run . . . For a while I let go. I wasn't having any crazy Michigans. I realized I didn't have to dig every single workout, I was just having solid days."

But on another level, he had yet to answer whether he could still go deeper, to that special place you go when you go beyond what you think possible. In late April, before the Penn Relays, Webb got his answer.

It was Webb and Raczko, out on the track in Virginia on a hot and muggy afternoon, running a series of 400s that involved arduous pace changes on each interval. At one point, Webb told Raczko he could do no more. Raczko responded with another two intervals. It was gut-check time, and Webb passed the test. In the process, Webb earned the knowledge that, in the toughest of circumstances, with 200 meters separating him from the tape, he, like the greatest of runners, could find the strength he needed for one final charge.

Yet as much as Webb points to that workout as a confidence booster, it's indicative of his maturation as an athlete that he places it in the context of a larger training program: "I know now that I don't have to [go to the well] every time, but I have to be willing to. That's different from what I used to think. As much as I want to have the Prefontaine mentality, blasting it every time, I realized it's too much. There's a fine line between doing it and being willing to do it, and you have to make sure you save a bit for those bigger races."

For Webb, those bigger races began in earnest on May 22, 2004, at the Home Depot Invitational in Carson, California. In the time since his monumental quarter workout at Virginia, he'd won both the invitational mile and the invitational 5000 meters at the Penn Relays, confirming for Webb yet again that he was on track. And now, after two years of struggle, here he was, ready to tackle a tough race and get the job done.

The race was billed as an attempt to gain the Olympic "A" 1500-meter qualifying standard of 3:36.2, and when the field emerged into the first turn, Alan Webb surged and tucked in right behind rabbit Milton Browne of Barbados. He stayed there for 1000 meters, until Browne stepped aside, and Webb found himself out of earshot of his closest competitor with a sea of tartan to navigate before he hit the wire. "At that point," he says, "I was so physically ready that it didn't matter if I had any negative thoughts, I was still going to run well. That's what happened. I'd finally gotten back to the point where I could lose myself in a race, and I lost myself in the moment."

Webb ran unheeded to the line to win by 3 seconds and secure the Olympic "A" standard, with a massive PR of 3:35.71.

Alan Webb had returned.

Ever since that race, Webb has continued to test his limitations—consequences be damned—and his courage has been rewarded in spades. In Ostrava, Czech Republic, on June 5, 2004, Webb repeated the strategy he'd executed at Home Depot, shadowing the rabbit until he dropped with a quarter to go before boldly assuming a lead he would never relinquish. In the process he shocked a top international field that included such stars as Kenyan Bernard Lagat (fourth) and Olympic champion Noah Ngeny (sixteenth), establishing a new PR of 3:32.73.

But it was weeks later, when he ran the mile at the Prefontaine Classic, the same race that had earned him the tag of "Next" in 2001 when he broke Jim Ryun's high school mile record, that Webb announced to the world that his time was now. Drawing on the strength he'd gained since August and the knowledge he'd accrued since April as to how deep he could go, Webb ran away from the field once more to win the mile in 3:50.83. The time was fast enough to erase another of Jim Ryun's seemingly intemperate records from the books, this time for the fastest mile ever run by an American on U.S. soil.

Perhaps it's fitting then that we end with Ryun, the miler who set the standard for Webb. It is Jim Ryun who earned the last Olympic medal by an American in the 1500 meters when he took home the silver from Mexico City in 1968. By the time you read this, that standard, too, may have fallen: As of this writing, Alan Webb is a legitimate threat to walk away from Athens with a medal around his neck.

Had Alan Webb not tasted Ryun's "necessary failure," we may never have witnessed the brilliance Webb has exhibited this spring. Success can mask a lot of flaws: Until the spring of 2002 at Michigan, he never had to examine how his need to test his limitations could hurt his progress. And until his failures of a year ago, he never had to confront the compulsions that, once washed away, would clear the path for his success in 2004.

The journey certainly hasn't been easy, but in hindsight, I'd have to agree with Congressman Ryun. It was necessary.

Chris Lear
July 2004

INDEX

Warhurst and, 20, 109, 111
Webb and, 2, 26, 79−80, 100, 183,
186, 188
Wetmore and, 127
World Track and Field
Championships, 20
Sylvester, Marc, 190−93

Tjiroze, Mao, 178
Tolman, Jeremy, 32, 35
Torres, Jorge, 208
Townsend, Sean, 87
Track and field
Americans' interest in, 5
outdoor track specifications, 2
Turner, Brian, 91−92

University of Michigan. *See also*
specific athletes and coaches
Big Ten Outdoor Track and Field
Championships team (2002),
169
Brannen and
first year at, 1−2, 22−23, 25−29
recruitment by, 26
Broe and, 20−21, 70−72, 90−91
McMullen and, 21−22, 215
Penn Relays team (2002), 108−12,
113−16
Sullivan and
career at, 20, 53, 169
professional training at,
19−20, 215−16
recruitment by, 20, 52
Webb and
first year at, 1−2
leaving, 205−10
recruitment by, 19, 53−54
USA Cross Country
Championships (2002), 21
USA Indoor Track and Field
Championships (2002), 21
USA Outdoor Track and Field
Championships (2002), 58,
215−217
USA Track and Field (USATF), 2

Van Swol, Jason, 159−61
Vermillion, Rob, 185

Walker, John, 4
Warhurst, Kalli, 16, 96, 157, 120, 170
Warhurst, Ron
athletes coached by, 2, 20, 51
Berryhill and, 217
birth of son, 96, 108, 156−57
Brannen and, 30−34, 36−37, 47,
59, 83−84, 104, 118−19,
189−90, 193
Broe and, 71−72, 111
collegiate track program and,
51−52
Cross and, 50
dependency problems, 52−53
Diemer and, 52
McMullen and, 22
Meyer and, 51
Raczko and, 19, 110, 182−83
start of 2002 season, 55−56
Sullivan and, 20, 109, 111
Vietnam War experiences,
47−49
Webb (Alan) and, 18, 38−41,
44−47, 53−54, 64, 72−73, 79,
92−94, 102−3, 118, 120−21,
126, 188, 198−201
Webb (Steve) and, 121
Webb, Alan
Achilles tendon injury
effects of, 17, 39−44
rehabilitation for, 63
recovery from, 17−19, 39−40,
44−45, 56−58, 63−68
Arb workouts and records, 39,
70−73, 84
Big Ten Cross Country
Championships (2001), 17, 56
Big Ten Outdoor Track and Field
Championships (2002)
early heats of, 156−58, 160−64
workouts prior to, 138−40,
149−50, 154−55
Blincoe and, 115−16, 200
Brannen and, 73, 118, 138−40,
154−55, 206
Broe and, 2, 26, 70−72, 139,
142−43, 167
comeback, 84−87
El Guerrouj and, 9−11, 127, 211